THE COLLECTED WORKS
OF HERMAN DOOYEWEERD

Series B, Volume 17

GENERAL EDITOR: *D.F.M. Strauss*

Essays in Legal, Social, and Political Philosophy

Series B, Volume 17

Herman Dooyeweerd

PAIDEIA PRESS

Library of Congress Cataloging-in-Publication Data

Dooyeweerd, H. (Herman), 1894-1977.
  [Lecture Series in the US. English 1960 / Edited 1999]
  Essay in Legal, Social, and Political Philosophy / Herman
  Dooyeweerd
  p. cm

  Includes bibliographical references, glossary, and index
  ISBN 978-0-88815-219-0
  1. Philosophy. 2. Legal Philosophy. 3. Social Philosophy.
  4. Political Philosophy. I Title

  This is Series B in the continuing series
  The Collected Works of Herman Dooyeweerd
  (Initially published by Mellen Press, now published
  by Paideia Press)

  ISBN 978-0-88815-332-6

  The Collected Works comprise a Series A, a Series B, and a Series C
    (*Series A* contains multi-volume works by Dooyeweerd,
    Series B contains smaller works and collections of essays,
    Series C contains reflections on Dooyeweerd's philosophy
      designated as: *Dooyeweerd's Living Legacy*, and
    Series D contains thematic selections from Series A and B)

  A CIP catalog record for this book is available from the British Library.

The Dooyeweerd Centre for Christian Philosophy
Redeemer College Ancaster, Ontario
CANADA L9K 1J4

All rights reserved. For information contact

©PAIDEIA PRESS 2012
Reprinted 2023
Jordan Station, ON.
www.paideiapress.ca

Printed in the United States of America

Translators and Editors

Essays in Legal, Social, and Political Philosophy

Under the above title this volume brings together the following six separately titled essays by Herman Dooyeweerd:

1) "Calvinism and Natural Law." This essay appeared in 1925 under the title: *Calvinisme en Natuurrecht* (Amersfoort: Wijngen, 32 pp.).
Translator: *A. Wolters*; Editors: *John Witte, Jr. & Alan M. Cameron*

2) "The modal structure of jural causality." The Dutch text appeared as a reprint of a paper presented at a meeting of the Royal Dutch Academy of Sciences, Literature Department, in 1950: "Overdruk uit Akademiedagen III," published in Amsterdam by the N.V. Noord-Hollandsche Uitgeversmaatschappij. The same article appeared in: "Mededelingen der Koninklijke Nederlandse Akademie van Wetenschappen, Afd. Letterkunde, Nieuwe Reeks, Deel 13, No. 5. Amsterdam, N.V. Noord-Hollandsche Uitgeversmaatschappij." It contains references to literature and jurisprudence also incorporated in the second volume of the Encyclopedia of Legal Science.
Translator: *D.F.M. Strauss*; Editor: *Alan M. Cameron*

3) "The relationship between Legal Philosophy and Sociology of Law." This article appeared in Dutch as: *"De verhouding tussen Rechtsfilosofie en Rechtssociologie,"* in *Album Professor Ferdinand van Goethem* (Leuven, 1964, pp.557-576).
Translator: *Robert Knudsen*; Editor: *Alan M. Cameron*

4) "The relation of the individual and community from a legal philosophical perspective." This article appeared in the "Algemeen Nederlands Tijdschrift voor Wijsbegeerte en Psychologie," Year 39, Number 1, October 1946, pp.5-11 – under the title: *De verhouding van individu en gemeenschap rechtswijsgeerig bezien* (The relation of the individual and community from a legal philosophical perspective).
Translator: *D.F.M. Strauss*; Editor: *Alan M. Cameron*

5) "The contest over the concept of sovereignty." Rectorial address, delivered on the occasion of the 70th anniversary of the Free University on 20 October 1950. This oration – considerably enlarged – was published in Dutch by J. H. Paris, Amsterdam: *De Strijd om het souvereiniteitsbegrip in de moderne Rechts- en Staatsleer* (The contest over the concept of sovereignty in modern Jurisprudence and Political Science) (62 pp.).
Translator: *Robert Knudsen*; Editor: *Alan M. Cameron*

6) "The Christian Idea of The State." (*De Christelijke Staatsidee.*) Presented at a day for Anti-Revolutionary youth on October 3, 1936 (Apeldoorn, Rotterdam-Utrecht, Libertas-Drukkerijen).

Translator: *John Kraay*; Editor: *D.F.M. Strauss*

Table of Contents

Foreword: .... (vii)

I
ESSAYS IN LEGAL PHILOSOPHY

Calvinism and Natural Law
Introduction: 3
The historical development of the law-idea 6
   The Aristotelian law-idea................................ 7
   The Christian church comes into the picture............. 10
   The Reformation 13
The Calvinist law-idea...................................... 15
Sphere-sovereignty as a philosophical consequence of the
Calvinistic law-idea.. 18
Natural law in its twofold significance..................... 19
The significance of primary natural law..................... 20
The doctrine of authority as central doctrine of primary
natural law... 22
Political natural law in the light of the Calvinist law-idea
and of the principle of sphere-sovereignty 25

The modal structure of jural causality
Introduction 39
Legal causality – a basic concept of Legal Science.......... 39
The two dominant theories 40
   Conditio sine qua non (von Buri)........................ 40
   Adequate causation (von Kries).......................... 40
      The "typical causal course" (Traeger)............... 41
      The "objective ex post prognosis" (Rümelin)......... 43
      Other Considerations 43
Continued reflection on the problem of jural causation 43
   The antinomy in van Eck's approach 44
   Four examples 45
The persistent prejudice concerning causal and normative
perspectives.. 48
   Causality in the deterministic sense of the natural
   science-ideal... 49
   The obstacle of freedom................................. 50
The inability to account for the causal jural relation 51

An intimate coherence and irreversible order 52
The modal diversity of causal relationships 54
The jural relation of causality within the modal
structure of the jural aspect 55
The modal structure of a causal legal fact 56
   The numerical analogy. 56
   The spatial analogy 57
   The physical analogy 57
   The biotical analogy. 58
   The psychical analogy 58
   The logical analogy: subjective and objective
   imputation 59
   Formation of law: the historical analogy 61
   Jural interpretation 63
   Legal intercourse 64
   The economical handling of legal means and interests 65
   Jural harmony and disharmony 66
The place of fault within the jural causal relation 68

II
ESSAYS IN SOCIAL PHILOSOPHY

The relationship between Legal Philosophy
and Sociology of Law
   Introduction 73
   Confusing constant structural principles
   with changing societal forms 73
   The important typology of legal spheres 74
   The impasse of an extreme nominalistic orientation:
   Gurvitch. 75
   Modal jural and typical jural relationships 80
   Transcendental categories of our social experience. 85
   Conclusion. 87
The relation of the individual and community from
a legal philosophical perspective
   Individualistic and Universalistic conceptions of Law 91
   Civil Law and the idea of the State 93
   The State as Public Legal Institution 98

III
ESSAYS IN POLITICAL PHILOSOPHY

The contest over the concept of sovereignty

Introduction 101
The History of the Dogma 103
   Bodin's concept of sovereignty and the humanistic
   doctrine of natural law 103
   The historical interpretation of the concept of
   sovereignty and the doctrine of state-sovereignty 108
   The doctrine of the sovereignty of law
   (Rechtssouveranität) and its presumed victory over the
   traditional dogma of sovereignty 113
   The traditional concept of sovereignty and the
   doctrine of sovereignty in its proper orbit 115

The Christian Idea of The State
   Emil Brunner rejects the Christian idea of the state 121
   National-Socialism and Fascism and the idea of the
   Christian state 122
   The ever new, inspiring idea of the Christian state and
   the causes of its decline 122
   Synthesis and Antithesis 123
   Actually, there is but one radical and Scriptural idea of
   the Christian state 123
   The contrast of "nature" and "grace" is
   non-Scriptural. Scripture posits the heart as the
   religious center of human existence 123
   The pagan view that "reason" is the supra-temporal
   center of a person's being 124
   The effects of compromise of Christian and pagan
   views. The scheme of "nature" and "grace" as a
   result of this compromise 125
   Thomas Aquinas on human nature. "Nature" as portal
   of "grace" 125
   Aristotle: the pagan idea of the state. The state as the
   highest bond of human society, of which all other
   societal relationships are but dependent parts 126
   The pagan totalitarian idea of the state and its revival
   in National-Socialism and Fascism 126
   The truly Christian view of the state takes its stance in
   the supra-temporal root-community of redeemed
   humanity in Christ Jesus 127
   All temporal societal relationships ought to be
   manifestations of the supra-temporal, invisible church
   of Christ 127
   The kingdom of God as the all-embracing rule of God 127
   The Christian idea of sphere-sovereignty over against
   the pagan view that the state is related to the other
   societal structures as the whole to its parts 128

Contents

The Roman Catholic view of the Christian state – Thomas Aquinas – is a falling away from the Scriptural conception 128
Infiltration of the pagan totality-idea in the Roman Catholic concept of the church 129
A false view of the Christian state: the state is subject to the temporal church-institute 129
Penetration of this view in modern denominational political parties 129
The Reformation over against the Roman Catholic view of Christian society 130
Nominalism in Late-Scholasticism 130
The nominalistic conception of the law as subjective arbitrariness and the Thomistic idea of the law as rational order 131
The nominalist dualism of nature and grace 131
This dualism was perpetuated in Luther's law-gospel polarity 132
Melanchthon's synthesis 132
Brunner continues Luther's dualism 132
Calvin breaks with the dualistic nature-grace scheme 133
Calvin's Scriptural view of law 134
The law as boundary between God and creature 134
Calvin's view of the divine creation-order contrasted with Thomas Aquinas 134
The principle of sphere-sovereignty: Calvin and Althusius 135
The greater influence of Melanchthon's synthesis predominates 135
The rise of the modern humanistic world- and life-view 136
The overpowering influence of the new mathematical science-ideal upon modern culture 136
The humanistic ideal of science continues in the modern individualistic idea of the state 137
Relativizing character of modern individualism in its view of society 137
Humanistic natural law over against its Aristotelian-Thomistic counterpart 137
Two mainstreams in humanistic natural law and the idea of the Rechtsstaat in its first phase of development 138
The old-liberal view of the Rechtsstaat and the separation of Church and State 138
Tolerance in State-absolutism 138

The Calvinistic view of sphere-sovereignty has
nothing in common with the humanistic freedom-idea
of natural law 139
The truly Christian idea of the state cannot be
separated from a recognition of sphere-sovereignty 140
The radical difference between sphere-sovereignty
and autonomy 140
Autonomy is proper only to parts of a whole;
sphere-sovereignty does not allow for such a relation 140
Sphere-sovereignty and antithesis go hand in hand in
Kuyper 141
Kuyper broke with nature-grace and distinguished
between church as institute and as organism 141
Elaboration of Kuyper's views the first meaning of
sphere-sovereignty, the sovereign law-spheres 142
Temporal aspects of reality in distinct law-spheres 142
The religious root-unity of the law-spheres 143
As sunlight diffuses itself in prismatic beauty 143
Common grace and the grace of rebirth (palingenesis):
no dualistic doctrine 143
Sphere-universality of the law-spheres 144
Succession of the law-spheres and the organic
character of sphere-sovereignty 144
Disclosure and deepening of the meaning of a
law-sphere 145
The second meaning of sphere-sovereignty:
individuality-structures in things and in societal
relationships 145
Concrete things function in all law-spheres indiscriminately. The
significance of the typical qualifying function 146
The first meaning of sphere-sovereignty (law-spheres)
is not voided in the individuality-structure of things.
The thing as individual totality 146
The basic error of humanistic science: the attempt to
dissolve the individuality-structure of a thing in a
pattern of lawful relations within one aspect of reality 147
The individuality-structure of societal relationships 147
The typical founding function 148
The structural principle of the state. The state an
institution required because of sin. This Scriptural
view not maintained by Thomas Aquinas 148
One-sided action for national disarmament is a neglect
of the structural principle of the state 149
The indissoluble coherence of the typical foundational
function and the typical qualifying function of the state 149

The "common good" (public welfare) as jural
principle and as absolutistic principle of power............ 150
The old-liberal idea of the Rechtsstaat proves
powerless to control the absolutism of "common
good" 150
The humanistic idea of the Rechtsstaat in its second,
formalistic phase 151
Only the Christian idea of the state, rooted in the
principle of sphere-sovereignty, is the true idea of the
Rechtsstaat 151
The task of the state cannot be limited externally by
excluding the state from certain aspects of reality 152
The state, with its function as political
faith-community, may not be subjected to an
ecclesiastical creed 152
Christian faith deepens the typically political
principles of justice. The Roman and the Christian
idea of justice 153
The liberal-humanistic and the Fascist views of justice 153
All non-Christian theories of the state are essentially
theories of power (Machtsstaatstheorieen) 154
The true relation of state and church: not a mechanical
division, but sphere-sovereignty 154
The inseparable, interwoven texture of the various
structures of society 155
The prophetic task of Christianity in these times 155
Glossary 157
Index 167

Foreword

That these philosophical essays have been appropriately grouped according to the headings legal, social and political cannot disguise the fact that all of them display an emphatic juridical bias. This in turn reflects the fact that Dooyeweerd's entire systematics grew out of reflection on his specialist discipline and that it was the problems of legal theory which he had particularly in mind throughout all his theoretical work. Yet it is Dooyeweerd's great achievement that his systematic philosophy is of general application to every field of theoretical inquiry.

On the other hand the first essay under the heading "legal," *Calvinism and Natural Law*, could also have been grouped under either of the other two categories as the social and political significance of the Calvinist and natural law theory traditions are attested to in the essay itself. Nevertheless, the strong connection between the juridical sense of "law" and the broader sense of natural law is more than coincidental and an acquaintance with jurisprudence in its narrower sense of legal concepts is indispensable for an understanding of the natural law idea in its various historical manifestations.

This essay is important because, although it was written before his philosophical framework was substantially in place, there can be no doubting even on a casual reading where his thought was heading. Already in 1925 when this work was published Dooyeweerd was well on the way to developing a "Christian" philosophical perspective that was consciously attempting to break not only with "humanistic" philosophy but with synthetic Christian traditions. In so doing he eventually produced a philosophy that is possibly unique in the history of Western philosophy. Yet one cannot help but notice at this stage in his development the strong affinities with the natural law tradition from which even at this stage Dooyeweerd was trying to distance himself. He has yet to find many of the philosophical concepts and the distinctive "Dooyeweerdian" terminology to express them though the germs of such original parts of his systematics as the modal theory and theory of individuality-structures are already present. Hence he refers to the structure of the social institution of the state as grounded in "political natural law."

The second of the legal essays, *The modal structure of jural causality*, is of quite a different order. Though there was at least still one important respect in which Dooyeweerd's systematics had yet to be developed (introduction of "kinematic" as an aspect distinct from the "physical" in the temporal order of the modal law-spheres) we have here in this 1950 article the application of the almost complete philosophical framework of the systematics to a special topic in his specialist field of study. It is for this reason that the essay on jural causality is possibly the most important not only of this collection but possibly of all the essays he wrote. For it seems that Dooyeweerd has taken this jurisprudential topic in particular to demonstrate the explanatory power of his theoretical method and his entire philosophical framework within his own field. The fact that he had already written a long article on the same topic in 1928 and that it is also subjected to extensive analysis when setting forth his account of the "basic" concepts of law in his *Encyclopedia of Legal Science* (to be published in subsequent volumes in *The Collected Works*) supports this view.

This essay, however, not only provides a model of the application of his systematics to the conceptual foundations of jurisprudence but a model for its application to every other field of theoretical inquiry. Furthermore the history of his treatment of jural causality also provides firm evidence of how closely connected was the development of Dooyeweerd's most acclaimed accomplishment, the Philosophy of the Cosmonomic Idea, with the development of his relatively unknown legal philosophy from the very beginning of his theoretical inquiries.

Despite the gap of almost two decades between the appearance of the two social essays they complement one another in a conceptually compatible way. Both have the sociological dimensions of juridical problems especially in mind. The more substantial essay, *The relationship between Legal Philosophy and Sociology of Law,* shows how, even in the recent development of legal sociology where there is a recognition of the importance of a philosophical account of the nature of social forms for an explanation of the different types of law and their historical manifestations, there is still lacking a proper structural analysis of these social forms that can be fruitfully applied to jurisprudential problems. The shorter of the two, *The relation of the individual and community from a legal philosophical perspective*, is no less penetrating in its insight. One could find no more succinct statement of Dooyeweerd's critique of the philosophical foundations of the history of modern social theory and its implications for the analysis of legal typology and its classifications. Nor can there be a more complete single example of the close interconnections between general philosophy, social theory, legal history and jurisprudence which the "encyclopedic" method of his "new critique" demands.

The final two essays under the "political" heading do not display the same degree of mutual compatibility at least not in a purely theoretical sense. *The Christian Idea of the State* is more a popular tract addressed to those who share the deepest faith convictions on which Dooyeweerd's theoretical work was based than a work of pure theory. Nevertheless it is still of considerable theoretical interest for it draws upon and expounds in some detail the elements of his theory of state in a manner which must have stretched the understanding of many of those to whom this account was first addressed even in the reduced form of a lecture.

It is also significant for at least two other reasons. First, its shows Dooyeweerd's political theory to embody a theory of the state as a community of public justice where justice is given a highly specific meaning but with a very broad social relevance. In this essay the idea of the state functioning according to the "rule of law" receives a *substantive* meaning by contrast with the idea of *formal* legal protections of the then prevailing liberal political theory at a crucial time in world history when fascism and Hitler's national-socialism were on the rise. Secondly, this essay shows how far his thought had already developed between this collection's first essay of 1925 and the date of this particular article which was published in 1936.

The other essay, *The contest over the concept of sovereignty,* deals with an aspect of political theory which is receiving as much attention in political and legal theory and practice today as possibly it has ever had. Also based on a public lecture there is no better example of the practical relevance of Dooyeweerd's critique of the Western theoretical traditions and of his philosophical ontology than this plea for a proper structural analysis of the idea of sovereignty. Nor is there a more powerfully articulated account of the differentiated character of state power and its juridical delimitation than in this theoretical flowering of the reformational principle of sphere-sovereignty. For those who recoil at the thought that there could be a distinctively Christian political philosophy and that one's deepest religious convictions can and should be brought to bear on the details of political life this essay shows why this is not only possible but an urgent necessity.

Alan Cameron
(Victoria University, Wellington, New Zealand)

I

ESSAYS IN LEGAL PHILOSOPHY

Calvinism and Natural Law[1]

Introduction

IN HIS STANDARD work *Die Philosophie des Rechtes*, Stahl is of the opinion that the great antithesis in the area of political thought can be characterized as the opposition between the principle of the revolution and that of legitimacy. The different shades of opinion on both sides of this boundary are many. In the anti-revolutionary camp, over which in Stahl's view the banner of the principle of legitimacy is raised, the nuances are many and of many kinds, but the adherents of this principle have in common, over against the revolutionary principle, a strong founding principle, which he describes as follows:

> Legitimacy: i.e. the authority that rests on its own prestige (in a higher sense, on divine sanction) in contrast to popular sovereignty; the original unity of the state in contrast to its establishment by the agreement of individuals and by contract; organic construction in contrast to abstract democracy and a constitutional mechanism; corporate associations in contrast to the absolute atomization of citizens; order rooted in tradition versus overthrow and construction by one's own reason: These are indeed indestructible truths, they are the foundations of the structure of the state.[2]

Today, few anti-revolutionaries will find this description of the principle of legitimacy as the motto of the anti-revolutionary school of political theory to be entirely satisfactory. As a strict Lutheran, raised in the milieu of German Romanticism and German historicism, Stahl was an admirer of the Prussian system of government as represented by the personal style of government of *Seine allerhöchste Majestät* the King and still deeply committed to the hierarchy of social ranks and stations as this had flourished in accordance with Lutheran standards under the *ançien régime* in Germany. Therefore, when he felt it to be his vocation to direct politics into Protestant anti-revolutionary channels in opposition to the principle of the counter-revolutionary Restoration movement (Von Haller, Van Jarcke and others), Stahl could hardly have been expected to have conceived of his new doctrine in terms other than those of the peculiarly German and Lutheran milieu, the atmosphere in which he himself had been so fully immersed.

---

1 Dutch ed.: *Calvinisme en Natuurrecht*. Amersfoort: Wijngen, 1925. 32 pp. *Translator:* A. Wolters; *Editors:* John Witte, Jr. & Alan M. Cameron.
2 Stahl, *Die Philosophie des Rechtes* I, 1, p.548/9 (Fourth edition, 1870).

Nor is it surprising, in the fierce battle which the anti-revolutionary party in this country[1] had to wage for its principles, that the more the influence of Von Haller and his school waned, the more Stahl's political ideas found ready acceptance. The danger of the Lutheranization of our own party which lay in the reliance on the great anti-revolutionary philosopher did not escape our eminent party leader, Groen van Prinsterer. "Stahl was a Lutheran; I remained a Calvinist," Groen wrote in his well-known *In Memory of Stahl*.

However, Groen was more of a historian than a philosopher. He had probably not fully realized the deeper connection between Stahl's practical governmental politics and the philosophical foundations of his whole system; as a result, his critique of Stahl was restricted to a rather incidental opposition to the Prussian-Lutheran glorification of the personal government of the King. Added to this was the circumstance that Groen, by his own account, did not consider the relevance of Calvinism to constitutional law and political theory to be so great that he personally felt keenly the need for a complete system of constitutional law and political theory which bore a specifically Calvinist stamp. To be sure, he had a high appreciation for Calvinism as the basic genius of our national character, and he looked to this Calvinist core for the power of his principled political theory, yet this was a far cry from positing Calvinism as a political slogan.

In the 1870's with the coming of Dr. Kuyper, the Calvinist element in the anti-revolutionary party began to come more strongly to the fore, elements nurtured in the *Reveil*, and looked for its own formula and system, in theory as well as practice. Increasingly, there arose on the part of the Calvinists resistance against the Lutheran doctrine of authority, as this had been defended in the Netherlands in Lohman's work *Our Constitution*. There was an intuitive sense that the personalistic doctrine of authority could not be reconciled with the Calvinist world- and life-view. Dr. Kuyper, himself, in his broad theological elaboration of the doctrine of common grace, in his positing of the principle of sphere-sovereignty, and in his *Lectures on Calvinism*, gave a panoramic view of the possibilities which Calvinism opened up as an independent political principle. As the same time there also began outside of the Netherlands a new period of scholarly interest in Calvinism. The sociological research which achieved such brilliant results in the studies done by Elster, Wiskeman, Weber, Troeltsch, Sombart and others, illuminated in unsuspected ways the influence which Calvinism has exercised in the development of social life.

Nevertheless there continues to be a void which urgently needs to be filled. If we compare the Roman Catholic world- and life-view with the

---

1 *Editorial note* – (DFMS): i.e., The Netherlands.

Calvinist one, we can hardly escape the impression that the Calvinist edifice is not yet completed, that various wings have been left unfinished, as though in a rough draft, that the great architectonic line has not been carried through consistently, but is in many places broken through by motives drawn from the world view of others.

If we compare the Calvinist edifice with the rounded-off massivity of the Roman Catholic one, founded on the canonized philosophical system of Thomas Aquinas, in which Aristotelianism, and in part Augustinianism, has with incomparable virtuosity been fitted into the doctrine of the church and the sociological pattern of the Roman Catholic hierarchy of ranks and stations, we cannot help but note the unfinished state of the former. In this regard there is indeed a weakness in our world- and life-view. In theology we have succeeded in developing a solidly founded dogmatics, but in the other academic disciplines the development of a distinctive Calvinist perspective has in many respects lagged behind.

What we lack is a philosophical systematics which weaves the fundamental concepts of the system through the embroidery of the whole, like a colorful motive giving to each component its character and special style, and encompassing the whole in the synthesis of the great governing idea.

This lacuna also becomes evident in our conception of constitutional law and political theory. That conception presents the picture of a collection of partially unrelated concepts, a complex of notions for the most part intuitively forged in the heat of the political battle and mixed up with foreign additions from the storehouses of Scholasticism and German scholarship. Professor van der Vlugt once compared anti-revolutionary constitutional law with a Christmas tree hastily hung with gifts from many shops to surprise the waiting children. This image indeed captures to some degree the impression which anti-revolutionary constitutional law makes on outsiders. To be sure, it testifies to a failure to understand the great intuitive elements in our theory of law and the state, yet at the same time it identifies the lacuna in our systematics. Many of the philosophically gifted among us, unsatisfied with this lack of systematic conception, have already turned away from Calvinism as a world- and life-view, in order to look to Kant or Hegel to find what they believed was lacking in Calvin.

In this essay I wish to put forward with great conviction the following counter-thesis. Calvinism, as Dr. Kuyper demonstrated in his Stone Lectures, is not merely a theological system, but it contains within itself the tremendous vitality of a complete world- and life-view. It encompasses a profound philosophical life perspective, offers the basic contours of a distinctive epistemology, a distinctive theory of science, a distinctive psychology, a distinctive view of history, a distinctive legal theory, a distinctive political theory. And the root of this vitality does not reside in Calvin, but in the immeasurable depth of God's Word and, as recognized by Calvin, in a very special and pregnant sense, of divine sovereignty over the whole of creation.

Within the brief compass of a lecture I can do no more than give an overall survey of the main contours required to bring us to a philosophical systematics of Calvinist inspiration and to bring to our consciousness, also in constitutional law and political theory, the close connection between the fundamental idea and the individual doctrines.

If such an attempt is to have any chance of success, we must not begin with the sophomoric claim that we are now going to think up something entirely new. We build on the foundations laid in history, and inquire how thinkers throughout the ages have looked for a synthesis in their world- and life-view.

The historical development of the law-idea[1]

If we do this we discover that "the organon" of every well-rounded world- and life-view is a leading cosmological principle which we can call the law-idea. Already in Plato and in Stoicism we meet the notion of a law of nature (lex naturalis) which is understood as the ultimate ordering principle in the entire creation. We could compare this lex naturalis with the blueprint of an architect, who has given a special character to each component part of his design, so that it forms a beautiful harmony with the other parts and with the whole. Now this ordering principle undergirds one's entire view of life and the world, and depending on the specific meaning and specific content assigned to this principle, one's world- and life-view varies. For Plato, for example, the law-idea is idealistic, for Greek Stoicism it is materialistic. And now we observe how ethics and legal theory were also founded in the lex naturalis which orders the entire creation. In the inflexible ethics of Greek Stoicism, for example, it is essentially the thought of an all-encompassing law of cause and effect which restrains the wise persons from giving in to their sensual desires, and which admonishes them to live in the freedom of rational judgment in accordance with that natural law.[2]

This is also the case in the domain of law, where Stoic philosophy demands of the legislator to formulate positive law in accordance with the eternal principles which are contained in the causal-material natural law. This was in fierce opposition to the philosophies of Cynicism and Skepticism which denied the existence of such an eternal natural law.

---

1 *Editorial note* (DFMS): Since the appearance of *A New Critique of Theoretical Thought* the Dutch term *Wetsidee* is translated as *Cosmonomic Idea*.

2 The fact that Stoic materialism actually does not accord with Stoic morality is a point that we will not pursue at present.

The Aristotelian law-idea

The law-idea acquired an entirely different character in Aristotle. This intellectual giant was brought by his extensive biological studies to a very special law-idea, in which he managed to combine Platonic idealism with empiricism. He discovered in the biological organism a purposeful interdependence, a subservience of all the organs to a governing goal.

He identified this goal as the essence (*substanz*) of the organism and called it *entelechy* (essential goal). Aristotle transposes the Platonic ideas, of which the empirical world was only a shadowy reflection, as *entelechies* into the essences of the empirical things themselves. In his view the essence of all existence now became the motive principle of the goal which is built potentially (i.e. germinally) into matter and, towards which goal, matter according to the law of nature, strives to reach its perfection. Aristotle expanded this law of *entelechy*, which he had discovered in biology, into a universal cosmological principle of the movement of the lower to the higher, matter to form, means to the end. The crown on this entire teleologically ordered cosmic plan was God, the Absolute which moves everything, yet is unmoved itself, the first cause and the final goal of all things.

In the domain of the finite, Aristotle saw humankind as the final goal, towards which the whole of the lower creation strove according to the pan-teleological law of nature. Whatever belongs to lower levels of being, according to that law, is adapted to human needs as to what is higher. Whereas irrational nature strives towards its goal or good by virtue of the necessity of the urge created within it, the human being must do this in rational freedom. An individual cannot reach his final goal (the highest good, moral perfection and happiness) alone in isolation.

God in his plan for the world has adapted humankind to the collectivity; every person inherently has the drive to live together in society (*zóon politikon*), to reside together in *the state*. Thus the state is for Aristotle the highest, "perfect community," composed of the biologically conceived cells of nuclear family, extended family and tribe, which are all organically adapted to each other.[1]

For Aristotle, the state, as the perfect community, also acquires the character of a perfect moral organization, in which all citizens must be led to their final goal: happiness or moral perfection. Aristotle gives a psychological proof of why the state community is necessary for this moral goal. The will for him is not an *einheitliche Substanz* (unitary substance), but rather a conglomerate of rational and sensual activity. The motivation of the *activity of the will* resides in the *appetitive*, the

---
1 This conception of the state must be clearly distinguished from our modern idea of the state; it was based on (*geborduurd op*) the Greek *polis* or city community.

motivation of the *decision of the will* in the *rational* part of the soul. The rational part of the soul, put on its own, can only choose the good (the ultimate moral goal), but the irrational part of the soul can never do this, because, being interwoven with sensual matter, it can only know the criteria of pleasure and pain. Therefore the human soul is the continual battle-ground of reason and desire. If moral activity is to be guided by the norms of virtue, then a compelling power from outside is necessary to restrain the sensual activity of the will and to accustom it to the guidance of reason. Only the state, according to Aristotle, qualifies as such a compelling power. The state is consequently necessary for the attainment of a person's destination. And thus the pan-teleology of Aristotle's law-idea, which had threatened to be broken through by his doctrine of the freedom of the will, finds its capstone in the purposeful necessity of the state, which directs the will by compulsion toward the goal (the good).

Human beings attain their full spiritual destination only as citizens.

Natural law was also permeated by this pan-teleogical law-idea. Law became the formative principle of the state organism, but was itself made subordinate to the goal of the moral perfection of the citizens. Thus the Aristotelian idea of justice is automatically *relative*, it is the material of ethics, in whose service it stands as means to an end. Aristotle looks for the stability of law in this relationship of relativity to morality, in the teleological law of nature itself, by virtue of which the moving principle remains constant in the midst of all movement. The principle of *suum cuique tribuere*, one of the basic rules of ancient natural law in antiquity, is permeated by the teleological law of nature.

This basic rule is for Aristotle the objective principle of the virtue of justice in its narrow sense as the distribution of goods, by which the interest of the subject (called "desire for profit" by Aristotle) finds satisfaction. As examples of this subjective interest he mentions self-preservation, wealth and honor.

These goods are allotted to individuals by the teleological law of nature as the necessary means for the attainment of their ultimate goal. Now with reference to these goods, the virtue of justice consists in the following: in the striving of all toward those goods, everyone taking into consideration the rights of others, and doing so specifically in keeping with the objective principle of equality, which must be realized partially in accordance with a *geometrical* relationship, partially in accordance with an *arithmetical* relationship (*justitia distributiva* and *commutativa*).

In the case of distributive justice it is the evaluation of the quality of the claimant which is decisive, so that equals are apportioned an equal measure and unequals an unequal measure (of offices, honors); in the case of commutative justice, which ought to hold for the regulation of treaties and legal offenses, it is only a matter of quantitative distribution. Here the amount due to the claimant is exactly equal to the amount which had accrued to the other party from the claimant's possessions.

In accordance with these two immutable basic principles of justice (*haplōs dikaion*), to which is added the *justitia legalis*, by which the community, too, "must be given its due," the state ought, according to Aristotle, to apportion to its citizens those goods which have been assigned to them by the law of nature as a means to the attainment of their ultimate goal and which they cannot acquire individually or in the community of the family. These are therefore communal goods.

In this way it was natural that the notion of the general welfare entered the idea of justice, the notion of the good or goal which humanity must attain in the state community. As it was later formulated:

Salus publica suprema lex esto!

At this stage the doctrine of a natural law founded in the *lex naturalis* was reinforced by its combination with the power-individualism of Rome. The Romans, the fathers of an independent science of jurisprudence, looked upon law as essentially power, as the will of power. Imperialism, the drive for world dominion, considered by all true Romans to be the great goal of their state community, permeated this view of law and caused them, in distinction from the Greeks, to view law as a realm apart, distinct from ethics. Fundamentally, Rome looked upon law as a conglomeration of self-contained spheres of will, within which the citizen, the *pater familias*, was absolute lord and master. This then became what is properly the domain of private law; (this notion of power comes to expression in the vocabulary of Roman law: *patria potestas, manus mariti, dominium* etc.).

Alongside of this, and independent of it, the Roman doctrine posited a second sphere of power or will, that of the *populus Romanus*, which is public law, properly speaking. The doctrine of the will held unrestricted sway also in public law. Law was the expressed will of the *populus*, the community of *cives Romani*, and when the principate had gradually secured all power for itself as plenipotentiary of the *populus*, the rule was: *Quod principi placuit legis habet vigorem, et princeps legibus solutus est.*

The combination of this positivistic doctrine of power and will with the Stoic-Aristotelian theory of natural law in the later or Roman-Stoic school (Cicero, Seneca) and in the Roman jurists, gave rise to the remarkable conflict in legal politics between the idea of law and that of the common good. The idea of law was then represented by the peculiarly Roman power-individualism (individual freedom within the will-sphere), albeit checked and directed by the natural law of Stoicism; whereas the idea of the common good was chiefly represented by the Aristotelian idea of the good or the goal which humanity must attain in the state-community, in order that the citizens may strive after their ultimate goal: happiness or moral perfection. In practice this dualism meant simply that the idea of law was restricted to the domain of private law while the "common good" became the exclusive criterion for public law. Natural law in this restricted sense acted as limit (*Schranke*) for the legislator.

The Christian church came into the picture

At this point the Christian church came into the picture, with her doctrine of sin and grace, her view of the infinite value of the human soul and the supremacy of the kingdom of God. She was faced with the problem of formulating a response to this secular natural law. The church fathers up to Augustine wrestled with the topic. We do not find a specific law-idea in their writings. As a rule they adopted the distinction, especially prominent in Seneca, between absolute and relative natural law, according to which the former was the original natural law as this was valid in the sinless Golden Age with its liberty, equality and fraternity, while the relative natural law was natural law as it had been altered by sin (property, slavery, inequality, governmental coercion, etc.). In Tertullian we even find, generally speaking, the Old-Stoic law-idea of a law of cause and effect which governs the entire creation – a law-idea which implied the view that the essence of all things (including the soul) is matter.

Generally speaking, Christians adopted a neutral, at times even hostile attitude, to the pagan state, which they accepted as the result of humankind's sinful condition, and they proclaimed all the more emphatically the independence of the church and the freedom of the Christian's conscience.

Ambrose, the bishop of Milan and the teacher of Augustine, voiced a protest against the Stoic formulation of the basic rules of natural law: *suum cuique tribuere, alium non laedere, honeste vivere*, in which he tasted the leaven of Roman power-individualism; he sought to permeate natural law with the Christian principle of charity. Nevertheless, it was really Augustine who first ventured a bold attempt at formulating a law-idea which corresponded to the Christian world- and life-view.

In this he was far from being free of pagan philosophy. The Greek-Jewish *logos* doctrine of Philo and especially the neo-Platonic doctrine of a hierarchical emanation of the highest, absolute idea (the One) provided him with the basic material for his law-idea. However, he sought to purify this Jewish and pagan doctrine of its pantheistic features in order to permeate it in a brilliant synthesis with an idea that was so very profoundly rooted in his thought, namely the idea of the absolute sovereignty of God and of the boundary between the finite and the infinite. The neo-Platonic philosophers conceived of the cosmos as a hierarchical emanation of the One (God), in which intellect (*nous*), as the sum total of the ideas, constituted the first stage, the soul the second stage, and matter in its infinite forms the third stage. Replace in this conception emanation with creation in the Christian sense, replace the neo-Platonic *nous* (intellect) with the Philonic *logos* (the Word),[1] and you have in rough outline the content of Augustine's law-idea.

This conception of law, called *lex aeterna* by Augustine, therefore has a twofold implication:

(1) The conception of a hierarchical ascent and descent in the whole creation from the lower to the higher to the absolute unity of God and *vice versa*, in which everything has its appointed place, and the whole, as one voice, sings the praises of God its Creator, and

(2) the attribution of this hierarchical creational order to the will of the personal God of revelation, the Creator of heaven and earth (the doctrine of *providentia*).

Augustine did not entirely succeed in reconciling these two lines of thought (the neo-Platonic and the Christian-theistic one) in his conception of law. For the first line easily led to an identification of the eternal law with the being of God, so that law would be made binding on God himself; the second line, on the other hand, presupposed a boundary between the Creator and the creature, a boundary which Augustine accordingly attempted to carry through strictly in his theology (doctrine of predestination, Christology, etc.), but which was partially lost again in his neo-Platonic mysticism.

Now into this idealistic law-idea (idealistic because it assumed the supremacy of the spiritual over the material, of the soul over matter, of the idea over its concretization) is interwoven Augustine's Christian view of history, which takes as its point of departure the opposition through all ages between the *civitas Dei* (kingdom of God) and the *civitas terrena* (the kingdom of the evil one). Evil consists in apostasy from the divine Creator, from the absolute ground of being, and is therefore a negation, not a positive "being." The secular state, which is not guided by the absolute justice contained in God's *lex aeterna*, but restricts itself to the pursuit of its own temporal well-being and that of its citizens, remains enclosed in the *civitas terrena*. If the state wishes to participate in the *civitas Dei*, then it must put itself in the service of the church (by eradicating heresies). Even the secular state, however, continues to occupy a very modest position; it is situated below the church, as the lower under the higher. Consequently, it is absolutely stripped by Augustine of the all-encompassing position which it occupied as "perfect community" in the thought of both Plato and Aristotle.

The Augustinian *lex aeterna* is the cosmic plan of God's law. Humankind participates in this eternal law by means of the *lex naturalis* (law of

---

1 By the *logos* (the Word) all things were made. Cf. the beginning of the gospel of John.

nature), which is God's law as it is by nature written in the hearts of the heathen (Paul). Now it is in the *lex aeterna*, with its subjective counterpart, the *lex naturalis*, that positive law (*lex temporalis, humanum ius*) is founded.

Characteristic of Augustine's law-idea with its neo-Platonic hierarchical structure is the manner in which he bases natural law on it. Augustine gives a Christian formulation of the content of natural law by defining it as the treatment of others as one would wish to be treated oneself. For him this law of nature coincides with the *ius gentium* of the Romans and the moral law of the Jews. If this law of nature is an idea, then its concretization or shadowy reflection is found in human law, the way the body is the shadowy reflection of the soul.

Albeit in rudimentary fashion, Augustine made a distinction in their essential natures between this human law (*recht*) and morality. Law is maintained by coercion, morality is observed in freedom; law is binding when it conflicts with natural law, provided there is no divine commandment to the contrary. But his law-idea did not allow him to look for the standards of the legal order (*recht*) anywhere but in morality. For the jural (*recht*) in his thought is the concretization (shadowy reflection) of God's moral law. Augustine, like the Stoics, legitimates the harshness of positive law (*recht*), with its governmental coercion, slavery[1] and inequality of wealth, by an appeal to the relative natural law which has been altered by sin; the absolute natural law, on the other hand, the natural law of the sinless state, in his view, coincided with the Decalogue. The hierarchical ordering of the universe according to the *lex aeterna* could in some sense be reconciled with the view that the relative natural law was a lower stage underneath the higher one of the absolute natural law.

This Augustinian-Platonic law-idea also continued to dominate, by and large, the whole period of early Scholasticism. It was only forced to retreat when, after considerable conflict inside and outside the church, in the period of High Scholasticism, Albertus Magnus and his famous disciple Thomas Aquinas brought to new life the Aristotelianism which had long been condemned by the church (largely due to ignorance of the original system), and reconciled it with the church's doctrine of grace. This was a process in which especially Augustine, but also other church fathers made a contribution. Aristotle's pan-teleological law-idea was now adopted once again and clothed in the Augustinian garment of the *lex aeterna*, of which the *lex naturalis* was the subjective counterpart. The Augustinian-Platonic conception lived on only among the Francis-

---

1 Schilling has pointed out that Augustine actually bases slavery not on relative natural law, but on a hypothetical natural law. The distinction does not seem to me to be one of principle, however.

can monks, while the Dominican order adhered to the strictly Aristotelian-Thomistic line.

In time the Roman Catholic church was to adopt the philosophical system of Aquinas as canon, and to this day we find that the Roman Catholic world- and life-view is based on the solid foundations of this philosophical system, in which the architectonic line follows the Aristotelian-Thomistic law-idea in literally every part – very strongly in the Roman Catholic view of natural law. This law-idea, with its *vermittelnd* or mediating character, reconciled nature and grace insofar as natural life became the matter which was elevated by the church's sacramental means of grace to the stage of highest perfection: fellowship with Christ. Church and state no longer needed to stand in a hostile relationship to each other, as they had in the days of the early church fathers. From the time the state had been Christianized the thought arose of the *corpus Christianum*, the one body of Christ with its spiritual and secular sides, while the teleological law-idea assigned to the state a place beneath the church, as the lower under the higher.[1]

The entire ecclesiastical hierarchy of Roman Catholicism is based on this law-idea. Also the characteristically Roman Catholic division into clergy and laity could find its synthetic unity in this teleological law-idea. Just as the church by its means of grace consecrated all of natural life and elevated it to the goal: happiness, so she also reconciled the natural life of the laity with the life of grace by representing the clergy as the higher stage of perfection. The Thomistic law-idea was the philosophical embodiment of the concept of *Vermittlung* or mediation which the Roman Catholic church had pursued in its sociological paradigm since the Christianization of the secular institutions. The old distinction between absolute and relative natural law receded into the background in favour of the reconciliation of "nature and grace" that had been achieved by the teleological law-idea.

The Reformation

On this state of affairs the Reformation had the effect of a spiritual revolution. Luther broke with the Thomistic law-idea as "organon" for his world- and life-view. With this the philosophical underpinnings of the entire reconciliation between nature and grace, as the Roman Catholic church had conceived this in her sociological paradigm, fell away. The salvation of the sinner by the grace of faith alone, the central religious idea of Lutheranism, destroyed the whole ingenious system of mediation of High Scholasticism. The opposition between nature and grace became unbridgeable. It became an inexorable "either-or." And now Luther failed to seize the opportunity of giving the law-idea a new con-

---

[1] This is therefore different from the view of Aristotle, who considered the state to be the highest, perfect community, a complete ethical-juridical organization.

tent, by which he could have given to his world- and life-view a governing synthetic conception.

His point of departure was the human personality in its state of perdition and its state of salvation. The law for him acquired the incidental significance of the Decalogue and for those regenerated he attributed to this moral law a merely pedagogical function in their daily failings, and a condemnatory function with respect to the lost.

But there was in his thought no conception of a law for the life of grace, let alone for a comprehensive cosmological law-idea. In his "table talk" Luther inveighs against the slaves of the law who also place regenerate life under the law, and he compares the regenerate with fig trees, which bring forth their fruit by an inner impulse, apart from any law which drives them to it. Here lies the seed of Lutheran naturalism, which for lack of a normative concept of law can so easily degenerate into quietism. For his conception of natural law, Luther returned to the distinction between absolute and relative natural law, which had by now receded into the background. In this relative natural law – the domain of property, government and punishment – he saw especially the idea of power, God's avenging hand against sin. In this dualism of power and gracious love, of relative and absolute natural law, the unity of his world- and life-view was forfeited once and for all. To be sure, Luther attempted a reconciliation by his doctrine of the spiritual penetration of natural life by the life of grace in one's calling; he argued that the offices of the secular order are as much a divine calling as the spiritual vocation; he restored the secular state to its divine value; nevertheless, he nowhere provided a synthetic conception. His doctrine of official and personal morality, which he himself later abandoned – a doctrine which destroyed morality itself by bringing both legal and ethical ordinances under the morality of grace – is a telling example of the impotence of a world-view which lacks a universal law-idea.

Soon we will encounter the same dilemma, the same unreconciled opposition between the idea of power and the morality of grace, in the philosophical system of Stahl, which is completely built on the foundations of the Lutheran conception of personality, as this is carried through in his personalistic doctrine of authority.

The idea of power in the secular domain, the core of the irrationalistic natural law of Lutheranism, leads to a *historicism* in which history is accorded, as in Stahl, a secondary normative significance.

And here the danger looms of the absorption of the idea of right by that of might, as that can be traced, not without a shudder, in the politics of Lutherans like Bismarck and Treitschke, Von Bernardi and Kaufmann.

The Calvinist law-idea

If Lutheranism, for lack of a cosmological law-idea, demonstrates a questionable brokenness and incoherence in its world- and life-view, the unity of the Protestant paradigm is rescued by Calvin. Calvin, a more penetrating thinker than Luther, sensed the necessity of a universal law-idea. In contrast with Melanchton and Zwingli, who sought to fill the gap with speculative elements from Stoicism and Aristotle, he conceived, in his profound doctrine of divine providence and predestination, a new law-idea, differing *toto caelo* from both the Stoic law-idea and the Thomistic-Aristotelian one. To penetrate to the true origin of this law-idea we must not look for metaphysical speculations, but sense the deeply religious spirit which animated the entire grand intellectual structure of Calvin's system. The absolute sovereignty of God and the concomitant absolute dependence of all that is created is the fundamental religious idea of Calvin in distinction from the more anthropological-soteriological one of Luther.

Now we must understand this well. In itself the recognition of the sovereignty of God is common to Christendom as a whole, but there is a significant difference between recognizing the sovereignty of God in dogmatics and making it, as Calvin does, the *cor ecclesiae* and the cornerstone of his system.

In his doctrine of divine *providentia* and *praedestination*, which is so often misunderstood, Calvin gathers together what the speculative systems had understood by *lex aeterna*. But how different the pattern of thought is in the two cases. Both the Stoic and the Aristotelian-Thomistic systems were speculative. The Thomistic one presupposed a rational commonality of being between God and humankind; the *lex aeterna* in Aquinas was the divine *Vernunft* (reason), part of the being of God and therefore binding on God himself. The *ratio* of humankind participated in that of God in the *lex naturalis*. In this way, therefore, humankind was capable, in the conception of a pan-teleological law-idea, of conceiving, albeit imperfectly, the unity of God's cosmic plan after him. Accordingly the doctrine of providence in Scholasticism was a part of *theologia naturalis*, which could be understood by natural reason itself. Only in the case of the truths of grace did Aquinas insist on the exclusive competence of *fides* (faith).

Calvin in his *Institutes* takes sharp issue with this scholastic metaphysics, as he does with the fatalism of Stoicism, which carried through its pan-causal law-idea in its doctrine of the *fatum* (*heimarmene, tyche*), which governs the world-process with blind necessity. Both systems detract from the sovereignty of God, which does not brook any blurring of the boundaries between himself and the finite. There is an absolute, impassable boundary between God and creature. Calvin expresses this *boundary* in general (cosmological) terms as *the concept of law*. He does this because God in his inscrutable providential cosmic plan has ordained everything according to fixed rules; he has put his holy ordinance over everything; which, being dependent only on God's will, is not binding on God but only on the creature. No creature, nothing in heaven or on earth, can call Him to account for his deeds, but everything outside of Him is bound to His law.

Thus we find in the cardinal doctrine of Calvinism a new conception of law, of a purely religious character: A law-idea as boundary-concept (*grensbegrip*) between the infinite and the finite, the Absolute One and the creature that is in everything dependent on Him.

In Calvin's conception this law-idea is not at all given the content of a pan-causality or pan-teleology, as in Stoicism or Aristotle and Aquinas. Calvin does speak repeatedly, both in his *Institutes* and in his treatise on predestination, about God as *prima causa* in distinction from the *causae secundae*, but by this divine causality he is far from interpreting it as the natural category of cause and effect.[1] Thus he fulminates against the Stoics, who identify the *providentia Dei* with a pan-causality, thus relegating God's governing of the world to the narrow confines of an *influxus naturae*, and think that his government "drives the celestial frame as well as its several parts by a universal motion" in that they dream up "a necessity out of the perpetual connection and intimately related series of causes which is contained in nature" (Inst. I, 16,8).

God is not subject to the causal law of nature, nor to the Thomistic law of means and ends, which in essence are related to each other again by necessary causality. When we read of *prima causa* and *ultimus finis* in Calvin, this has to do exclusively with a religious turn of phrase, a terminology which expresses the absolute dependence of all that is created on the Creator.

Thus we find that Calvin conceives of law (*wet*) as a universal boundary line between the finite and the infinite.

The content of this law-idea is that of divine ordering, the ordaining of all that is created according to the unity of an *einheitlich* (unitary) and providential cosmic plan – a unity which is unknowable to our reason.

Calvin often expresses this content with the words *ordre de nature, ordo naturae, lex naturae, etc. etc.*

Formally speaking, therefore, the Calvinistic law-idea is a limiting concept, but materially it is given content from the doctrine of *providentia*, to which predestination belongs.

In the light of that doctrine, this law-idea thus comes to stand squarely opposed to that of nominalism (Occam and his followers), which like Calvin teaches a universal boundary line between creator and

---

1 This distinction is derived from Greek Stoicism (Chrysippus), which sought in this way to preserve human freedom over against the law of nature (cf. Cicero, *De Fato* 18, 41).

creature, yet at the same time bases the content of the ordering of the world on the arbitrary whim (*willekeur*) of God, completely independent of divine reason and divine wisdom, so that the essence of the law-idea is in fact itself violated (nominalism is consequently empiricistic in its epistemology).

Calvin's law-idea also stands squarely opposed to that of deism, which also posits an essential boundary between God and creature, but at the same time fails to honor the steady dependency between creature and creator that is grounded in the plan of creation.

In summary, we can recapitulate Calvin's law-idea in its thetical and antithetical significance in three elements:

1. *formally* it posits a universal boundary between the being of God and the being of creation.
2. *materially* its content is that of ordering, the product of God's wisdom in his providential cosmic plan, in which it also finds that unity which reason cannot comprehend.
3. *materially* it also posits in Augustinian fashion a continuous dependency between *Creator and the creature*. (God's upholding of creation is a continuous creation.)

The implications of this religious law-idea are decisive for every part of the reformational world- and life-view. In this context we can only mention in passing its fundamental significance for epistemology and philosophy. Calvin's law-idea is transcendental, drawing a boundary line. Consequently it also imposes on reason the boundary of the law. This means a verdict against *speculative* metaphysics of every kind, which time and again bases itself on a speculative law-idea. Human thought is bound to lawful fields of vision,[1] which are given to us and each of which also delimits a field of formal categories and essential characteristics.

There are two kinds of relationships in the world of creation: the absolutely dependent creation relationship between God and his creation, a relationship which also encompasses human reason; and the relationship, founded in the first one, between reason and its objects. The first relationship encompasses the domain of the *kosmos;* the second that of the *logos*. Thought does not create its *Gegenstand (object)*, but the *Gegenstand* is given to thought in the field of vision, which only comes to our consciousness by intuition (*schouwend*). This field of vision is made by thinking into a field of thought, and in this field of thought the *Gegenstand* becomes object (*task*) insofar as it must be determined here in a system of relations (e.g. the system of nature). In this way every epistemology based on Calvinist principles should occupy a middle ground between the Thomistic-Aristotelian speculative epistemology, on the one hand, which presupposes a rational community of being between

---

1 *Translator's note:* Dutch: *wetmatige gezichtsvelden*.

God and the rational creature, and the critical idealism of Kant, on the other hand, which presupposes the sovereignty of the *logos*, and therefore makes the *Gegenstand* dependent on the creative function of thought. Calvinist epistemology must be a *transcendental* realism. We cannot elaborate on this point here.

In the meantime, to explain the significance of the Calvinistic law-idea for natural law, we must point out a second distinguishing characteristic of this conception.

Sphere-sovereignty as a philosophical consequence of the Calvinistic law-idea

Calvin's law-idea grounds its unity on the providence of God, which is unknowable to reason. God has ordained everything according to his decree and also guides everything for our salvation and the glorification of His name.

Beneath the boundary line of the law, however, we behold God's wisdom as a multiplicity. As Calvin himself expresses it:

> Because on account of the sluggishness of our understanding God's wisdom appears manifold (or "multiform" as the old translator renders it), ought we therefore to dream that there is any variation in God himself, as if He either may change his counsel or disagree with himself? (Institutes I, 18,3)

Calvin's law-idea, consequently, is pluralistic. It must be because it is transcendental-realistic, and by virtue of its non-rational character it cannot reduce the given multiplicity in God's inscrutable providence to a unity for the sake of human reason. In his law or ordinance, God's wisdom encompasses the entire creation, but the lawfulness of nature is one thing, that of history another, and that of the normative fields of law (recht) and morality still another. Under the boundary-concept of the law, the cosmos unfolds into a multiplicity of sovereign spheres. Separate ordinances, founded only and exclusively in divine sovereignty, hold for each of these spheres. Reason may not force the many spheres of these sovereign ordinances into a speculative unity, as Aristotelian-Thomism does in its entelechistic law-idea, or as Stoic metaphysics does in its law of causality.

But in our actions, too, our will must conform to the specific ordinances which God has laid down for them.

Calvin distinguishes between *voluntas* and *praeceptum Dei*. It is not simply the difference of hidden and revealed will of God that is given in this distinction; rather, it is *in nuce* the normative sphere that is placed as sovereign over against all the other law-spheres.

Here lies the point of connection with the important doctrine of sphere-sovereignty. The elaboration of this doctrine is undoubtedly still rudimentary in Calvin, but thorough reflection on his transcendental law-idea will necessarily lead to its complete elaboration.

This principle of sphere-sovereignty must, however, not be misunderstood. It must not be conceived as a sovereignty of finite subjects within certain spheres of life. Such a conception compromises God's honor.

Sphere-sovereignty is merely the sovereignty of the law-spheres distinct from each other. God's sovereignty is resplendent in the sovereignty of his ordinances. That is also why the Calvinistic law-idea opposes a personalism which construes the unity of the ordinances organically as a harmony in the personality, essentially seen by Stahl as an act. Law is not the essence of personality, as both Lutheranism and Thomism hold, albeit in different ways, but it is the sovereign will-ordinance of God, which as such is imposed on and placed above human personality. It is purely heteronomous, or rather theonomous, and not theonomous-autonomous (Aquinas and Stahl), much less an autonomous lawfulness of the will (Kant).

Across the board the Calvinist rises to the defence of a purely theonomous law-idea, which unfolds itself in a multiplicity of purely theonomous ordinances. He is intransigent in his opposition to every attempt to make human reason or the human will a co-legislator, because such an attempt invariably finds its origin in a speculative view of a community of reason or will between God and creature.

The fierce attack on heteronomy by Kant and Schopenhauer need not disturb the Calvinist.

For Kant understands by heteronomy merely the heteronomy of the necessity of nature, and he comes to the autonomy of the will in order to secure moral freedom over against natural causality. This is the result of positing the sovereignty of reason. But Kant has no appreciation for Calvin's religious law-idea with its pluralistic character. Those who accept this law-idea, together with its implication, sphere-sovereignty, do not need the autonomy of the will in order to secure the normative field of morality and law over against that of the lawfulness of nature.

Natural law in its twofold significance

Once we have understood sphere-sovereignty as a theonomous principle, the way is cleared for an investigation of the relationship of Calvinism and natural law. We distinguish two senses of natural law.

1. Primary natural law, i.e. the nature of positive law or the totality of essential properties which every legal order as such must exhibit if it is to lay claim to the name of law. Natural law in this sense does not provide the criterion for an evaluation of the positive legal norms as to correctness or incorrectness. Primary natural law only expresses that which is the unchangeable essence of every legal order according to the divine ordinance, which is independent of our will.

The field of investigation is here formed partly by the formal essential characteristics of law in distinction from the other spheres of ordinances (law is the normative ordering of the community, whereas morality concerns the regulation of attitudes), partly by the material essential characteristics of the concrete concepts of law (property, contract, misdemeanor, guilt and punishment, law and bylaw etc. etc.).

To this area also belongs the doctrine of governmental authority, which, in whatever form it manifests itself, is inherent in every legal order.

2. Political natural law, i.e. the totality of the normative principles to be observed in law formation, in order that this may take place in accordance with the divine idea of law.

First a remark about the connection between primary and political natural law. The erroneous conception of the older theories of natural law, from Grotius to Kant, was threefold:

(i) The distinction between both kinds of natural law was neglected, but a rationalistic code of political natural law was presented as primary natural law.
(ii) In connection with this latter point, the relationship between positive law and natural law was an embarrassment. The most consistent school declared positive law that did not accord with political law to be non-binding; the more moderate school did not give positive validity to political natural law until it had been taken up into positive law.
(iii) The changing character of positive law was not taken into account.

The significance of primary natural law
The Calvinist law-idea must consistently lead to the distinction of the two kinds of natural law. To begin with, anyone who accepts this law-idea cannot concede that positive law does not rest on immutable ordinances. Law is in essence not a creation of human beings, but has been ordained by God to have its own essential character. Law by its nature has authority, because it is an ordinance of God for the regulation of the human will. Law is therefore normative in nature. It holds its subjects responsible for the observance of its norms. Calvinist legal theory can therefore only be normative legal theory. However, such a normative legal theory is something quite different from the modern theories of legal sovereignty of Kelsen and his school.

It differs from the Kelsenian view both in point of departure and in method and object. The point of departure for Kelsen is that of critical idealism, the sovereignty of reason. Reason creates the *Gegenstand* of legal theory. It accomplishes this creative work functionally; it may not accept anything "given," but in pure legal theory it must reduce everything to functions of thought, *a priori* conditions of our legal knowledge. Such a legal theory is misleadingly formalistic: it does not appreciate the essential character of multiplicity; it can comprehend all legal phenomena in their juridical essence only according to their forms, which lack content. Its real object is only the logical method. For that reason it commits the second mistake of making law according to its formal concept into a quasi-logical task. For us that logic is only the "organon" of thought, but law, both in its formal concept and in its essential character, is given to thought in intuitive consciousness. Law for us is a closed field of vision with its own formal and essential character. For us the given *Gegenstand* determines the method; the method does not create the *Gegenstand*. It is for that reason that the object is different for us than for the neo-Kantians.

When we define law as the heteronomous-normative ordering of community we have only delimited the *Gegenstand* formally. It is only after this *actio finium regundorum* that the most important task of primary natural law begins: the investigation of the essential structure of the various legal concepts. The unchangeable essence of property law, for example, includes complete title for the establishment of rights to the object of ownership (the unity of material law). A positive legal order can regulate this kind of law in many ways, but it cannot violate its essential character without abolishing ownership itself. Whether the latter can be necessary in certain cases is a question of political natural law (expropriation, etc.)

Such a view of ownership as being grounded in natural law is of course something quite different from the Roman Catholic view that everyone by nature has a right to acquire property and that *private* property is an institution of natural law. The Roman Catholic view of natural law deduces such a right out of the teleological order of nature, in which instruments are fitted to human personality as means to an end. However, this view places the right not in the domain of primary natural law (in ancient times a slave could not acquire property, yet this was a regulation of positive law), but in that of political natural law.

Another example of primary natural law in a material sense is the well-known adage *pacta sunt servanda*.

The positive legal order can regulate contracts in many and various ways, but it cannot violate the essence of the *pactum*, namely that it cannot be arbitrarily broken by one of the parties, without abolishing the very idea of contract as immediate legal ground of agreements. A Bolshevist government that would decree for example, that laborers might unilaterally break a legal labour contract when that is in their interest, would decree a juridical non-entity, because its decree would be in conflict with primary natural law.

The core of primary natural law, however, is the doctrine of legal authority which we must here subject to a closer, if very brief, scrutiny.

The doctrine of authority as central doctrine of primary natural law

The doctrine of governmental authority has always been considered the foundational tenet of anti-revolutionary political theory. However, it can lay claim to this significance only if it is considered as direct consequence of the anti-revolutionary doctrine of authority in general. Now anti-revolutionary political theory does not at all constitute a consistent unity. There are chiefly two views which stand in sharp contrast to each other, and which I would like to designate as the *personalistic* and the *transpersonalistic* views.

The personalistic doctrine of authority has appeared in the course of history in various forms. It received its sharpest formulation in the voluntarist doctrine of Roman law. The church fathers gave this doctrine a theocratic twist. In Scholasticism it received the support of nominalism (Occam, Gerson), which denied the existence of an eternal natural law and simply conceived of positive law as the decree of the government. In the course of time the personalistic doctrine of authority would find its scientific elaboration in the sovereignty theories of Bodin, Graswinckel, Salmasius and Filmer.

In modern times the opposition between personalism and transpersonalism in the anti-revolutionary doctrine of authority has come to a head especially in the antithesis between the Lutheran and the Calvinist conception. Our concern at present is especially the connection between these different conceptions and the fundamental idea of Lutheranism and that of Calvinism as world- and life-view.

We have already seen that Luther's fundamental idea was to distinguish between human personality in its state of misery and in its state of redemption. In modern times it is Stahl who builds on the foundations of this idea. Taking as a point of departure the Christian idea of the personality of God, he saw throughout creation a propensity for personality, and now is diligent to carry through that idea of personality in all parts of his system. Motifs from Schelling's romanticism play a tangential role in this intellectual edifice,[1] but the basic line of Lutheranism is maintained throughout. Now, according to Stahl, earthly authority must also exhibit this propensity for personality. Authority everywhere is, according to the image of God, *personal* authority. Consequently the

---
1 For example the places where Stahl sees the essence of personality in the act. Compare also Faust's words: *Im Anfang war die That* ("in the beginning was the act").

authority of the government is also personal. Hence Stahl's defence of monarchy as the best form of government: "In monarchy the state becomes personal."

Of course Stahl grants that this personal authority does not belong to the government *suo iure*, but only by virtue of divine delegation "by the grace of God." Nevertheless it is a personal, albeit public, right of government to issue legally valid commands by its own authority *according to its title*, independently of the positive legal order (the laws of the land).

In Stahl's view, the state is a *moral realm*, just as the kingdom of God, in the highest sense of the word, is a moral realm. Now, just as in the kingdom of God the personal dominion of the personal God holds sway, so also in the state a personal dominion has been established over human beings. In the state the dominion is exercised by an organ of the state and it is most natural that this dominion should also have its center in a natural personality (the king). Here too, however, we are dealing with a dominion according to moral intellectual goals and here too men ought therefore to obey in freedom, because the order placed over them at the same time also *constitutes their own true essence and will*. Since the state has a real and free power of dominion, albeit on the basis of a moral-rational *ordering*, that dominion according to Stahl has two components, namely (1) the personal authority of the government, or state authority (*imperium*), i.e. the power which is exercised by men, and (2) the factual dominion of the law (*lex*).

Stahl conceives the relationship between these two authorities (government and law) to be organic. Both have a title of their own and are equally original, but they are also mutually dependent on each other. (The law regulates the personal sovereignty in the state, but that sovereignty is itself the foundation and condition for the law). For that reason the subjects must also obey (always within the limits of the law) *the personal will of the sovereign*, not because he executes what the law prescribes, but because he is king. Stahl therefore rejects the ancient adage *princeps legibus solutus est*, but on the other hand is a forceful advocate of the personal regime of the sovereign alongside the law. This whole authority scheme is confused; those who accept a personal dominion in the state involve themselves in contradiction if they also assume an equally original factual authority of legal norms.

Lohman and Van Idsenga, the two Christian-Historical theorists on authority in this country, are therefore more consistent than Stahl insofar as they maintain the principle *princeps legibus solutus est* in a juridical sense, and assume only an ethical duty of the government to protect the legal order.

Opposed to this personalistic doctrine of authority stands the Calvinist one. The latter can best be studied by way of the reformational doctrine of the church. The Calvinistic law-idea works itself out here more clearly than anywhere else. Whereas Luther allowed for a personal regime of the princes in the church, Calvin does not tolerate any personal authority in the church of Christ. Here only the law of God may rule, that law which Christ uses instrumentally to rule his church.

Ecclesiastical authority, according to the Calvinist church order, does not just find its limit (*Schranke*) in the law of God – no, that law is the foundation and exclusive norm for the entire system of church government. And we see Calvinism, with the supra-personal concept of authority in ecclesiology as a point of departure, struggle also in the doctrine of governmental authority for a theory which is in accordance with its supra-personal law-idea. In Calvin himself a remarkable development can be detected in this regard. In his humanistic period, when he wrote the commentary on Seneca, a work of his youth, his position is still completely the personalistic one of Roman law, which looks for the characteristic feature of the sovereignty of government in the maxim *princeps legibus solutus est*. But in one of his last works, his commentary on Samuel, the reformational position on law has broken through in all its clarity. Now we read that the ancient maxim *princeps legibus solutus est* is the slogan and hallmark of the government of tyrants. Only God is sovereign, only He, the almighty One, is not bound by laws, but all earthly governments have been subjected to the law of God and the human laws *which are based on* it. We can properly appreciate this conception only when we observe that it is coupled with an irrevocable rejection of the Scholastic doctrine of popular sovereignty.[1] Calvin rightly considers this later doctrine to be irreconcilable with his own position on law, which ascribes sovereignty only to God, but not to individuals (whether government or the people).

Considered in this way, Calvin's doctrine of authority can have no other meaning than this, that all authority on earth finds its foundation in God's law, more specifically in the ordinances of God which have been instituted for the special sphere in which that authority is exercised. For the moral authority in the relation between parents and children these ordinances lie in the moral law of God, for the juridical authority in the relation between government and subjects they lie in God's appointment of the legal order itself. The ordinances of the legal order are normative according to their divine nature, because they are

---

[1] It is well-known that in this matter the Reformed monarchomachians (Beza, Hottomannus, Languet, Althusius, and others) ended up on a mistaken, uncalvinist track, in that they believed, in conflict with Calvin's law-idea, that they could combine the doctrine of divine sovereignty with the Scholastic doctrine of popular sovereignty.

directed to the rational will and have simply been imposed on that will by God. The Lutheran doctrine of authority is nothing more than the old voluntarist doctrine in theocratic dress. The Calvinist doctrine, on the other hand, is based on a theonomous natural law. It belongs pre-eminently and centrally to primary natural law, because it is rooted in the essence of law, viewed in the light of the theonomous law-idea of Calvinism. Law, according to its divine nature, is normative. The authority of government is an authority of office which is exclusively rooted in the essence of law, and is therefore also bound to the entire positive legal order insofar as this is founded on primary natural law. The authority of government is therefore a supra-personal authority of a supra-personal normative legal institution (the government)[1].

Since the Calvinist doctrine of authority is rooted in primary natural law, it provides by itself alone a guarantee against transgression of official competency with reference either to natural or positive law. But Calvinism places the whole of life under God's law, and must therefore also provide the guidelines for *law-formation*. The formulation of positive law, too, may not be left to the arbitrary decision of a governmental institution. For every measure that it must take, for every norm that it must issue, the government must place itself before the face of God and before his holy law. The burning question is simply this: what is the nature of that law which God has established for government?

Political natural law in the light of the Calvinist law-idea and of the principle of sphere-sovereignty

With this we make the transition to political natural law. The existence of such a political natural law is disputed from various sides. On the one hand we have the neo-Hegelian school (Kohler, Berolzheimer and others), who in common with sociological positivism (Comte, Durkheim, and their school) reject out of hand the existence of ideal standards for law-formation (the evolutionistic standpoint of *Kulturfortschritt!*). Furthermore we meet, in the neo-Kantian circles of the Baden school (Windelband and Rickert), the relativism of Radbruch and Jellinek, who deny the existence of an objectively valid idea of law, and who allow the subjectivity of conscience to choose from among the possible standpoints within political natural law.

In Christian circles, finally, the vast majority of those who still hold to a natural law seek to found this in the moral law of God. Such is the

---

[1] Surely we need hardly demonstrate the difference between this doctrine of authority based on natural law and Krabbe's doctrine of legal sovereignty (*rechtssouvereiniteit*). Krabbe takes as point of departure the psychological consciousness of what is just (!) (*rechtsbewustzijn*) and ends up via pseudo-psychological ways in the old revolutionary majority principle. The worst of it is that this doctrine makes an explicitly political claim. Accordingly, we would have to classify it under political natural law. And the result of his theory is that Krabbe ends up in positivism!

case for Stahl[1] and Roman Catholic natural law theory, and essentially also for the neo-Kantian Stammler.

Political natural law then in fact becomes social *ethics*. This is strongly evident in Stammler, who desires, in neo-Kantian manner, a purely formal natural law "with changing content" and who constructs this entire natural law on the basis of Kant's idea of the autonomous moral (or pure) will. Stammler attempts to distinguish his idea of law from ethics by combining the idea of moral personality with the concept of the "community of freely willing individuals." But it is already evident in the first deductive step that the purely ethical domain has not been left behind. Stammler incorporates his community concept in the purely ethical category of "the neighbor."

All schools of this latter type, which want an ethical natural law, can be comprised under the name *ethical personalism*. They take their point of departure in the moral personality of a person as *Selbstzweck* (end in itself).

As an illustration of ethical personalism in natural law, as this is found among the Lutheran anti-revolutionaries, we may take the following quotation from Stahl's major work *Die Philosophie des Rechtes*:

> Law and morality, the two sides of the total human ethos, consequently stand in a bond of unity. For it is the same ethical (or world-economic) ideas which constitute the content of law and the content of morality, insofar as the latter refers precisely to the conditions of common existence. ... We can express it plainly and definitely as follows: law as much as morality is based on the Ten Commandments, and only on them.[2]

And if we desire an expression of ethical personalism from the neo-Kantian side, we should read what Stammler writes in his last chapter about Christ's teaching on love. In his view the commandment "love your brothers" is in the first place a rule of objective *richtiges Recht* insofar as it norms the mutual relationship between human beings as "neighbors."[3] We see here the characteristically ethical standpoint in political theory, which is of a peculiar character in Stammler only in the sense that he does not relate it to God's ordinance in the moral law, as do Stahl and the Roman Catholic natural law theorists (Cathrein, Von Hertling, Von Pesch, Beyssens and others), but to the sovereignty of practical reason.[4]

Many objections may be raised against this ethical standpoint, both in the area of immanent and in that of transcendent critique.

---

1 Stahl rejects only the name of natural law, but not its essence.
2 *Die Philosophie des Rechtes* 2, I, p.206.
3 *Lehrbuch der Rechtsphilosophie* (1922), pp.203-204, note 6.
4 It is noteworthy that Stammler is ecclesiastically Lutheran.

From the point of view of immanent critique the untenability of the ethical standpoint can be demonstrated as follows:

1. It is generally conceded nowadays that there is a difference in *concept* between law and morality. However, both orders are taken together under the higher order of ethics and it is claimed that morality and law express the same ethical norms of the moral law, only in formally different ways: morality, subjectively as *regulation of attitudes*, law, objectively as external regulation of the *community*. Considered in this way, therefore, the thesis would only apply to a purely formal difference in modality. With this thesis, however, ethical natural law theory comes into conflict with itself insofar as it must concede that morality does finally require something quite different from what law requires (love and respect between husband and wife, the sacredness of the bond of friendship, love of neighbor, etc.)[1]

    The difference between law and morality is therefore not just a formal difference in modality, but *omnium consensu* a material difference in *nature* and *object*. There is an entire sphere, in a formal and material sense, which the legal order must keep inviolate. But if the material difference is granted, how can the same moral law be a guideline for both morality and positive law?

2. In connection with this difficulty we observe that ethical personalism takes a most dangerous turn in its theory of political natural law.

    Its idea of the jural is restricted to a guideline for those departments of private and criminal law where the material to be regulated also exhibits a moral side (marriage, property, law of succession, etc.) and declares the whole of public law to be purely *formal* law, in which the criterion of the common good must apply (Stahl). This dualistic doctrine of the idea of justice versus the common good, and *vice versa*, is then often shored up by a theocratic-personalistic doctrine of authority, according to which the public legal restraints which are imposed on individual freedom are binding as positive law on the basis of the will of the government ruling by the grace of God.

    This is indeed another smuggling in of the old dualism in Roman law between the idea of justice and the common good. The "common good" however, has at all times been the slogan of state absolutism, from Hobbes via Rousseau to the German Hegelian doctrine of state-sovereignty. As long as we allow the common good to stand

---

1 In Roman Catholic natural law (theory) the difference between law and morality is characterized (defined) as a difference in *Gegenstand*. The highest principle of the natural moral law is: "do good; avoid (*laat*) evil." Under this "good" falls both community good (object of justice) and the individual good (object of morality). This unity scheme is however purely formalistic. The Roman Catholic synthesis is in principle found in its teleological law-idea.

unreconciled alongside the individualistically conceived idea of justice, we allow the vulture and the dove to live in the same cage. Refuge is sought in the ancient *Schrankentheorie*, which is indeed the theory of arbitrariness, because an "ethical" idea of justice is not an idea of justice, and the "common good" is no criterion.

3. The ethical standpoint in political natural law consequently gives rise to a very concrete threat to the rights and freedoms of citizens, and in general to the maintenance of the divine idea of justice in political theory. Once again we will give a number of examples by way of illustrations.

First of all, a few from the practical politics of the Lutheran Conservative Party make it clear that various politicians of this persuasion have themselves realized the impossibility of an ethical politics. So now, for lack of a *genuine political natural law*, they publicly and shamelessly proclaim the naked idea of power.

It was Bismarck, in private life a convinced Lutheran, who spoke the notorious words: *Wenn ich nicht lügen soll, kann ich nicht auswartiger Minister sein.* ("If I may not lie, I cannot be foreign minister.")

In the *Reichstag* session of December 12, 1900, the Conservative Chancellor, Prince Von Bulow, stated:

> The politician is not a censor of morality. He is only to safeguard the interests and rights of his own country. I cannot engage in foreign policy from the standpoint of pure moral philosophy; Prince Bismarck did not do this either.

The conservative Rümelin writes in *Ueber das Verhältnis der Politik zur Moral*:

> In one word, the whole chapter concerning the duties of love, and with it the major part of all morality, does not apply to States. They must have recourse not to the love of others, but the love of self, to the maintenance and development of their own power and welfare, and if one wants to use the rather inappropriate word egoism, well, then egoism is the basic principle of all politics.

The Christian periodical of the Conservative Party, *Die Kreuzzeitung*, expressed itself in a similar vein in 1885:

> The true Christian must aspire to rid himself or herself of all egoism, whereas a body politic which would seek to observe this principle, especially in foreign policy, would perish without fail.

Who does not think, upon reading such statements, of the ancient conflict in the bosom of Lutheranism between the morality of love and natural law, for which Luther gave the pseudo-solution of distinguishing official and personal morality?

In unreconciled juxtaposition to such expressions of the idea of power stands Ludwig van Gerlach's demand for an ethical politics, and Stahl's idea of a Christian state, though the formulation of the latter is restricted to a number of *desiderata*, which the Calvinist can certainly not accept without qualification.[1]

Nor should we forget that the same *Kreuzzeitung*, which in 1885 had so bluntly advocated the idea of power in politics, in 1902 defended the demand of state socialism for a right to labour and did so on the basis of the idea of the Christian state, which it asserted ought to take the moral law as its foundation!

The foregoing examples of the precariousness of an "ethical politics" will perhaps be dismissed with the remark that a few snowflakes do not make a winter.

In that case I refer you to an ethical-personalistic utterance from an entirely different quarter, namely that of the individualistic neo-Kantianism of professor Rudolph Stammler, who in his *Lehre vom richtigen Recht* (p.59), in all seriousness asks himself why the legal order could not also regulate, for example, friendship relationships with reference to bequests and the law of succession. What confusion ethical personalism creates in natural law theory is evident, finally, in our own country, where not only Tolstoyan Christian anarchists, but also serious scholars like Professor Heeres, rise in opposition to the military draft and defend as a matter of principle the idea of non-resistance on the basis of God's moral law.

The same confusion is even more pronounced in the endless debates which have recently been held about the moral permissibility of the repeal of Article 40 of the Salary Resolution – an Article which was untenable from the point of view of both natural and positive law.

We will come back to these last two practical questions below.

The transcendent critique of ethical personalism provides a natural transition to the Calvinist standpoint on political natural law.

This standpoint can be approached only in terms of the Calvinistic law-idea and the theonomous principle of sphere-sovereignty which we discussed briefly earlier.

If we deny the applicability of God's moral law with respect to political natural law, our reason for this must not be to now put human standards in its place. No, political natural law must also rest on a divine law, but here we are dealing with a law *sui generis* with its own ordinances. The difference between political natural law and the moral law of God is twofold: (1) the former only has the character of a complex of normative *principles*, while the moral law offers a complex of entirely

---

[1] For example, Stahl, in his *Der Christliche Staat*, p.314, makes confession of the Christian religion a requirement for the holding of public office and the participation in national defence.

concrete and well-defined *norms*; (2) political natural law covers the sphere of community order while moral law covers that of the entire inner life in the relationship between God and humankind, as well as the external life in the relationship between individuals and their neighbors.

Ad primum. The character of *principle* which is proper to political natural law belongs to the nature of the jural itself. For the positive legal order is by its nature a *temporal* order. It enters into all the vicissitudes of temporal conditions and places. Consequently it cannot be a code of eternal and concrete natural law norms which positive law would only have to "transcribe," so to speak. The latter was the position on dogmatic natural law theory from Grotius to Kant, which had emancipated itself from divine sovereignty. No, God avails himself instrumentally of the institution of government in all its normative organs (including the administration of justice), in order to institute a positive legal order in accordance with the essential nature of a given time and place. The totality of these divine normative principles of natural law constitutes the material content of the Calvinist idea of the jural, which in its formal character is a community-idea. We must therefore conceive this idea of justice in the light of the reformational law-idea, and its corollary the principle of sphere-sovereignty.

According to this latter principle, God's moral law is distinct from political natural law. The idea of justice in political natural law manifests its sovereign character very clearly in the reformational *doctrine of retribution in criminal law*. Paradoxical as it may sound, this doctrine of retribution is the bulwark of the reformational principle of sphere-sovereignty as applied to political natural law, and in this capacity it is also the bulwark of our political rights and freedoms, as we shall see.

The doctrine of retribution is the big obstacle for ethical personalism, and is consequently rejected by most ethical theories. One cannot base the doctrine of retribution on God's moral law, the summary of which is the love for God and one's neighbor. From his spiritual-ethical standpoint, Luther did not know how to deal with the divine commandment to punish homicide with death.

It is well-known how he initially sought a way out through his doctrine of official and personal morality. As Christians, he argued, we must love our neighbor, but in the office of government God's moral law requires us to hang the criminal, to burn him and to break him on the wheel! However, quite apart from the impossibility of two kinds of morality, what commandment of the moral law here justifies Luther's thesis? Stahl, too, is at a loss with respect to the doctrine of retribution. He cannot and does not want to disregard God's explicit commandment. Therefore he introduces a construction (based on his personalistic doctrine of the moral kingdom) in which the personal dominion of God cannot tolerate a rival dominion which is sovereign (*selbstherrlich*). The latter must be cast down. But where is the appeal to the Decalogue to justify this construction, if by Stahl's own account the entire legal order rests only and exclusively on it? Stahl is here inconsistent with his point of departure; he in fact makes an appeal to the Lutheran idea of power. As a result the doctrine of retribution becomes an absolutely foreign component in a system based on an ethical view of natural law.

The consistently ethical standpoint must reject the doctrine of retribution. The Roman Catholic natural law theory, with Thomas Aquinas at its head, in fact does this, adopting a *relative* theory, in which punishment, insofar as it is necessary for the attainment of the good of the community (the common good),[1] is justified in terms of its *goal*. But such a relative theory is not just of *incidental*, but of *fundamental* significance; it necessarily presupposes the relativization of the whole idea of justice. We need only read what Aquinas and more recently Cathrein writes about the *goal of the state*. The goal of the state, completely in line with their pan-teleological law-idea, is at the same time the moving cause and the essence of the state. The moving cause is the circumstance that prevents individuals from attaining in isolation the temporal goals which are subordinate to their ultimate goal, but allows them to do so only in the community of family, tribe and finally the state as *perfect* community. The cause of state formation, consequently, is "the insufficiency, the inadequacy, the need for fulfillment of the isolated individuals and families".[2] Now the goal of the state lies in this moving cause, which Cathrein seeks to advance as the provision of all those goods which the individual and the family cannot attain in isolation. The Roman Catholic teaching summarizes this goal of the state in the Aristotelian concept of the "common good." Included under this common good are also legal security and legal protection, which liberal natural law from Thomasius to Kant had considered to be the only task of the state.

And then the common good is defined as "the totality of conditions that are required in order that all members of the state can to the maximum extent possible freely and spontaneously attain their true earthly happiness".[3] In these *Bedingungen* two components are distinguished: the *Rechtsschutzzweck* (the goal of legal protection) and the *Wohlfahrtszweck* (the goal of welfare).

---

1 Augustine's ethical doctrine of natural law had already preceded Scholasticism at this point. Augustine, too, holds a relative theory of criminal law.
2 German: *"das Ungenügen, die Unzulänglichkeit, das Ergänzungsbedurfnis der isolierten Individuen und Familien."*
3 German: *"Gesammtheit der Bedingungen, die erforderlich sind, damit nach Möglichkeit alle Glieder des Staates frei und selbsttätig ihr wahres irdisches Glück erreichen können."*

Now Cathrein immediately concedes that the concept *Bedingung*, and therefore also the concept of "earthly well-being," is relative. The legal goal of the state is therefore also subject to this relativity, and with this the relativization of the idea of justice altogether, in line with Aristotelian Thomism, is complete. Amidst this relativity Roman Catholic theory may still hold fast to a number of individual rights, but this is no more than a weak dam against the rising tide of the incalculable influence of the common good, which (as we saw earlier) cannot be checked by the assertion of the partial validity of moral law for the state. As a matter of principle, relativization of the idea of justice is a continual danger for the rights and freedoms of citizens and institutions. The situation is no different in the case of the natural law theory of Krause and Ahrens, who consciously break with the old dualism of the idea of justice versus the common good. They give a comprehensive cultural content to the idea of justice itself, but at the same time reduce that idea to a *subservient value* below the ultimate goal of humankind (the idea of culture or humanity). In this way law (both in concept and idea!) becomes "the organic whole of those conditions dependent on the activity of the will which serve to realize the overall purpose of human life, and of the individual essential life goals that are contained therein."[1]

Krause and his school make a distinction, following Aristotle, between the immediate and the ultimate goal of the state. And in his legal theory it is only a corollary of his speculative entelechical law-idea that a sphere of divine ordinances, namely law, is put as a lower subservient sphere below the other law-spheres (morality, the spheres of culture, etc.). Human reason sets itself up as judge of the value of divine ordinances. But thereby it violates God's sovereignty.

This is evident once more from the position which the ethical personalist Krause adopts with reference to criminal law. He does not want to have anything to do with the doctrine of retribution, in whatever form it is put forward. Law in a jural sense is not an absolute idea, but a subservient value, a value in service of personality and, in a higher sense, in service of the cultural idea of humanity. An absolute law of God, which threatens the sinner with eternal punishment, thus becomes an absurdity.

Punishment can justify itself before the forum of reason only as a means to the *improvement* of personality or, in a higher sense, of humankind. In this way the so-called idea of humanity violates the righteousness of God. Moreover, the tender mercies of the wicked are cruel. For the moment righteousness ceases to be an absolute law of God, hu-

---

1 German: *"... das organische Ganze der von der Willensthatigkeit abhängigen Bedingungen zur Verwirklichung der Gesammtbestimmung des menschlichen Lebens und der darin enthaltenen einzelnen wesentlichen Lebenszwecke."*

man law is made unstable, and the door is open for the absolutism of the idea of humanity, the tyranny of the common good!

A glance at history can teach us what this means. The spiritual father of the idea of humanity is the philosopher Christian Wolff. Well, Jellinek, who himself does not recognize an absolute idea of justice, has to admit in his *Allgemeine Staatslehre*,[1] that it was precisely Wolff's doctrine that gave rise, in its practical application, to the greatest danger to individual freedom.

It now becomes plain why earlier we called the doctrine of retribution the bulwark of our political freedoms. For that doctrine of retribution in its reformational sense of heteronomous law (*heteronoom-wettelijken zin*) (it is God who commanded that crime should be punished retributively!) testifies to the absoluteness of the idea of justice. It is also a living testimony to the divine truthfulness of the fundamental reformational principle of sphere-sovereignty.

For it was not in his moral law, which forbids murder, that God commanded the government to mete out punishment as retribution, but in his divine natural law, and it is not for any human being to be the arbiter between moral law and a legal stipulation of natural law!

The burning question is now, where does government find the basic ordinances which constitute political natural law, and what are those principles?

Our answer is as follows: those principles are many, indeed we do not even know them all as yet. Here too there is a progressive revelation of God through the ages. Thus the principle that the human personality ought as such to be legal subject (*rechtssubject*) and never legal object (slave) has only prevailed after an arduous struggle. The early Christian church did not yet recognize this principle, but defended slavery on the basis of relative natural law in our sinful state.

God has revealed himself on this point partially in his word, partially in the law of righteousness which by nature is written in the hearts of humankind, partially also in the legal customs as they have been formed in history (this latter source of knowledge, however, may never, by reason of its subjectivity, be considered an independent source of knowledge, not even in a secondary sense; for it must always be tested against the revealed law of God).

Within the brief limits of this essay we cannot begin to enter into a complete investigation of all the principles of political natural law. We will therefore conclude with only a few remarks of a general nature, illustrated by a number of practical issues.

On the basis of God's law itself we assert with great conviction that the only normative guideline for government is political natural law,

---
[1] Third edition, 1919, p.243.

comprised in the idea of the jural; and that this idea of the jural is absolute, transcending human evaluation. We have described this idea of the jural in a formal sense as community-idea. This community-idea, however, must again be tested against the law-idea. When this is done we observe that Calvinism has always occupied a middle position in its social scheme between liberal individualism and socialistic state absolutism. That middle road is only possible for Calvinism because its community-idea is in turn a supra-personal law-idea; it does not take its point of departure in human personality or in the common good of society, but in God's legal ordinance, which has given a place to every person, with an independent purpose and an infinite value, in the midst of a society in which the community-idea must be realized.

Let us illustrate this point with an example from Calvin's own works. Calvinism acknowledges social inequality as an ordinance of God. Calvin points out repeatedly that the predestination of God's sovereign will is revealed in this inequality. And this predestination must not only be understood from an individual perspective in the sense that God destined A to wealth and B to poverty, but first of all as a supra-personal legal ordinance, which government may not meddle with in bad faith. However, Calvin immediately adds to this: God is the supreme owner; over against God individuals only have their possessions on loan, and they must use these possessions to the honor of God according to his ordinances.

This holds not only in ethical life (engaging in works of charity), but also in economic life (investing one's talents in a God-pleasing manner), and in legal life (contributing to community costs according to one's means). Thus we see in Calvin a view of property which ascribes the *dominium supereminens* to a sovereign Creator who has ordained inequality among individuals, and on that account looks upon private property at one and the same time as a principle of political individual natural law while also imposing a social legal duty. In this way the unity in the idea of the jural between private and public law is also maintained. Property is not an absolute power of will (the conception of Roman law), nor a right which only belongs to the community (the social conception). No, it is a supra-personal legal function, in which the individual and the social element are reconciled.

What this means, therefore, is not the *Schrankentheorie*, which sets apart the authority of government and individual private law, and puts them in opposition to each other, but a harmonious, supra-personal unity in God's ordinance, in which private and public law are reconciled.

The Calvinist doctrine of natural law requires that government, for every measure which it takes, for every legal directive which it issues, identify a positive basis *in natural law*, in God's ordinances for communal life. Since in our view political natural law only comprises a complex of normative *principles*, the natural law principle must in each case be related to a certain complex of facts, and the *necessity* of the legal measure to be taken must be demonstrated. The primary principles of political natural law (for example, taxation according to means; punishment as retribution for actions qualifying as misdemeanor which violate natural law; social regulation of property law; regulation of marriage on the solid basis of the divine legal institution, according to which marriage is an enduring and complete life's community between one man and one woman, which excludes dissolution by agreement; protection of life and other legal goods of citizens against injustice or natural hazards which threaten the community order; maintenance of the legal subjectivity of the human person) are of course of an absolute character. The so-called hypothetical principles, however, are based on these absolute principles; these must also be related to a divine ordinance, but they only emerge from the application of an absolute principle to a particular complex of facts.[1]

These last mentioned principles of political natural law are of course of a *hypothetical* character. They are formulated as follows: "If the factual situation is such and such, than the legal order ought in principle to make provision in the following manner." The government has only the freedom of reasonable judgment in the manner of working out the principle (the requirement of efficiency in law formation), but the principles themselves are fixed in the divine natural law.

Ad secundum: and then the reformational principle of sphere-sovereignty, in its application to (political) natural law, guards inexorably against state absolutism.

Once again, sphere-sovereignty must not be seen as a personal sovereignty of an individual or institution over against the state. This naive conception runs aground on every observation of reality and is in principle false, since it attacks God's honor. No, only from the point of view of a supra-personal law does this principle provide a genuine divine bulwark against state absolutism. It is the sovereignty of law-spheres which the government must honor. That is why there must be no interference by government in spiritual life and the spiritual organization of the church, which stands directly under the law laid down for it by Christ and the apostles, and there also must be no church as secular state within the state, by which the unity of the legal order, and therefore the legal order itself would be done away with.

That is why there must be no intervention by the government in the ethical law-sphere which stands directly under the authority of God's eternal, unchangeable and completely delineated moral law, but also no

---

[1] Thus the derived principle of the state's individual duty of defence emerges from the absolute principle of retribution (here taken in a broader sense) applied to the factual situation in which no authority other than the individual state possesses the means to oppose a breach of international law.

withdrawal of external life in the sphere of natural law in the community from legal regulation(s) under the pretext of the demands of conscience.

This last point requires a brief commentary. We here touch upon two controversial areas:

(1) the relationship of the government to so-called "public morality" and
(2) the attitude of the government over against so-called conscientious objections.

Ad primum. Does not the interference of the government in public morality show most clearly the untenability of the principle of sphere-sovereignty, which forbids the blurring of boundaries between moral and (political) natural law? We are brought somewhat closer to the answer to this question if we take a look at private law, where the *Civil Code* (*Burgerlijk Wetboek*) leaves to the so-called free discretion (*freies Ermessen*) of the judge the judgment of whether or not an agreement is in conflict with public order and good morals (cf. article 1373०, article 1356 sub 4o of the *Civil Code*). We find the same principle also in article 1690 of the *Civil Code*, article 1 sub 3,20 of the law of April 22, 1855 S. 32 etc. etc.). Stammler has already pointed out that such criteria as equity and good morals are not ethical criteria, but exclusively criteria of *richtiges Recht* (just law).

We are therefore standing here with both feet in the domain of what Calvin, following classical dogmatics, calls the *usus politicus* of the law.

This view is increasingly being accepted by our students of civil law (especially in the so-called *Freirechtsschule*, although the latter's fundamental negation of the objectivity of (political) natural law does put a deep chasm between them and Calvinism), and appears to us to be, for reasons we need not go into at present, the only correct view.

Indeed, the old maxim – *de internis non judicat praetor* – is still valid for the judge in its full meaning: he must have objective criteria of *justice*, and by "good morals" in our positive law is meant nothing more than just such a criterion!

Matters are different in public law. We should not let ourselves be confused by the rather infelicitous terminology "public morality" (compare also the curious phrase "moral bodies" in our *Civil Code*). When according to our anti-revolutionary principle the government must guard against prostitution, pimping, public drunkenness and the giving of public offence in other ways, then it does not do so as upholder of God's moral law – a task which God has not assigned to it and which it is also not *capable* of fulfilling – but only as upholder of natural law. For prostitution and pimping, which degrade a person from legal subject to legal object, are attacks upon (*political*) natural law, just as public attacks on decency violate the public order in society, and thereby God's ordinance.

We do not wish to be misunderstood. We do not propose a separation of justice and morality in the form of "watertight partitions" between the two, to use the telling phrase of the Christian-Historical statesman van Idsenga. We acknowledge the tremendous influence of Christian morality on our legal life, which, without the support of morality, is doomed to perish despite the best provisions of the law. Nor are we going to split human activity into a moral, an economic, a juridical activity, etc. The activity is a unity, but the law-spheres are distinct, and government only has one of these spheres, namely natural law, as its domain.

Ad secundum. Calvinism has always in its historical development championed the freedoms of the people. The declarations of human and civil rights of the American constitution may have been partially influenced by ideas of the French revolution, but the fundamental character of these "declarations" is a Puritan-Calvinistic one (cf. Kuyper, Hundeshagen, Troeltsch, Jellinek and others). At the same time Calvinism does not conceive of these "freedoms" as a freedom of personal choice, but as a lack of competency of the legal sphere in areas where other ordinances of God (laws of thought, moral law etc. etc.) govern life immediately. Therefore, with regard to the question to what degree government must yield to conscientious objections (against military service, etc.), it would be a mistake, in principle, to take our point of departure in the *conscience* of a person, as the modern ethical tendency does (over against professor Herring and others).

Calvinism with its heteronomous law-standpoint can only approach the question in terms of the law of God; its solution is fundamentally *an objective*, not a subjective one. As to the question of conscientious objectors, for example, the Calvinist asks what God has ordained in his natural law. He accepts the state as an institution of God, as the institution of the legal order, and accepts God's ordinance that injustice must be resisted with the secular arm. As long as no institution of a league of nations, which stands above the individual states, has sufficient means of power at its disposal to protect the international legal order, every state is individually called by God to protect its rights in every area (including the area of trade) – in the first place to protect its integrity as legal institution against attacks from outside, but also to reject the personalistic principle of non-intervention and to resist assaults on the integrity of other states, insofar as it is called by God to do so by virtue of its position of power.

Over against this explicit ordinance of God, which stands on the same footing with the right to taxation, the government must *in principle* not yield to conscientious objections. The conscience which has scruples on this point, errs; God cannot contradict himself when on the one hand he commands us in his moral law to love our neighbor, and on the other hand commands government in his natural law to punish the murderer with death. Nevertheless, government can look for the *modus* not to violate the erring conscience in individual cases, to the degree that this is possible, and with due observance of national security.

In this connection we also want to make a few remarks about the notorious question of whether or not the repeal of Article 40 of the *Salary Resolution* was morally permissible.

The discussion of this thorny issue, both within parliament and outside it has become entangled in a thorn bush of confusion by bringing this question to the area of ethics.

Assuredly, we do not wish to invalidate the moral law for the *person* of government. Every cabinet minister as well as every member of Parliament is conscience-bound to the full moral law of God. Not a jot or tittle of that law, according to the words of Christ, is inapplicable to him or her. A person will have to give an account before the judgment seat of God for every vain promise. But by framing the question in this way we do not get a step closer to solving the question of whether or not the repeal of the notorious Article 40 is permissible. For this question lies exclusively in the area, of (1) positive law and (2) natural law. Once it has been established that article 40, *iure constituto* and *iure constituendo*, was a monstrosity, then it must not put the wagon of government on a dead-ended track once more by raising the ethical question.

The government as institution is *supra-personal* and finds its only guideline for the formation of law in (political) natural law. Actually this thesis is so self-evident! Can we seriously bind a later administration for ethical reasons to a promise that is untenable in terms of natural and positive law, and thus reinforce injustice with an appeal to God's moral law? To ask the question is to answer it.

* *
*

With this we take our assignment, within the limits of a lecture, to be completed. Our purpose was to give an overall survey of the Calvinist law-idea as the synthetic-architectonic line of our world- and life-view, and to show that in a proper carrying through of this law-idea, the alpha and omega of which is the absolute recognition of divine sovereignty in every sphere of the world and life, there lies for political theory: the origin and guarantee of our constitutional freedom.

The modal structure of jural causality[1]

Introduction

IN SPITE OF the fact that the problem of jural[2] causality has already been the subject of extremely thorough and penetrating special studies for nearly 150 years, it has not lost any of its scientific appeal today. Those who take the trouble to work through the vast literature dedicated to the subject will make the slightly disconcerting discovery that legal science has not managed to come to a consensus about it. The well-known statement of Immanuel Kant, that "jurists are still in search of their concept of law," could with complete justification be equally applied to the problem of legal causality.

Legal causality – a basic concept of Legal Science

If, as I wish to argue in this presentation, legal causality indeed belongs to the *basic concepts* of legal thought, it may not be that surprising, for the fundamental concept of law shares with all general basic concepts a dependence on a philosophically determined theoretical view of the experiential world. A critical analysis of such a theoretical view shows that it is ultimately determined by the supra-theoretic, religiously rooted starting point of thought.

---

1 The Dutch text appeared as a reprint of a paper presented at a meeting of the Royal Dutch Academy of Sciences, Literature Department, in 1950: "Overdruk uit Akademiedagen III," published in Amsterdam by the N.V. Noord-Hollandsche Uitgeversmaatschappij. The same article appeared in: "Mededelingen der Koninklijke Nederlandse Akademie van Wetenschappen, Afd. Letterkunde, Nieuwe Reeks, Deel 13, No. 5. Amsterdam, N.V. Noord-Hollandsche Uitgeversmaatschappij." It contains references to literature and jurisprudence also incorporated in the Encyclopedia of Legal Science (A-Series. Volume 10).
Translator: D.F.M. Strauss; *Editor:* Alan M. Cameron.

2 *Translator's note:* Dooyeweerd's philosophy is sensitive to the distinction between what is *ontically given* and what is the result of human intervention – be it through reflection or through giving positive form to ontic possibilities. We therefore prefer to translate the Dutch term "juridisch" with the word "jural" in order to convey more directly the sense (of the modal aspect) implied in the term "juridisch" rather than using the more common English terms "juridical" or "juristic." His own language use, however, is not consistent. Later on in this article, for example, he uses the Dutch equivalents of "biological," "ontological" and "psychological" where he actually had the ontically given "biotic," "ontic" and "psychical" phenomena in mind.

The two dominant theories

In the current situation there are two main contrasting theories. They are the *conditio sine qua non* and that of *adequate causation*. In particular, the latter again breaks down into a number of variants. Due to criticism, other conceptions have by and large collapsed.

Since both these prevailing theories have frequently been analyzed in the literature, I want to restrict myself here to a very brief indication of the way in which those formulating them have understood the problem of jural causality and the manner in which they have tried to bring it to a solution.

They have their shared basis in the so-called "philosophical" concept of causality, as it was developed in the previous century by the well-known British thinker, John Stuart Mill, in his *System of Logic*. Its essential formulation (Mill provides more than one circumscription) reads: "by the cause of an event one has to understand the totality of changing conditions, both positive and negative, which in their cooperation invariably and unconditionally result in the mentioned event." In particular and in a very positive sense Mill had a natural-scientific connection in mind, understood according to the classical deterministic concept of a natural law.

Conditio sine qua non (von Buri)

Pursuing this so-called philosophical concept of causality the German criminal jurist, von Buri, now developed the theory of *conditio sine qua non* in the sense of a so-called doctrine of equivalence. Since all cooperating conditions within the causal relation are equally necessary, no one of them could be eliminated without at the same time canceling the effect, and since determining their greater or lesser quantitative operations transcends human cognitive ability, he formulated the statement that all conditions are equal in value. By proceeding from this thesis, already to be found in Mill, von Buri then, in his second formulation, also concluded that every *conditio sine qua non* may separately be viewed as a cause, when all the others are given. This naturally flows from criminal legal considerations, since in the latter only human actions are considered as causes.

Adequate causation (von Kries)

While von Buri wanted to conceive conditions and consequences in their full concreteness, requiring theoretically that one should always in retrospect arrive at a judgment of necessity, von Kries, the physiologist and epistemologist from Freiburg, laid the foundation for the theory of *adequate causation* based on an analysis of the concept of the objective possibility concerning the prognosis of a causal course of events.

Where, in the *ex ante* perspective, not all conditions are known in their concrete particulars which may, in the future, lead to a specific consequence, and where one could know of only a few of all the factual particularities of the latter, it is not possible to come to a *judgment of necessity* but only to a *judgment of possibility* with respect to the causal relation. In doing this one should *generalize* the unknown (or presumed as unknown) conditions and particulars of only the subsequently occurring consequences.

Von Kries sharply distinguishes the concept of objective possibility from that of subjective probability as it was already employed by von Buri in the doctrine of fault in order to establish the required degree of determination of the intentionally envisaged causation. The concept of objective possibility is based upon the concept of leeway ("room to play") as developed in the calculus of probabilities.

The concept of an absolute possibility, which, in some cases allows for a calculation of the probability in a fraction, is totally useless in jurisprudence. As an alternative, von Kries developed the concept of the relative possibility, or rather that concerning the "condition that in general serves to enhance the effect." Such a generally enhancing *conditio sine qua non* then is called the *adequate cause* of the effect.[1]

The "typical causal course" (Traeger)

Though, in principle, totally different from the conception of *adequate causation*, the so-called "typical causal course" appeared often to be confused with the former. In the latter case the foundation of objective possibility is given up. In its stead the experience of a certain number of similar cases serves as the basis of the probability proposition. The following example given by Traeger may explain this difference (cf. his *Der Kausalbegriff im Straf- und Zivilrecht*, 1904:170):

> A, who has never been taught to fire a gun, shoots and kills B from a distance at which even an experienced shooter would be unlikely to hit the target.

According to the theory of the relative possibility, when both circumstances mentioned are incorporated in the calculation of chance, A has adequately caused the death of his victim. After all, his shooting is a generally enhancing condition of the effect, irrespective of how small the absolute degree of possibility of hitting his victim might have been. In this case the theory of the "typical causal course" would not acknowledge an adequate causal relation, since the causal process occurred quite abnormally.

---

1 Thus, for example, through the eccentric position of the point of gravity of a dice with six sides, the chance of a specific throw (normally one out of four), for which the "room to play" should be considered to be equal in an absolute sense, could relatively be increased. The degree of absolute possibility could then be expressed with the fraction 1/6.

There are two reasons why this difference of opinion concerning the doctrine of *adequate causation* is of particular importance for criminal law: (i) in the first place, one does not have the supporting tool of statistics; and (ii) the comparative material one has to work with comprising a concrete complex of conditions is relatively small in most cases. Von Kries pointed out that only when the comparative material is massive does the outcome of the doctrine of the *typical causal course* approximate that of statistical calculation.

Distinct from these two conceptions of *adequate causation*, which, in the case of most representatives of this theory, would be found alongside each other and sometimes even in combination, opinions divide sharply with regard to the question as to how the basis of the possibility or probability judgment should be determined in a more precise way. Three questions arise:

1. What are the factual ("ontological") elements that may be considered to be given and that may, consequently, be excluded from the generalization? For example, if a slight strike against someone's head may be considered the adequate cause of that person's death, does the fact that *ex post facto* it turned out that the deceased had an exceptionally thin skull have to be taken into account, or is abstraction from this condition required?

2. Which knowledge of natural laws and other rules that determine the factual course of events (von Kries mentions nomological knowledge) has to be taken into account as a basis for the calculation of the probability?

3. What degree of probability is required in order to speak about adequate causation?

Concerning the second question, all supporters of the doctrine of adequate causation agree that the totality of nomological knowledge of humankind has to be taken as a basis and not the lesser knowledge of the actor or only that of a normal human being. On the other hand, with regard to the first question there exists substantial disagreement. This is not surprising, since the choice of an ontological basis for the probability judgment is theoretically arbitrary, that is to say, as long as one wishes to safeguard the doctrine of causality from normative perspectives.

Von Kries prefers to assume as a starting point for criminal law the "action at fault." His intention is to understand "fault"[1] in a purely descriptive "psychological" sense. It implies that one then should only consider that knowledge of the circumstances a person possesses while

---

1 *Editorial note* (AC): The Dutch "schuld" as with German "die Schuld" can be translated either as "fault" or "guilt." In English-speaking Common Law jurisdictions "fault" is usually reserved for civil wrongs (torts) and "guilt" for criminal wrongs. Dooyeweerd uses "schuld" in this essay to refer to both types of wrong (i.e. to both

committing the deed, or that he or she could have had, considering the capacity of that individual to observe and to assess. This is known as the "subjective prognosis."

The "objective ex post prognosis" (Rümelin)

In opposition to this Rümelin defends the standpoint of the so-called "objective ex post prognosis" (*objective nachträgliche Prognose*). All circumstantial particulars present at the time of the deed should be taken into account, even if they may become known after the occurrence of the effect, for example through the investigation of a specialist.

Other Considerations

Finally Traeger taught that neither the subjective knowledge of the person committing the deed, nor knowledge of the circumstances only acquired afterwards should serve as the required basis. Only those facts accessible to, what he calls "the most insightful human being" (*einsichtigsten Mensch*), should form the basis. Still others are satisfied with the ontological knowledge of a "normal" human being.

Concerning the third question: "which degree of probability is required?," by and large only vague indications are given by authors – opinions which in practice make an appeal to the "value judgments and deliberations of the will in practical life." Only the theory of the "generally enhancing condition" manages to provide here a properly thought-through theoretical criterion.

Although the doctrine of adequate causation was recommended to legal science by von Kries and his followers owing to the fact that the theory of the *conditio sine qua non* in certain instances would lead to consequences that are contrary to one's intuition of what is just, the express aim nevertheless, was to safeguard the theory itself from all normative viewpoints.

As we have seen, the philosophical basis of the theory of the *conditio sine qua non* is not given up. In response to the criticism of von Buri and his followers, i.e. that the question concerning adequacy does not belong to the doctrine of causality but to the doctrine of *imputation*, it is repeatedly pointed out that this criticism confuses the concepts of "objective possibility" and "subjective probability."

Continued reflection on the problem of jural causation

In 1928, in an article entitled: *The problem of jural causality in the light of the cosmonomic idea*,[1] I had already opposed the above described ways in which the dominant theories approached the problem of jural

---

civil and criminal delicts) and it has been translated as "fault" used in a broader sense not specific to any particular category of legal wrong.

1 *Editorial note* (AC): "Het juridisch causaliteitsprobleem in het licht der wetsidee," (1928) 2, Anti-Revolutionaire Staatkunde, 21-121.

causality. I came to the conviction that this issue fundamentally involves a problem of structure, and as long as one proceeds from a view of reality which conceives of the latter as something structureless, it is not even possible to state this problem properly.

Since my perspectives in this regard in the areas of both philosophy and the special sciences have now matured, I would like to use the opportunity provided during my time in the Academy to focus once again upon the jural causal relation and shed light on it from the angle of my structural theory which in the intervening period I have fully developed and articulated.

The antinomy in van Eck's approach

The appearance of the dissertation of D. van Eck, *Causality and Liability for Effects in Criminal Law* (2 Vols., 1947, University of Nijmegen), serves as a special motivation and justification for reflecting anew on this theme because this author reached the conclusion that the genuine questions concerning causality do not belong to the domain of systematic reflection in criminal law. According to him the attention centered in the theory of causation upon the doctrine of the person committing the deed formed an impediment to the construction of an elaborated doctrine of liability conforming to the requirements of law. Criminal law should not be concerned with the cause-effect relation, but only be interested in the liability for effects. Consequently, the recommended radical therapy is to ban totally the whole problem of causality from the theory of criminal law.

In spite of this intention, it turns out that the recommended therapy is less radical than it appears to be.[1] For in his treatment of the factual connection between the deed and its effect, required by accountability, the theories of causality – that of the *conditio sine qua non* and *adequate causation* – which were expelled through the front door, were invited back in again through the back door. They were only required to leave behind the tag of theories of causality. The effect is that this dissertation, which in other respects is quite meritorious and carefully elaborated, is permeated by a remarkable antinomy. This antinomy springs from the fact that the author proceeds from the prevalent conception which claims that the question of causality does not evince any normative facet. This implies that in the determination of a causal relation one is never allowed to apply a normative criterion. The truly praise-worthy guiding idea of his study is his rejection of a naturalistic-causal mode of thought in the theory of criminal law, serving his emphasis on *anti-normativity* as the central concept of the so-called objective side of a punishable fact.

---

1 Kohnstamm pointed this out in an article that appeared in the *Journal for Criminal Law*.

This guiding idea is opposed to the rejected naturalistic conception of the person committing the deed. Nonetheless, as a consequence, the above-mentioned antinomy manifests itself in a strict *either/or* relationship between the doctrines of causality and that of accountability.

In order to do justice to the doctrine of accountability, the problem of causality had to be banished from the domain of criminal law. But since this attempt was not successful, the position taken by the author forced him once again to incorporate the predominant theories of causation, stripped of all normative viewpoints, in his doctrine of accountability.

We have here an antinomy holding the entire domain of juridical thought captive and beyond that all those other disciplines investigating reality from the perspective of an aspect with a normative structure. This antinomy concerns the generally accepted prejudice, rarely critically questioned, that causal explanation and a normative mode of viewing reality are mutually exclusive. This opposition then is linked with another one, that between "is" and "ought," – pure factuality and normative evaluation. Using some examples, I now want to demonstrate that this actually involves a prejudice that cannot stand up against the test of undeniable states of affairs.

Four examples

1) A burglary is undoubtedly a social fact with many aspects. However, it is totally impossible to determine this fact without applying legal norms. Jurists proceed by saying that, in a case like this, it involves a so-called *material delict* where the causing of a specific effect belongs to the constitutive elements of the legal definition. But the effect also cannot be determined without applying legal norms. It can only exist in an infringement of a property right, which is only capable of being caused when someone not possessing a thing unlawfully withdraws it from the rightful owner with the aim of unlawfully laying claim to it. This whole legal fact, in all its concrete jural details, is normatively qualified throughout. Every attempt to relinquish these normative realities in determining the so-called *Tatbestand*[1] of this damage to property is doomed to be unfruitful. This *Tatbestand* can never exist purely in a psychically willed physical taking away of something or other which would, in its reality, fall outside the normative jural field of view. It is possible for a person to steal something without raising as much as a finger, for example, when it is arranged that another person commit the deed on behalf of that person. When abstracted from the normative jural aspect, the *taking away of something* is a mere combination of words without specific meaning. Only legal objects can be intended in theft. And the concept *legal object* cannot be understood in an a-normative way.

---

1 Factual state of affairs.

2) Let us consider another example, this time taken from the domain of civil private law.[1] The owner of a house sells it and hands it over to the buyer. Recording this contract in the public registers, or, as held by P. Scholten, concluding the prior business agreement (and only at that point in time concluding it in the relation between the buyer and seller),[2] presupposes that the seller really was the owner. Without any doubt we are here confronted with a factual social event, which inherently displays a many-sided relation between cause and effect. Within the *jural* aspect of this event the transfer of property implies a change in the factual legal state of affairs. At this level an explanation is just as much required, similar to the psychical explanation required to explain the emotional shock aroused by hearing an approaching bombardment, or to the physical explanation of the transformation of heat energy into mechanical energy.

In this example I have done something quite unusual in modern legal science. I have extended the question concerning causality to also include those changes in legal life which completely conform to positive legal norms without causing, in a legal sense, any damaging effect. In doing this, I have brought the issue of causality within the same perspective as that mentioned in the previous example.

After all, the relation involved in a factual agreement or legal conveyance concerns that of a *legal ground* and its *legal effect*. Normally this relation, as a purely normative one, is presented in sharp contrast to the genuine causal one as something purely factual. The assumption is that the first-mentioned relation would be completely determined by legal norms, whereas the second-mentioned one, on the other hand, would be completely determined by natural laws, viz. a-normative rules of experience. However, this line of argumentation completely ignores the fact that a concrete transfer of property belongs to the *factual side* of legal life, and, consequently, cannot, as such, embody an "ought" in the sense of a claim simply posited by a legal norm. Obviously, the legal order specifies the rule according to which the transfer of property can take effect. But a particular transfer of property is not in and of itself a norm, or even an abstractly defined condition in the norm concerning the legal effect, since it is a factual legal event which has, in its turn, its jural cause in an obligatory agreement. It is a subjective legal fact, similar to a killing or a theft.

---

1 *Translator's note:* Dooyeweerd distinguishes between *civil* and *non-civil private law*. The latter concerns the *internal legal competence* of those societal institutions and organizations *distinct* from the state, whereas the former relates to the legal protection of the domain of *personal individual freedom* in inter-individual legal intercourse in a differentiated society. Relations on equal footing between societal collectivities also belong to the domain of civil private law.

2 Which, according to Dutch civil law, causes the change of ownership.

In the meantime the factual side and the norm-side of legal life remain indissolubly related to each other. This implies that no single legal fact, irrespective of whether it concerns a lawful act, a delict, or a so-called objective legal fact, such as a strike of lightning, can be empirically established apart from legal norms. Not even the strike of lightning can be so viewed, because, as an objective legal fact, it is not a purely physical phenomenon, but a possible condition for the occurrence of legal effects. And this objective legal fact could only be such in dependence upon specific subjective legal relationships, for example, concrete property rights, the relation between those insured and the insurance company, etc.

An objective legal fact is therefore always a *dependent* legal fact. In its legal consequences it is dependent upon subjective legal relationships. And since the latter cannot be determined apart from legal norms, the same applies to the former. At stake here, is a subject-object relation belonging to the *jural structure* of this legal fact.

3) I now select a third example, in this case derived from private insurance law. On December 6, 1939, a German ship, carrying coffee from overseas, received an official navigation order to alter its set course. This change directed it through a dangerous ice area. On January 10, 1940, this blockade-breaker was damaged so severely that the crew sank it as they abandoned ship, causing its contents to be lost. In the decision of November 28, 1941, the *Reichsgericht* had to address the question whether the loss had been caused by the crew or by the dangerous ice, or possibly by a combination of both. It was impossible to avoid this question, since, as a rule, loss caused by the crew and that caused by the sea were independently insured. Furthermore, the claim for payment resulting from peril of the sea, owing to the addition of profit in the mentioned insurance policy, was 188,000 German marks higher than that which could have been claimed on the basis of damage caused by the crew. That the loss was caused by the war was implied in the order to change direction – which order, legally viewed, the captain had to obey. This change of direction did not, as a matter of natural necessity, in any way cause the ship to encounter the dangerous floating ice.

The captain misjudged the danger of the ice, without being at fault in the legal sense of the term.

The *Reichsgericht* decided that even when, based on the insurance agreements, the "adequate cause" cannot be sought in the peril of the sea, but instead is sought in the danger of riot, the misjudgment of the captain has to be seen as the decisive *proximate* cause, since it "gave the course of events its definitive direction, making the accident inevitable." And this cause belongs to the category of "peril of the sea."

Regardless of the way in which the complementary application of the doctrine of the proximate cause and its motivation by appealing to the "code of sea traffic" and reasonableness are viewed, *neither* the concrete facts, *nor* the causal relation in question could have been determined without a legal standard. Damage caused by the war, an incorrect assessment of the danger of sea ice by the captain, the sinking of the ship and the damage caused are not natural facts. The causal relation here evinces a duality of *possible* legal constructions that cannot be ignored by the judge, because there were two possible causes of damage.

4) The fourth and final example is once again derived from private insurance law. According to article 291 or of the Dutch *Commercial Code (Wetboek van Koophandel)*, loss covered by insurance includes loss caused by water, loss caused through damage or theft during the extinguishing of the fire, as well as loss caused through the partial or total destruction of what is insured as the result of a superior's order so as to prevent the fire that had arisen from continuing. In this case it is clearly incorrect to speak of a natural causal relation, even in the sense of a possible connection.

The factual nature of loss intended in this example could only be established within the context of legal relationships. Apart from this legal context, it is not possible to detect any causal connection among the summarized facts. In this case even the facts themselves disappear. If it is said: "the fire is after all factually a condition *sine qua non* of the loss caused by the water, the property damage, the theft and the destruction as an effect of the superior's order," this statement could only be meaningful if the expression *conditio sine qua non* is understood in a normative legal sense, and is not, as is usually the case, associated with a natural-causal connotation. After all the expression *conditio sine qua non* is just as multivocal as the term causation or causal relation.

It is precisely this trap of multivocality that misleads jurists when they believe that the theory of *conditio sine qua non* expresses nothing more than a self-evident truth that is, in a logical sense, the only possible doctrine of causality. Thus, in the second example given above, the transfer of property was the *conditio sine qua non* for the transfer of property, without leading any one in this context to attach a natural causal meaning to the concept of *conditio sine qua non*.

The persistent prejudice concerning causal and normative perspectives

How then, is this persistent prejudice concerning causal and normative perspectives to be explained? In my work *De Wijsbegeerte der Wetsidee (The Philosophy of the Law-Idea)*[1] and various other publications, I have shown that this is the outcome of a religious ground-motive which since Kant is known as the motive of *nature* and *freedom* that has taken modern scientific thinking captive since the Renaissance. The

---

1   *Translator's note:* This work appeared in a translated, revised, and extended form under the title: *A New Critique of Theoretical Thought*. The English text used the term *Cosmonomic Idea* as translational equivalent for *Law-Idea*. This work forms part of the *A-Series* of Dooyeweerd's Collected Works – Volumes A1, A2, A3, and A4 – currently being published by *The Edwin Mellen Press*.

ground-motive has a dialectical character. This means that it is constituted by two mutually exclusive motives, entangled in an absolute, central religious antithesis. Philosophical thought rooted in this ground-motive is successively driven into polarly-opposed directions. The freedom-motive, embodied in the modern humanistic personality-ideal, is aimed at the emancipation of the human personality from the bondage of heteronomy. Humankind claimed unrestricted autonomy within the domains of scholarly reflection, morality and religion, finding its only foundation in human reason. This freedom-motive called forth the modern nature-motive, propelling scientific thought in the direction of complete control of empirical reality and emancipating the prevailing view of nature from the grip of faith in supra-natural influences.

Causality in the deterministic sense of the natural science-ideal

Driven by this motive of an autonomous control of nature, philosophy forced itself upon the modern natural sciences. Since Galileo and Newton, it has developed a new, purely functional concept of causality in terms of a new concept of natural law, which, as such, was completely unknown to Greek antiquity and the scholasticism of the High Middle Ages. Initially it was solely concerned with the demonstration of a functional coherence between all phenomena of nature, superseding the earlier conception regarding the difference in principle between what does and what does not transcend the level of the celestial position of the moon. For this reason abstraction from the individuality-structures[1] of reality is required by this approach. The functional concept of causality thus acquired, to the extent that the state of scientific reflection at that time was reliable, remained that of material energy-operation, or whatever other phrase one would use to describe the same concept. Given the fact that, at this stage, notions such as quanta and Heisenberg's relation of uncertainty were lacking, this concept of causality possessed an unmistakably deterministic character. It was rooted in the conviction that the concrete phenomena of nature could be dissolved into a system of lawful relations, leaving no room for the play of individuality, in spite of the necessity of introducing a merely statistical concept of law since the development of the kinetic theory of gases.

In the meantime this philosophy, under the influence of the above-mentioned ground-motive, elevated the new scientific method to the level of a universal model of thought that, insofar as it was consistently carried through, left no room for the autonomous freedom of humankind. The deterministic form of the natural-scientific concept of causality now was extended to the theoretical idea of a universal law of causality determining all phenomena irrespective of their inner nature and structure. The theoretical view of reality constructed along these

---
1 *Translator's note:* See Glossary.

lines completely abandoned the architectonic structural design of reality. It aimed at a *continuous* world-view in which the discontinuity of the modal aspects and individuality-structures would be conquered by sovereign thought. In the *lex continui* of Leibniz one finds this desire in its classical expression. Mill's formulation of the so-called philosophical concept of causality was also completely determined by this classical science-ideal.

The obstacle of freedom

Only one obstacle stood in the way of this science-ideal: the problematic relationship between the physical and the psychical. Pre-Kantian metaphysics identified this issue with that concerning the relationship between "body" and "soul." After subjecting the "bodily" world completely to the mechanistic-causal perspective, the issue of whether the validity of the law of causality also applies to the human "spiritual life" became a burning question. At this point the freedom-motive openly came into conflict with the nature-motive and its inherent tendency to govern everything deterministically. It gave the contest between determinism and indeterminism its modern face.

Kant located this struggle in a different context. In his *Critique of Pure Reason* he denied the possibility of freedom within the domain of *theoretical metaphysics*. Instead he transposed it to the realm of practical reason. The concept of causality is now seen as an *a priori* category of the understanding, which, in its scientific validity, is limited to empirical phenomena (both physical and psychical) as they are given in space and time. These phenomena are co-ordered by the category of causality into an "objective world of experience." The autonomous freedom of the human personality emerged as a practical idea of reason, that should be completely divorced from the sensory nature since it belongs to the supra-sensorial realm of the "ought." In this domain the categorical imperative has its validity for the moral will. It could no longer find asylum in the "empirical world," identified with "sensory nature."

Along with this demarcation between nature and freedom the exclusive opposition between is (sein) and ought (sollen), causal explanation and normative evaluation was introduced. For Kant it coincided with the opposition between science and rational faith. And even though post-Kantian freedom idealism attempted to resolve this tension along dialectical lines in order to re-unite nature and freedom, within the domain of science it was accepted as an indubitable dogma. It found general recognition also within the areas of dogmatic legal science and sociology.

In principle nothing really changed when, under the influence of H. Rickert and Weber, the pseudo-natural scientific mode of explanation for social actions was increasingly replaced by a "cultural-scientific" interpretative mode of understanding, supported by so-called ideal-typical models. Within this circle of reflection causal explanation and normative evaluation remained strictly separated.

The inability to account for the causal jural relation

My thesis now is that under the influence of this whole trend of thought legal science remained incapable of critically accounting for the modal structure and nature of the causal jural relation itself, as well as for the causal relations that manifest themselves in the non-jural aspects of reality.

To this day the problem of jural causality has never been viewed as a general foundational problem for legal science, but only as a particular issue for specific areas, such as criminal law, the civil theory of the unlawful act (tort law), the failure to perform the obligation of delivery in the execution of contracts, private law concerning the insurance of loss, and social insurance law. And because jurists often find themselves confronted with typical manifestations of the jural causality relation, which reveal important (mutual) differences, the unity in the peculiar legal way of posing the problem remains completely concealed. The general concept of causation, which is adopted as a theoretical basis and which often attempts to accommodate special legal requirements, was not in itself jural in nature. It corresponded, as we have seen, with a structureless theoretical view of reality, known as the "physical-psychic," in which all normative modal structures are eliminated. Accompanying this un-jural concept of causality is an un-jural concept of action as well as an un-jural (conceived in a psychological sense) will-concept and fault-concept. Only in retrospect is an attempt made to recombine these concepts once again with normative-jural concepts such as accountability, unlawfulness, and responsibility.

This creates a web of antinomies within legal scientific thought. In order to camouflage them it is necessary to take recourse to different kinds of theoretical fictions.

There is nothing to be gained by attempting the impossible, as Van Eck did, by totally banning the problem of causality from the normative jural field of view. Truly radical therapy in this regard should start out with the acknowledgment that the problem of causality evinces just as many modal aspects as are present in our experiential world prior to any theorization. The place of the normative is just as legitimate as those of the non-normative aspects.

In a theoretical-scientific attitude of thought these aspects, which in pre-scientific experience are grasped in their integral coherence, are distinguished and put over against each other. They then constitute the abstracted modal fields of research of the different disciplines. Each special science investigates empirical reality through the gateway of one modal aspect. Within each viewpoint, which surely cannot deny its inner coherence with the other aspects of reality, the general field of study of an academic discipline may be "specialized" in different ways. The present state of scholarship allows a distinction between the following aspects: that of quantity (number) and spatiality, the aspect of energy-operation,[1] the bio-organic aspect, the psychic aspect (or aspect of feeling), the logical-analytical aspect, the historical aspect (of cultural development), the lingual aspect (of symbolic signification), the social aspect (in which social reality is subject to norms of courtesy, style, tact, hospitality, fashion, etc.), the economic aspect, the aesthetic aspect, the jural aspect, the moral aspect (of normative relationships of love) and the pistical (faith) aspect.

As I have shown extensively in my work, *De Wijsbegeerte der Wetsidee*,[2] all these aspects are mutually interwoven in an indissoluble temporal coherence and are set within an irreversible order of succession.[3] It is only in the theoretical attitude of thought that we can abstract them.

An intimate coherence and irreversible order

This intimate coherence and irreversible order comes to expression in what I have called the *modal structure* of these aspects. Empirical reality simultaneously functions in all these aspects and it is only accessible to us in the typical totality-structures of things, events, societal spheres, and so on. The latter embrace all modal aspects, though the aspects are grouped and individualized into an individual whole in typically different ways.

These typical totality-structures are therefore the *structures of individuality*. They show within the modal aspects the *typical* structural differences which are not to be explained purely in terms of the modal character of the aspects themselves. For example, it is impossible to derive the typical differences between constitutional law, civil private law, internal business law, internal ecclesiastical law, etc., from the general modal structure and nature of the jural aspect. These typical legal spheres of law are instead determined by the typical totality-structures of societal spheres such as the state, the firm, the church, etc. Though all the legal spheres are *jural* in nature, each bears a *typical* legal character.

The modal aspects should never be identified with empirical reality. Nowhere does there exist a separate physical, psychical, historical or an economic reality. In the totality-structures of existing things, processes or events, the physical-chemical or some other aspect plays a typically qualifying role. A strike of lightning, for example, is typically qualified as a phenomenon of electrical discharge in which the physical-chemical aspect of energy-operation is the qualifying function. This does not

---

1 *Translator's note:* Soon after the appearance of this essay Dooyeweerd introduced his distinction between the *kinematical aspect* of *uniform motion* and the *physical aspect* of *energy-operation*.

2 *Translator's note:* English version *A New Critique of Theoretical Thought* (Collected Works, A-Series, Vols.1-4).

3 *Translator's note:* Read the Glossary inscription on *Law-Sphere* (p.161) and look at the *Diagram* on page 165.

mean, however, that this fact of nature cannot also function *objectively* in other aspects of reality, such as the biotic, the psychical, the historical, and so on. We have already come to recognize this event as an objective legal fact which as such can only function in a jural subject-object relation.

As a real thing the nest of a bird displays a typical totality-structure that is qualified by its *typical biotic object-function*. It is an animal product which, as object, typically serves the organic life of a bird. The bird is a *subject* in the biotic aspect of organic life, it is a living being. Its nest does not live, but is a biotical *object* that functions in a typical structural relation to the bird as a living being. But this nest also functions in all other aspects.

A church building, to take another example, is typically qualified by its objectively being destined for service within the context of an ecclesiastical faith community. Its qualifying function is constituted by a typical object-function within the certitudinal aspect that is structurally related to the qualifying function of the church community as institutional Christian faith community amidst the organized service of the Word and Sacraments. But within the typical total structure of the church and the church building thus qualified, both function in all modal aspects of reality, including the jural.

These few examples may suffice to explain to some degree what I have in mind in the structural constitution of our empirical reality. For a more detailed explanation I refer the reader to Volume III of my *De Wijsbegeerte der Wetsidee*.[1]

Once we have substituted the structureless theoretical view of reality, to which the generally accepted philosophical concept of causality conforms, with an image of reality in which justice is once again done to the rich diversity of extremely complicated structural interlacements of our experiential world, the problem of causality acquires a totally different, and structurally varied character.

Firstly, it should be clear that the modal aspects cannot stand in a mutual relation of causality, since causal relationships can only represent themselves in the case of real events. The latter are only accessible to us in their typical totality-structures which in principle function in all aspects concurrently. One can only say that a causal relationship displays different modal aspects – aspects that exist in a mutual coherence while maintaining the irreducible uniqueness and laws specific to each one of them.

The modal diversity of causal relationships

The empirical disciplines can only attend to the causal relationships, that represent themselves in reality, within the aspects investigated by

---

1 *Translator's note:* English version, *A New Critique of Theoretical Thought*, Vol.III (A-Series, Vol.3).

them. An explanation given by a particular academic discipline presupposes that cause and effect should be subsumed under the same modal aspect as its denominator. In other words, cause and effect should be conceived within the structural coherence of the same aspect.

If we want to approach a total causal process within reality itself, then we should not order the facts in a sequence of *conditiones* lacking all structure, but rather we have to understand them in the typical interlacing of their structures of individuality which are themselves *totality*-structures. A tree, for example, displays an extremely complicated individuality-structure[1] within which physical processes also take place that are typically directed by the organic life-function of the whole and which one can only scientifically investigate through bio-chemical research. These processes within the individual whole only have a direct causal relation with the external world in so far as they belong to the bio-milieu (*Umwelt*) which, while also functioning within a typical individuality-structure, is interlaced with that of the tree. Within human society causal relationships can only be investigated in a meaningful way when the individuality-structures of social reality are considered.

Since the individuality-structures express themselves within the modal aspects of reality, one ought to respect the typical structural diversity present in a causal relation within these aspects themselves. This state of affairs also explains why within the jural problem of causality one discerns typical structural differences depending upon the context in which it reveals itself. It could relate to criminal law, civil private law, law of damages as a part of internal business law, or as part of civil private law, ecclesiastical law, international law, and so on. In the case of internal ecclesiastical law, for example, the causal jural facts are always certitudinally qualified in such a way that they indissolubly cohere with questions concerning faith and confession; in internal business law, on the contrary, they are typically economically qualified, a qualification expressing itself immediately in the question concerning the measure according to which the loss caused has to be calculated (market value, replacement value or otherwise).

---

1 Even this, in fact, is phrased too simplistically, because in reality a tree should be understood in terms of – as I have called it – an *enkaptic structural whole* in which very different individuality-structures are interwoven – comprising the *material constituents* and the *living organism* – while the whole is qualified by the highest (biotic) structure.

The jural relation of causality within the modal structure of the jural aspect

But first of all one has to understand the jural relation of causality within the *modal* structure of the jural aspect of reality itself. The structure of this modal aspect forms an architectonic whole. As with most other aspects,[1] it is constituted by an irreducible nuclear moment, which I have called the modal *meaning-nucleus*,[2] guaranteeing the inner coherence between the aspect concerned and all the others. It is placed in the same order as that prevailing between the different aspects. These latter structural moments partially refer back to those aspects preceding the jural aspect and partially point ahead to those aspects following the jural aspect.

Those structural moments referring backwards I have called modal *retrocipations* and those pointing ahead modal *anticipations*.[3] Both are qualified by the modal meaning-nucleus. *Only in their unbreakable coherence can these structural moments reveal their jural meaning.*

If we now understand the jural causal relation in terms of this modal structure, then we have to note in the first place that it could never be a selection from a physical or psychical causal series. Only *legal facts* relate to each other in a jural causal connection. But since *legal* facts are only the jural aspect of real facts, which also function in all other aspects of reality, and since the different aspects are mutually fitted in an unbreakable coherence, answering the jural question concerning the causal relation as a rule shows the most intimate connection with non-jural questions concerning causal relations.

According to the *law-side* of legal life the relevant legal facts mutually relate to each other in the normative causal relation between legal ground and legal effect. According to the *factual side* every legal fact indicates a causal intervention into subjective legal relationships, which form the *actual* legal ground for *actual* legal effects.

---

1   Only the two limiting aspects, namely that of quantity and the faith aspect, display a different structure inasmuch as the former does not have any analogical and the latter no anticipatory structural moments. Consult our subsequent exposition for an explanation of these terms. (See also the following translator's note – DFMS).

2   *Editorial note* (AC): Possible alternative translations for the Dutch expression "zin-kern" are "meaning-core" and "meaning kernel."

3   *Translator's note*: Soon after the publication of this treatise Dooyeweerd realized that one can explain the inter-modal coherence between the different aspects by subsuming both *retrocipations* and *anticipations* under the general category of *analogical structural moments*, implying that one should distinguish systematically between retrocipatory and anticipatory *analogies* (cf. *A New Critique of Theoretical Thought*, Vol.II, p.75).

The modal structure of a causal legal fact

The numerical analogy

Within the general modal structure of a causal legal fact we first of all discern a *numerical analogy* that is inherently present in every possible legal relationship.

The question, "Are we confronted with one or more than one legal fact, or are we confronted with one or more than one jural causal relation?", is an intrinsically *legal question* that can only be posed and answered according to a normative legal viewpoint. In criminal law especially these questions govern the doctrine concerning *forms of participation*[1] as well as the doctrine concerning *conjoint wrong-doing*.[2] In the law concerning the insurance of loss, we saw the same problem in the above-mentioned example concerning the case of the ship in icy waters. Failure to insure one's own goods, the fault of the party suffering loss, etc., are constantly occurring legal facts having an independent significance within legal life. The numerical analogy within the causal relation plays an important role also in civil legal doctrines concerning unlawfulness and failure to meet the requirements of a binding contract.

The jural character of the numerical analogy, as we have identified it above, is necessarily denied by a naturalistic conception of jural causality. The concept of conduct employed by the latter is intimately connected with a naturalistic action concept.

Von Kries mentions a case where a nurse, forgetting the medical prescription, unknowingly gives to a patient for the second time medicine that contains a poisonous mixture prepared by someone else. As a consequence the patient dies. If the causality question is posed *before* answering the question, "Is there one or more than one causal legal fact?," the legal domain is abandoned, von Kries argued. This is so, he said, even if an attempt is then made to solve the causality problem posed in non-jural terms according to the doctrine of the condition *sine qua non* or according to that of *adequate causation*.

In modern criminal law the actions of the nurse do not occur as an independent legal fact. Here we witness the *legal unity* of a legal fact comprising *two* actions – the so-called *instrumental commission* (*actual carrying out*) to be distinguished from that of *indirect wrong-doing* or the situation where someone is used to commit the offense, where the act of executing the deed, though unlawful with regard to the effect, does not qualify for punishment. *Legally viewed*, giving the poisonous medication to the patient is not an act of the nurse, but an act of the person who prepared the mixture, merely using the nurse as an instrument.

1 Dutch: *deelnemingsvormen*.
2 Dutch: *samenloop*.

In the case of joint commission we witness a jural unity of the causal relation on the basis of a multiplicity of legal facts directed at the same legal effect. In the case of instigating on the one hand and complicity on the other hand, it may concern legal facts where the legal causal relation is multiple. In the case where the instigator directly causes the main fact, for example a killing, the main perpetrator in law directly causes the death of the victim; the accomplice acts in helping the occurrence of the main fact which the main offender pre-meditated.[1]

In the case of the so-called true *double wrong-doing*[2] there is a *multitude* of legal facts and causal relations amidst a *unity* of action. For example, in his anger a visitor grasps an extremely valuable ornament and throws it at the head of his host. The latter acquires a bloody wound and the ornament breaks into pieces. *One action* here caused *two* delicts: *abuse* and *damage to property*, constituting a twofold causal relation.

The spatial analogy

M.E. Mayer, a German criminal law scholar, made the fitting remark: "The art of counting crimes is difficult, as long as one is uncertain about what actually should be counted."[3] If, however, we identify the concrete delict with the act, conceived of in a naturalistic sense (the willed movement of muscles), and conclude: *one act, one* delict, then we forget that it involves *jural* numerical relationships. The perpetrator's fundamental mistake cannot be light-heartedly dismissed with the remark that the opposite conception practices the art of counting in the sense of a "a magical one-times-one."

It has to be conceded that a particular legal order may arrange the jural numerical relations regarding causal legal facts differently from the way in which they may be arranged in another legal order. Therefore, the numerical analogy within the structure of the jural causal relation necessarily is connected with a *spatial analogy*: the *domain of jurisdiction* and the *legal location* of the legal fact. Outside *legal space* no causal relation in the jural sense can present itself. The concrete jural structure of the causal relation is dependent upon the sphere of validity of the legal norms, in subjection to which it takes place.

The physical analogy

The jural causal relation is, as we have seen, structurally tied to legal facts, be it subjective or objective legal facts, which exert a jural effect by altering the (subjective) legal relationships. This jural operation is a

---
1 The terms *direct* and *indirect* therefore, if they are understood in their *legal meaning*, definitely have their place in the legal adjudication of causality. Consequently, the attempt to ban them from legal practice, as required by the critique of naturalistic theories of causality, never succeeded.
2 Dutch: *eendaadschen samenloop*.
3 *Der allgemeine Teil der deutschen Strafrechts*, 1915, p.156.

true analogy of the energy-operation within the physical aspect of reality and is, therefore, not merely a "figure of speech".

After all, within the modal structure of the jural aspect itself, it guarantees inner coherence with the aspect of energy, in order that within empirical reality the jural causal relations are always based upon physical energy-operation, while fully maintaining their mutual uniqueness and sphere-sovereignty. It can never be the case that a physical causal relation fully coincides with a jural causal relation, although determining the latter frequently would be impossible without implicitly establishing the former. The jurist, however, should be conscious of the point where the jural causal relation begins and where the natural-scientific one ends. In case of doubt the latter should be presented to experts. However, the jurist cannot leave the question concerning jural causality to be assessed by the physicist or the chemist.

The biotical analogy

The physical or energetic analogy in the jural causal relation, in turn, is indissolubly tied to the *biotic analogy*. It is impossible for anything to be causal in the jural sense of the term, without interfering in *legal life*. Legal life, in turn, functions in the context of a dynamic balance of legal interests, maintained by competent organs regulated by legal norms. In this case also we are concerned with a true *modal analogy* and not with a mere figure of speech. To be sure, legal life could only function upon the ontic foundation of organic life in its biotic sense. Within the jural aspect, life and death are themselves fitted into the legal relationships aimed at establishing a balance between legal interests.

The commandment: "You shall not murder" is therefore, according to its jural aspect, never to be understood as a prohibition that forbids causing the death of a person in a purely biotic sense, but as a prohibition forbidding taking away life as a subjective legal interest by distorting the balance of legal interests. When a member of the fire brigade, for example, in order to save a child from a burning room has to break a window, that person does not cause any loss in legal life since the act does not breach the balance of legal interests. Life as a legal interest is more important than a concrete legal object. Legally seen the loss is only to be attributed to the fire and eventually will be covered by insurance.

The psychical analogy

The biotic analogy within the modal structure of the jural causal relation in its turn is indissolubly related to the *psychical* analogy: the jural will-function, in so far as it concerns subjective causal legal facts, i.e., human causal actions, according to their jural aspect. A subjective legal fact is always a *jural expression of will* that cannot be determined apart from legal norms.

The function of the jural will never coincide with the concrete act of will as it expresses itself within the aspect of feeling, but it does exist in an intrinsic ontic[1] coherence with the latter.

A legal expression of will as such always constitutes a causal intervention in legal life, carrying with it legal responsibility for the consequences.

You cannot disassociate yourself from these effects with the remark that you did not desire and envision them in a psychical sense. The legal order *demands* foreseeing the consequences of an intended act – that is essential for fulfilling your legal duties. Employing an a-normative psychological concept of the will always entangles legal science in antinomies and is intimately associated with the use of a non-jural concept of causation and action. The latter is unjural because it is conceived of in a naturalistic sense. Those who call the jural will-function a fictitious construction of "legal technique" proceed from an abstract naturalistic view of reality that eliminates all normative aspects. They should then, however, call legal life in its entirety a fiction, since nothing in it corresponds with a so-called "psycho-physical" view of reality. Legal norms can only direct themselves to the jurally normative will-function of the human being that is an indispensable factor in the reality of human society. These norms do not have any say over the non-jural aspects of the human will: they obey their own proper laws.

The concrete effects of objective legal facts, such as the collapse of a building, the event of a lightning strike, a dog's bite, etc., are always – in the sense of the jural subject-object relation outlined above – structurally focused upon those legal subjects who are, in their jural will-function, responsible for the damage.

The logical analogy: subjective and objective imputation

This implies that the legal causality question cannot be posed apart from *subjective* and *objective imputation* and – concerning subjective legal facts – apart from the question concerning the lawfulness or unlawfulness of causal actions. Here we touch upon the *logical analogies* in the jural causal relation.

Legal *imputation* (attributing to) is based upon the logical principle of causality, i.e. the principle of the sufficient reason (ground) in the logical conclusion. The jural opposition between *lawful-unlawful* finds its foundation in the logical principle of contradiction. These logical analogies, nonetheless, are not *logical* (analytical) in nature but rather have a jural disposition. They merely guarantee the unbreakable coherence between the logical and the jural aspects.

---

1 *Translator's note:* Although in the Dutch text Dooyeweerd here uses the equivalent of the term "ontological," his intention is to refer to an *ontic* relation. Compare footnote (2) of this article on page 39.

The issue of imputation does not primarily belong to the question concerning fault[1] but to that concerning causality. In the case of a subjective causal legal fact the legal question is always: Who caused the effect? This question would become meaningless whenever one were to employ a naturalistic concept of causality, for in that case one would not reach a point of closure – only a calculation through the entire series of conditions. If, in the instance of the person who mixed the poison, referred to by von Kries, the mixer, the nurse and the patient are all regarded as having caused the deadly effect, it no longer makes any sense *ex post facto* to raise the issue of accountability. Jural imputation cannot be based upon an unjural assessment of causality.

That jural imputation also forms an essential part of the question of causation of objective legal facts – a new proof against the argument for absorbing it into the fault question – already manifested itself in the mentioned example of damage caused by a fire. In this case the issue concerning the attribution of factual consequences to a cause also cannot be omitted, because the factual jural causal relation always shares in the feature of being a legal ground for legal effects. A causal legal fact as such cannot be determined without *attributing* it to that which is considered to be its legal cause.

In the case of insurance law, the fact that loss caused by water as well as other effects of human intervention are attributed to the fire as cause, in contrast to damage in the course of business which is not attributed to the fire as cause, is based upon (objective) jural attribution, without which no legal causal relation could occur.

Whenever the causal legal fact is present in a delict, then it is impossible to separate the question of jural causality from that of unlawfulness. Once one has distanced oneself from the naturalistic conception of the "factual state of affairs" (*Tatbestand*), this must be immediately clear. Accepting this would then eliminate the unresolvable antinomies which naturalistic theories of causality discern in legal causation through omission, the problem of the so-called *"non-genuine omission delicts"* where a certain effect belongs to the constitutive elements of the legal definition. Of course only those who are subject to a legal duty to act in a specific way can commit the delict of omission – and it is these very same naturalistic theories that want to disregard legal duties. Legal life, on the contrary, depends on the fulfillment of their legal duties by all legal subjects. A person who does not perform a legal duty has already disrupted the jural balance, and by doing that, has causally intervened in legal life. There is not a trace of fiction here. But naturalistic theories in this context can only save themselves with fictions!

---

1 *Editorial note* (AC): See *editor's note* on page 42.

All this does not mean that the question of jural causality can be absorbed by the question concerning unlawfulness. Although every unlawful act or omission implies a disrupting intervention in legal life in the case of material delicts, it is impossible to deduce the jural scope of the causal relation from unlawfulness. The person controlling the signals who disregards the duty to switch the signal from safe to unsafe, *causes* a dangerous condition on the railway lines through this neglect. The question whether that person would have caused a railway accident can only be answered by considering the course of events following the initial dangerous situation created by the omission. It may turn out that, in the meantime, new causal legal facts occurred to which the train accident wholly or partially must be attributed.

In any case it is clear that there does not exist any unlawfulness without a disturbing (damaging) causal intervention in the balance of legal interests. This perspective is consonant with the basic conception of the so-called doctrine of material unlawfulness. But this entails that the jural causal relation presupposes a balancing of these interests by the person *forming law*.

Formation of law: the historical analogy

At this point we touch upon a new analogy within the modal structure of the jural aspect: the *historical*, which once again helps to provide us with a closer specification of the general nature of the jural causal relation. On both the law-side and the factual side, legal life is not given to human beings in a definite and finalized form. Much rather, it requires *formation*. Those having the power to *shape* law give a positive form to jural principles. These principles are contained in the modal structure of the jural aspect as well as in the distinct structural types within society – for the greater part they rest upon a historical foundation. Those competent to form law also give positive shape to the causal relation of legal ground and legal effect by constituting certain types of causal legal facts to which they connect positive legal consequences. Jural form-giving in this sense is a true analogy of cultural form-giving within the historical aspect.[1] In the order of aspects, legal life rests upon a cultural-historical basis. Magical causal relations, which in earlier times – and even today in the case of the so-called "aboriginals" – played such an important role in legal life, no longer have any place in it. Through the immense development of scholarship and technology juridical causal findings in many respects have been subject to alteration and extension. Due to this

---

1 The modal meaning-nucleus of this aspect is *power* or *control*. As to its law-side it concerns power over persons, and according to this factual side it reveals itself as power over objects. In the controlling mode of form-giving, occurring according to a free design, one discerns the difference in principle between cultural and animal form-giving. Within the jural aspect *legal* power is an analogy of *historical* power. This explains why the formation of law presupposes competence, i.e. legal power.

development one may now detect many causal legal facts that were simply unthinkable in earlier times. A jural causal relation is therefore never a natural phenomenon. It always rests upon a historical foundation.

The relativity of the jural relation of causality and of unlawfulness is intimately connected with this historical analogy. Relativity here is meant in the sense that the jural relation would assume different shapes dependent upon the typical character of the legal spheres in which they manifest themselves within the very differentiated nature of modern society. Thus, for example, there is a typical structural difference between the criminal legal and the civil legal forms of unlawfulness and causality. The nature of modern criminal law, in so far as it rests upon the principle that there is no liability to punishment without the existence of a legal stipulation of punishment preceding the occurrence of the factual event concerned (compare article 1 of the *Dutch Criminal Code*), carries with it the sense that unlawfulness and causality here are always bound to distinct and more or less exactly circumscribed definitions of law concerning the typical delictual forms. In other words, not every unlawful act is illegal in the criminal legal sense of the term, but only those that answer to the delictual forms prescribed by criminal law.

Due to the internal nature of criminal law, which is interlaced with the structure of the state, this implies that the unlawfulness and causality of a human action here has the typical meaning of a disrupting intervention affecting the public legal interest of the whole political community, implying that it never only concerns an act that is unlawful and causal over against and in respect of an individual person. In the case of a civil legal delict, on the contrary, it always involves a causal intervention in the civil legal sphere of interests of a particular legal subject, standing on an equal footing over against the person who committed the deed. Here *every* unlawful act, in so far as it is damaging to the interests of the person affected and in so far as the damage is caused through fault, results in the liability of the person committing the act.

Here the jural form-giving to the causal legal fact – pending supplementary rules regarding some particular delicts – is left to the jurisprudence of the Courts, since the legislators restricted themselves to a general liability formula.

Consequently, no contradiction exists when an act, considered from the perspective of the public interest, is assessed to be perfectly lawful (for example the construction of a new railroad embankment or the withdrawal of ground water by a municipal water supply firm), while, at the same time, when viewed from the perspective of specific individuals, is said to be unlawful as a result of the damage caused to an object of their property rights (for example through causing neighboring areas to be elevated, through cracks in the walls of houses on those premises, or through causing the drying out of particular areas), in spite of reasonable precautionary measures taken.

Of course, in the process of jural form-giving, the judge may also choose another construction regarding the causal legal fact, for example as was done by German jurisprudence that found a legal risk independent of the unlawful act, or, in line with the *Dutch Supreme Court* (compare its decision of May 3, 1946 N.J. 1946, 323), the civil legal unlawfulness may be sought in an infringement of a legal duty caused by the act respecting third parties who are adversely affected. But these constructions or "acts of giving shape" do not detract from the relativity of the assessment of unlawfulness and causality alluded to above. They are contained in the structure of the jural causal relation itself by virtue of the historical analogy of jural form-giving.

Jural interpretation

This historical analogy in its turn is indissolubly connected with *the lingual analogy* that constitutes the subsequent sphere of analogies within the modal structure of the jural aspect. The meaning nucleus of the lingual aspect can be described as "symbolic meaning." Since legal life as a whole in the ontic order of aspects rests on a symbolic basis, jural form-giving always implies the determination of the legal significance of the causal intervention. Every fact of which the legal question concerning causality can be asked immediately demands *jural interpretation*.

Seen from a scientific point of view, therefore, it is an unjustified limitation of the problem of jural interpretation to restrict it merely to the words used in the expressed jural declarations of will. The lingual aspect itself is not necessarily restricted to the use of *words*. At the same time one should keep in mind that the jural interpretation is not identical with the lingual one. What is at stake is the *legal* and not the lingual meaning, although the latter shows an inner coherence with the former.

The legal meaning of a causal fact is connected with the entire modal structure of its jural aspect. *In every legal problem of causation a legal problem of interpretation conceals itself.*[1]

When, in the case of foggy conditions, two cars are involved in a collision and some of the passengers are wounded or killed, then the question whether the accident was caused by the careless driving of one or both drivers (one or two subjective legal facts), or whether the fog as

---

1 In the law governing the insurance of loss one may consider the interpretation of the damage clauses. In various countries the interpretation may turn out to be somewhat different. This problem of interpretation entailed in every problem of causation governs the question how one should understand risk of "riot" as an insured cause of loss.

objective legal fact primarily caused the accident, is one of jural interpretation of the incident which, in the nature of the case, could not be answered apart from legal norms.

Legal intercourse

These legal norms are co-determined by the requirements of *legal intercourse*. This represents the social analogy in the modal structure of the jural causal relation, through which the earlier discussed biotic analogy receives a more precise meaning. We have portrayed legal life as a dynamic balance of legal interests, maintained by competent legal organs regulated by legal norms and in which interventions, be they the outcome of subjective expressions of will or objective legal facts, are attributed with being the legal grounds for legal consequences. We have seen how these causal interventions could only manifest themselves in historically-founded legal forms and also found that their legal meaning should be determined by legal interpretation. Since legal intercourse always manifests itself in a *correlation of legal coordinational and legal communal relationships*,[1] it thus gives a further specification to the balance of legal interests. With the term *coordinational* we intend to capture all those legal ties in which the functioning of legal subjects is co-ordinated in a side-by-side relation. These legal subjects do not act in a capacity of members of a societal whole. The term *communal relationships*, on the other hand, exactly captures the latter case, namely where legal subjects are, indeed, considered as members of a larger whole. This explains why, in this case, a causal intervention in the balance of legal interests always would imply an intervention in the communal legal interests.

In our discussion of the *relativity* of the jural causal relation and the unlawfulness relation we implicitly became aware of this state of affairs. Legal interaction requires a balance of communal and coordinational interests because every communal relationship has as its counterpart some coordinational relationship and vice versa. If then, for example in the earlier mentioned case of the construction of an embankment, where the public communal interest is served concurrently with a loss-causing intervention in the private property right of civil legal coordinational relationships, then one ought to find a balance between communal and coordinational legal interests with regard to the legal consequences of this causal legal fact. This explains why the judge did not forbid the activity of the railroad, accompanied by a directive to clean up the construction plant, but only ruled in favour of allocating compensation for the damage to those who suffered losses. The same ruling applies to

---

1 *Translator's note:* The Dutch term *maatschapsverhoudingen* does not have a direct English equivalent. It is meant to designate those social forms of peer interaction where individuals or societal collectivities are coordinated alongside each other.

beneficial firms that are granted a licence permitted under the law of insurance with the sanction of a concession legitimized by a law of nuisance[1] and that, nonetheless, cause damage to nearby neighbors. Another instance where the same ruling applies concerns the case where a mining company could not exploit a mine and at the same time avoid the risk of the sagging of the surface and the danger it entailed for particular houses, and so on.

The economical handling of legal means and interests

A new specification of the balance of legal interests in the correlation of jural communal and coordinational interests, in which causal legal facts intervene (be it damaging or not), is given by the economic analogy in the jural causal relation.

It is evident that within the economic aspect the relation of balance presents itself in an analogical sense. However, it is qualified by the meaning-nucleus of the economic aspect: the stewardly mode of interacting with relatively scarce means (directed towards ends chosen according to human needs).

The economic analogy in the legal relation of balance concerns the economical handling of legal means and interests of others within the context of alternative possible choices a person is free to pursue. Every excessive, every unrestrained exploration of one's own legal interest, within legal life, is an interrupting causal intervention in the legal balance of interests against which the legal order reacts with restorative legal consequences. The driver of a car, who, when another car approaches from a side-street, continues driving on a road that gives the first-mentioned motorist the right of way, does not cause the subsequent accident when the same driver had no reason to expect that the other motorist would not yield. However, if the first motorist still continues to drive on, while having had the opportunity to stop in time after realizing that the other driver had disobeyed the traffic rules, then the loss-causing effect should also be imputed to the former's act since it is in conflict with the principle of jural economy and constitutes as such an excessive pursuit of one's own legal interest. If, according to the theory of the *conditio sine qua non*, the jural imputation of the effect is only introduced in connection with the question of fault, it would essentially amount to a total elimination of the jural problem of causality. After all, the genuine jural question of *who* caused the accident no longer has any meaning – and without answering this question the issue of fault could also no longer be posed in a jural sense.

In the case of excessive force in self-defence, legal responsibility is excluded if the excessive action is performed under the influence of the

---
1 Dutch: *Hinderwetvergunning*.

serious emotional stress caused by the assault. This excess, nonetheless, continues to constitute a loss-producing causal intervention in the balance of legal interests, which is imputed to the person concerned as an unlawful action and against which self-defence is allowed in turn.

Jural harmony and disharmony

The last analogy within the structure of the jural causal relation is the aesthetic, i.e. the structural moment of jural harmony (and its contrary counterpart disharmony)[1] through which the relationship of legal balance – and also the causal relation in legal life – has its last modal analogical specification.[2] The relationship of balance among the legal interests requires that it should be harmonized according to the weighing of coordinational interests against communal interests.

The legal consequences, attributed by a legal order to a causal intervention in the balance of legal interests governed by this legal order, ought to be proportional to the jural significance of this causal legal fact. Furthermore, since the causal relation between a legal fact and its consequences within legal life can only be considered as legal ground for legal consequences, the scope of the factual causal relation also ought to be determined according to a jural norm of proportionality. In this way the interpretive function of the legal assessment of causality receives a further specification, as we have mentioned in the discussion of the lingual analogy.

With regard to the scope of the causal relation, the legal order, due to the principle of proportionality, can only orient itself to the *ex ante* standpoint. Then it can only take into account those consequences which stand in relation to the nature of the causal legal fact and which follow from it with a certain degree of probability. This also follows from the structural relation between the causal legal fact and legal normativity. The legal norm, in its command or prohibition, always positions itself on the *ex ante* standpoint. This is the kernel of truth in the doctrine of *adequate cause*, which, however, as we have seen in the theoretical development of its foundation, went off the rails, juridically speaking, by supporting the theory of the *conditio sine qua non* in its untenable separation of the question concerning causality and that concerning normative imputation. In its practical application and specifi-

---

1 *Translator's note:* Calvin Seerveld questions Dooyeweerd's placement of the aesthetic aspect as well as his designation of the meaning-kernel of the aesthetic mode (harmony). This issue was discussed at the first international Conference arranged by the Dooyeweerd Centre for Christian Philosophy in June 1996. The Proceedings of this Conference will appear as the 1997 Yearbook of the Collected Works of Dooyeweerd. Compare also Duncan Roper: "The Reformational Contribution to Aesthetic Theory," *Issues*, November 1992, no.7, pp.3-31.

2 *Translator's note:* This expression refers to the succession of aspects in the modal order of time.

cally in jurisprudence it has always been positioned intuitively within the modal structure of the jural aspect. As a consequence this jurisprudential practice never fell prey to an unjural conception of the possibility or probability question.

In the application of the jurally defined concept of adequate cause one cannot dispense with the condition *sine qua non*, as long as the latter is also transposed into a normative jural sense, as we have remarked in an earlier context. Viewed from the perspective of criminal (or tort) law, it does not avail someone committing fraud to deny the causal relation between that person's deceitful act and the handing over of the goods, by making an appeal to the declaration of the victim that the latter would have handed over the goods even if the wrong-doer had spoken the truth (H.M.G. June 12, 1925 M.R.T. Vol.193, p.189). In a jural sense this delict was an adequate *conditio sine qua non* for this effect, because the relation between both flows from the very nature of the legal offense, at least in so far as no new legal facts positioned themselves between the deed and the effect. But in the causation of human acts one is never justified in speaking about a naturally necessary effect, as required by the theory of the condition *sine qua non*. Speaking in this context about "psychical causality" one has to realize that it cannot replace the antecedent questions of the assessment of jural causality to which it belongs.

The degree of probability required to assume a factual causal relation in legal life wholly depends upon the typical context within which the question of causality manifests itself. The jural principle of proportionality demands the employment of the risk principle in social and private insurance law (and in modern times also in the case of the civil legal causation of damage to someone else's property). If the causal relation, providing the basis of liability, follows from the nature of the causal fact, the risk principle implies that a relatively low degree of probability for the occurrence of the effect is sufficient. This risk principle does not cover the insured's own fault or the lack of an insurable interest, at least not within the civil legal sphere.

When, by contrast in civil law and by and large in the criminal law of delicts, the principle of fault is used as measure of proportionality, then within jurisprudence formulations such as the "reasonable consequences or consequences expected according to the rules of experience" come to the fore, presupposing a relatively high degree of probability. This only shows how the principle of fault influences the jural causality judgment. Also, in the case of reasonable foreseeability of the effect, proof of absence of fault is conceivable (compare the case of the excess force in self-defence).

The place of fault within the jural causal relation[1]

This is an appropriate place to discuss briefly the place of fault within the jural causal relation. The structural element of fault cannot belong to the [retrocipatory][2] analogical elements in the structure of the jural aspect. In so-called primitive (I prefer still-undifferentiated and closed) legal life, this principle in general does not play a role in the determination of liability, although, since the investigations of Lowie (*Primitive Society*), one has to be careful with overly absolute statements in this regard. What is certain, at any rate, is that observing fault in the case of unlawful infringements in the balance of legal interests indicates a deepening and disclosure of the modal meaning of law, revealing an inner connection between law and morality. In order to avoid any vagueness with regard to the nature of the moral aspect and confusion in relation to the central religious root-unity of the human existence, it should be pointed out that the meaning-nucleus of the intended aspect is to be found in normative *love* within temporal relationships. In the ontic order of the aspects the jural precedes the moral aspect delimited in this way, as I have argued extensively in *De Wijsbegeerte der Wetsidee* (*The Philosophy of the Law-Idea*[3]).

Jural fault is therefore an anticipatory structural element, pointing towards a moral defect in the neighborly love of concrete behavior. In the nature of the case this structural element can only occur in unlawful subjective legal facts. Nevertheless, it cannot be reduced to moral fault since it remains an anticipatory moment firmly fitted within the modal structure of the jural aspect. It coheres also with the psychical analogies of this structure although it can never be dissolved into an a-normative psychical moment. Jural fault presupposes unlawfulness, imputation to the jural will-function as well as the causal intervention in the balance of legal interests.

Through this moment the legal meaning of all these analogical moments are deepened within the structure of a delict, since it implies a moral reproach that requires the causal unlawful act to be viewed in the light of *jural morality*. Therefore, one can never formulate the question concerning fault apart from those regarding unlawfulness and causality, though the opposite is possible. The contrary conception, holding that fault can appear apart from causality, constantly finds its origin in a naturalistic and therefore unjural concept of causation.

An explanation of why it is the case in jurisprudence that the question of causation is sometimes separately treated and at other times implic-

---

[1] *Editorial note* (AC): See *editor's note* on page 42.
[2] *Translator's note:* See the translator's note on page 55.
[3] Published under the title: *A New Critique of Theoretical Thought*, Compare Vol.II, pp.140-163.

itly answered in connection with the question of fault is due solely to the position of the moment of fault within the modal structure of the jural causal relation. As long as the attribution of fault is indeed understood in a jural sense, and its presence is affirmed, no practical objection can be raised because the attribution of legal causality is always implied in it. If the decision finds the absence of fault then there is no certainty that unlawfulness and causality would also be absent.

Within the limited scope of this essay I cannot deal in detail with this extremely important but also very complicated concept of fault. I have restricted myself to a location of the element of fault in the modal structure of the jural causal relation of a delict.

All the analyzed analogical and anticipating moments[1] in this structure finally have to receive their jural qualification through what I have called the modal meaning-nucleus of this structure. I adhere to the view that this meaning-nucleus should be described as *retribution* (the retributive mode), keeping in mind that its general modal meaning must not be identified with the typical way in which it reveals itself in the domain of criminal law. That this modal nuclear moment of jural evaluation is not to be found in the principle of proportionality, as Kranenburg for example holds, appears irrefutably from the fact that this principle has a mathematical origin – a point already appreciated by Aristotle and Hugo Grotius. Therefore, in its jural employment, this principle must have an *analogical* meaning. In the jural aspect it does not involve a *mathematical* but a retributive proportionality between cause and effect, both according to the law-side and the factual side of legal life which is subject to the former.

If the development of the concept of causality is traced, we come to the surprising discovery that human reflection grasped causal relations first of all in a retributive sense. Hans Kelsen once again amply demonstrated this insight in a thoroughly documented work on retribution and causality.[2] In the Ionic philosophy of nature it was the $dik\bar{e}$, retributive justice, that maintained a fixed proportionality between coming into being and passing away. Even in late modernity we see how a thinker like Hermann Lotze (*Logik*, par.364) traces all natural-scientific judgments of causality back to a metaphysical law of "aesthetic justice."

It stands to reason that the natural sciences and philosophy of nature should free themselves from this predominance of a normative-jural viewpoint. But legal science, in its turn, should not allow itself to be dominated by a quasi natural-scientific mode of thought that leaves no room for the normative jural aspect of the problem of causality. Within

---

1 *Translator's note:* See the translator's note on page 55.
2 *Vergeltung und Kausalität*, Den Haag-Chicago, 1941.

its modal field of vision all questions of causality remain focused upon retribution as modal meaning-nucleus of every possible legal relationship.

II

ESSAYS IN SOCIAL PHILOSOPHY

The relationship between Legal Philosophy and Sociology of Law[1]

Introduction
IN A FIRST, provisional attempt to delimit the area of sociology of law from other "modal"[2] branches of sociology, such as sociology of ethics, of "religion," of language, economics, art, etc., one is inescapably confronted with a problem of legal philosophy. This problem concerns the transcendental-juridical experiential mode of social relationships, both in its general modal distinctness from, and its inner coherence with, all other transcendental modes of experience (modal aspects) of these relationships.

Confusing constant structural principles with changing societal forms
There can be no doubt that real societal relations in the mutual coherence of their modal aspects can only be experienced in typical individuality-structures.[3] And the inner structural *principles* of the latter are of an invariant transcendental character. This cannot be otherwise since these principles condition the possibility of experience. The investigation of these transcendental principles of societal individuality-structures belongs to the task of social philosophy. What is needed first of all is insight into the *typical inner nature* of societal relations within the various societal spheres of life; and it is this very inner nature, determined by typical transcendental structural principles, that maintains its constancy in and throughout all the variable forms which humankind may give to them.

Influenced by positivistic and historicistic views of social reality, modern sociology began to confuse the typical inner character of the specific societal spheres with the changing societal forms in which the internal structural principles are positivized and realized. The result was that the inner nature of the different social life-spheres also came to be thought of as a changing phenomenon of history so that any attempt at

---
1 This article appeared in Dutch as: *"De verhouding tussen Rechtsfilosofie en Rechtssociologie,"* in *Album Professor Ferdinand van Goethem*, pp.557-576. Leuven, 1964. *Translator:* Robert Knudsen; *Editor:* Alan M. Cameron.
2 This term will be explained in the text.
3 *Editorial note* (DFMS): See the Glossary explanation on page 159.

typology seemed to lack a firm basis and the inner boundaries of these spheres became blurred. The reason is that the original forms of these societal spheres, as well as those into which they evolved, will vary depending on the historical development of a particular society. They are the central links of numerous intertwinements between various social relationships each having a quite different inner nature.

Consequently, the variable empirical forms in which societal relationships are realized cannot furnish reliable criteria for a typological distinction of the latter according to their qualitative inner character. For instance, in the concrete forms of existence of social collectivities, such as in the case of a farmer functioning in our differentiated Western society, the inner character of his natural family community is closely interrelated with that of agricultural enterprise. On the other hand, the inner character of the natural family community is radically different from that of the state or that of the church. Nevertheless, in our modern Western society the family is interwoven in many ways with the state and often also with the church. These latter intertwinements too are realized but in various other specific societal forms.

Now, the internal structural principles that determine the typical inner nature of the distinct societal spheres also determine the typical character of their internal legal spheres. The typical inner nature of the latter cannot be deduced from the general modal structure of the juridical aspect of our experiential world.

The reason is that this modal structure cannot contain any typical trait of a particular legal sphere, since it determines the general juridical character of all of them. The investigation of the typical nature of the internal legal spheres of the different social orbits belongs to the common task of legal philosophy and that of social philosophy. This inquiry should relate to the second transcendental dimension of juridical experience, namely that of the fundamental social types of legal spheres[1] which, however, presupposes the transcendental modal dimension.

The important typology of legal spheres

By the absence of this type of inquiry, the development of the sociology of law was poorly served. For the result of this oversight was that in "theoretical sociology of law" the fundamentally important typology of the special legal spheres according to the inner character of the distinct societal areas to which they belong either remained entirely left out of the consideration or was confused with a formal-logical classification of the specific legal spheres of "social groups." In the latter case, widely different arbitrary criteria were used, established without concern for

---

1 By fundamental social types of legal spheres I understand those which result from the invariable typical inner nature of the latter.

the inner typical-structural nature of societal life-spheres, and consequently were not fit to provide a real basis for such a typology.

It is especially noteworthy that this confusion can be seen in a sociologist of law like Georges Gurvitch, who, unlike many others, correctly insists on the intrinsic connection between sociology of law and philosophy of law. He repeatedly points to the need for a detailed typology of the distinct legal spheres, and he rightly considers its absence in many students of theoretical sociology of law to be a serious fault. "There is no sociology of law without a philosophy of law and vice versa," Gurvitch wrote in his *Sociology of Law*.[1]

But in the three-fold task that Gurvitch assigns to philosophy of law[2] one fails to find anything like "research into internal structural principles of the various types of legal spheres." The "jural typology of social groups" in Gurvitch lacks a transcendental-philosophical basis. He considers this typology only a schematic aid in the service of juridical sociography of the plurality and variability of the typical legal spheres ("frameworks of law") of specific social groups in the all-embracing society *at a certain historical point of time* (p.189). In his sociology of law there is no trace at all of a distinction between the internally invariable essential nature of the typical legal spheres of the social life-areas, and the variable forms given to them in the course of history from which originate the so-called variability types of these legal spheres. There is no place for such a distinction within historicistic views of human society prevalent in modern sociology. And in Gurvitch one meets with an "idealistic-realistic" version of this historicism, strongly influenced by Bergson's "philosophy of life," Hauriou's theory of the social institutions, W. James' pluralistic view of integral and immediate experience, and other philosophical trends.

The impasse of an extreme nominalistic orientation: Gurvitch

The foundations of sociology of law and of the study of legal history would clearly be undermined by a consistent application of this view to the typology of "social groups" since it implies an extreme nominalistic orientation. For if the essential typical inner nature of, for example, the natural communities of marriage and family, or of the state, the institutional church, the industrial community, etc. were subject to change in

---
1 Gurvitch, G.: *Sociology of Law*, London: Routledge and Kegan Paul Ltd., 1947, 1953 (no change in pagination).
2 a) Penetration behind juridical "constructs and symbols" to the "immediate jural experience"; b) Determination of criteria to distinguish juridical and other (moral, religious, aesthetic and "intellectual") experience; c) Distinction among juridical values, embodied in "normative social facts," between objectively valid ones and those that rest upon mere subjective illusions of the "collective mentality." p.243.

the historical development of Western and non-Western society, then every conceptual distinction of these types of social units (and their internally typical legal spheres) would lose its basis. In this case the very idea of their historical development would also lose any possible sense. Hence, in his typology of the specific social "groups" Gurvitch is forced to introduce criteria[1] that are evidently meant to be constant and universal, and, in combination, are intended to characterize these groups according to their typical general nature. This typology, for instance, is used in his conceptual description of the state regardless of its functioning in a Western or a non-Western society and independent of periods in cultural-historical development of the state.

The following definition (p.188) rests upon a combination of two of his typological criteria, i.e.

(a) "function" – specified as function of "the bloc of locality groupings" – and

(b) the (monopoly of) "unconditional constraint," which he also calls "political sovereignty."

But this definition lacks the structural-typological character that a conceptual description of the typical inner nature of the state or any other societal life-sphere should have. The two criteria used by Gurvitch, function and unconditional constraint, are completely independent of each other and are no more than just two amongst a series of unargued, unjustified criteria introduced for the purpose of a universal typological classification of all social groups. There is no evidence for an inner, typically structural coherence between these two. To define the state, they are externally connected; externally, because Gurvitch has to admit that "unconditional constraint" also occurs in vastly different types of communities, as for instance in the natural domestic family, the clan, the medieval church, the hereditary castes of India, the labour unions with unconditional membership in a totalitarian state,[2] and so on.

[1] These criteria are the following (cf. pp.182 ff.):
1) scope (particular and inclusive groups); 2) duration (temporary and durable groups); 3) function (explained in the text); 4) attitude (divisive and unifying groups); 5) ruling organizational principle (unorganized and organized groups); 6) form of constraint (conditional and unconditional); 7) degree of unity (unitary, federal and confederated groups). 8) The last criterion applies to organized groups only.

[2] The example given here by Gurvitch indicates, however, that he has no insight into the fundamental difference between the typical internal legal sphere of a trade union and its external function of compulsory organization within the public legal sphere of a totalitarian state. The union cannot derive this function from itself, i.e. on the strength of its inner character, but it has, in such a case, been imposed externally upon it by the state for the sake of its totalitarian ends. Only as "arm of the state" – a function intrinsically foreign to the trade union – can it display an "unconditional" coercive character.

But, if this is so, then "unconditional constraint" cannot have an intrinsic, required structural coherence with the criterion of "locality group." For this necessary coherence does not follow from Gurvitch's statement that "it is primarily locality groups based on proximity which have a tendency towards the organization of unconditioned constraint." (p.187)

According to Gurvitch, "locality groups" are connected by (static-social) "proximity." They are supposed to be one of six types[1] in which all "durable" particular (non-inclusive) groups can be divided and in which a uni-functional or multi-functional sociality predominates in their social balance. The criterion for this typological classification is the "general character of their function(s)," where "function" is understood, not as predetermined purpose, but as communal task, inspired by one or more "values" that become operative in a social *milieu* – a conception that is obviously influenced by Maurice Hauriou's doctrine of the "institution." However, one only needs to reflect a little longer to realize that these six "generically-functional" types of groups and their species have little if anything to do with a real structural-typological investigation of societal relationships.

Within the six "functional" basic types, for example, both differentiated and primitive undifferentiated "groups" are listed as sub-types, so that this "function" typology of social groups takes on an utterly arbitrary character. One wonders why the primitive, undifferentiated clan, based on "mystic parentage," together with the natural family, based on blood-relation, is classified under "kinship groups" (p. 185) and not, say, under "political groups" or under "mystic ecstatic groups," where churches, congregations, religious orders and sects, together with "magical brotherhoods" (!) are supposed to belong as sub-types. Indeed, one is left to wonder in vain, especially since Gurvitch explains that "in archaic society, the family is identical with the clan, which is itself identical with the church (!) and the political groups," while he identifies the "magical brotherhood" in this society with the *occupational group*, which he has characterized as a sub-type of "economic activity groups." In addition, the primitive clans or sibs, too, often display the character of this latter type. Later we shall show the fundamental error in Gurvitch's attempt to classify undifferentiated communities with the help of a functional criterion which he also applies to differentiated "social groups."

The "groups of non-lucrative activity" mentioned in his classification group (c), are simply catch-alls without any real structural-typological

---

[1] a) Kinship groups; locality groups; b) economic activity groups; c) groups of non-lucrative activity; d) mystic-ecstatic groups; e) friendship groups; or f) groups of table-companions, admirers or followers of one leader etc. (p.185).

meaning, just as are the groups under group (f), in which the common basic type seems to have been especially undetermined.

It is obvious that on the basis of such a shaky foundation there can be no question of a real structural analysis of the internal legal spheres of distinct types of differentiated or undifferentiated social areas.

It is not my intention – an impossibility in an article of this limited scope – to analyze every detail of the extremely complex sociology of law offered by Gurvitch. I referred only to that section of it that he called the "differential sociology of law" or the "jural typology of particular groupings," to show that a structural typology of the specific legal spheres of the distinct societal areas confronts us with transcendental-philosophical problems that cannot be disregarded with impunity. Which problems are these?

They are closely connected with the relation between the modal-aspectual structures and the typical individuality-structures of our temporal world of experience.

When Gurvitch calls upon philosophy of law to discover the criterion by which the field of investigation of *juridical* sociology can be delimited from *ethical* sociology, sociology of "religion" (*faith*),[1] *economic* sociology, *aesthetic* sociology, etc., it is immediately clear that he has not accounted for the transcendental-*modal* character of the relevant problematics.

For, as soon as he, in the Introduction of his *Sociology of Law*, introduces the juridical-philosophical problem of a "definition of law," he makes quite clear that what is at stake is to gain "non-dogmatical" insight into the "specificity of the complex reality of law" (p. 41). And because, according to him, sociology of law especially must investigate this complex social reality of law, philosophy of law should remain in close contact with sociology of law, also when the former seeks specific criteria of juridical experience and "jural reality." These sciences are "mutually dependent." The contradiction seemingly implied in this "mutual dependence" is supposedly resolved in his theory of the immediate, collective juridical experience,[2] the common basis for philosophy of law and sociology of law (and dogmatic juridical science as well), "infinitely variable in both spiritual and sense data and alone making it possible to grasp the full reality of law" (p. 241).

---

1 Cf. pp.183, 204. Here by "religion," Gurvitch meant the "religious community" which in the clans, as he wrongly supposes, is always of a totemistic character. But in reality totemistic clans do not always consider the totem as a god (cf. p.205). Lowie, in his well-known book *Primitive Society*, has already rightly warned against such a generalizing religious view of totemism.

2 According to Gurvitch this immediate, spontaneous juridical experience consists of collective acts of recognition of "spiritual values," embodied in social facts in which they are realized and brought together in a (variable) balance by means of "justice" (cf. pp.39, 241).

But what is to be understood here by "the full reality of law?" And in what sense can we seek a "definition of law" in the specific criteria of the "full reality of law," which supposedly can be grasped only in the immediate "integral" juridical experience?

A specific social reality of a *merely juridical* character does not exist. The "juridical" or "jural" is never more than a modal aspect of social reality, and this reality is given to us only in a great diversity of typical individuality-structures in mutual interwovenness. In principle these individuality-structures embrace *all* modal aspects of our temporal world of experience in an unbreakable meaning-coherence. It is within these integral structures, which show a gradual arrangement according to structural types or radical types and sub-types, that the modal aspectual functions of social reality are gradually individualized and placed within a *typical* structural coherence as "typicalized" (i.e. individualized in a typical way) modal functions of an individual whole. This typical structural coherence will be explained later.

Because of its purely modal character the juridical point of view, distinguishing sociology of law from economic, aesthetic, moral or religious (better, *pistical – Gr. pistis* = faith) sociology, can never grasp a "specific social reality." In other words, the fundamental concept of law, which Gurvitch correctly considers a necessary jural-philosophical presupposition of the sociology of law, can only be gained by way of an analysis of the modal structure of the jural mode of experience, which, as such, is strictly a transcendental *modus quo*, a general *how*, not a concrete *what* of our integral social experience.

Gurvitch, whose concept of this experiential mode is supposed to relate to a specifically juridical "social reality," is as a result of this erroneous supposition caught in inescapable contradictions. On the one hand he posits that "the most immediate data of jural experience are 'normative facts' and the 'justice' which governs them" (p.42). On the other hand he writes just a little earlier: "the social reality of law is neither an immediate datum of intuition nor a content of sense perception, but is rather a construct of reason, moreover, detached from social reality as a total phenomenon" (p. 41).[1] It happens that for Gurvitch the "social reality of law" consists primarily in exactly these "normative social facts" of a specifically juridical character. If such "facts" are construc-

---

1 This statement, which is far from clear, depends on the presupposition that the philosophical criteria for distinguishing the "jural," "moral," "aesthetic," and "religious," ought to make it possible "to isolate in the reality of collective conduct and external patterns the working of law, or morality, of religion or aesthetics" (p. 39). The "social reality of law" then is, in his opinion, an abstraction from social reality as it is given in its totality, just like a social reality of morality, or of religion, or of aesthetics would be. But then it can never be an immediate given of intuitive juridical experience in the sense meant by Gurvitch. The lack of clarity and the inner contradiction in this train of thought is rooted in his continually confusing the juridical, moral, pistical and aesthetic modes of experience, with abstracted "kinds of reality."

tions of reason and mere abstractions from the "social reality as total phenomenon," how then can they be the most immediate *data* of juridical experience?

Sociology of law ought to begin, he says, with the aid of philosophy of law, "by delimiting the jural facts from those social facts which, being equally related to spiritual values, are most closely akin to the facts of law, i.e. moral, religious, aesthetic and similar facts" (p. 41).

According to his further explanation he understands by "jural facts" or "facts of law" the "normative facts" which are the immediate sources of positive law and which he distinguishes sharply from secondary sources, for instance, the technical procedures for establishing such facts, such as statutes, sentences, contracts, etc., taken in a formal sense, which are usually called juridical originating forms of law. In contradistinction to Eugen Ehrligh's naturalistic conception of *Tatsachen des Rechts*, Gurvitch wishes to take these "facts of law" in a real *juridical* sense, i.e. as *legal* facts, in which values are embodied, balanced by "justice." Every social group where an active form of social life dominates and in which values are embodied in this way, and also every all-embracing society in which such groups function, constitute such "jural facts," and they produce their own law. The same is true, according to him, of the "micro-sociological elements" out of which these groups and societies are built up, and by which he means the ways of being bound to and by the societal whole, or the "forms of sociability."[1]

But for sociology of law "jural facts," too, can never be more than the *juridical aspect* of concrete societal facts. Certainly, there are societal facts that, according to their individuality-structure, are typically *qualified* by their juridical aspect, such as a summons, a sentence, an act of legislation, just as there are others of typically economic, aesthetic, moral, or pistical qualification. But even in the case of typical juridically qualified social facts, the "jural fact" is merely a modal aspect of an *actual* social fact. For the latter is not exhausted in the former. And, *a fortiori*, "social groups" and the "society" in which they function cannot be "normative facts" in a merely-juridical sense.

Modal jural and typical jural relationships

It is not possible to gain insight into the transcendental structural principles of the *typical internal* legal spheres of the particular societal areas without some understanding of the *modal* structure of the juridical aspect in its indissoluble coherence with the other modal aspects of our experience. Because the plurality of these typical legal spheres, to which Gurvitch has correctly called attention in his sociology of law, is

---

[1] It must be clear that by these "forms of sociability" Gurvitch means something quite different from what I have called the "societal forms" in which the typical structural principles of the societal spheres are realized.

possible only on the basis of the unity of the general modal structure of our jural mode of experience. It is on the strength thereof that we can attribute without reservation a *juridical* character to all these legal spheres, independently of their *juridical typicalness*.

A penetrating transcendental analysis of this modal structure on the part of the philosophy of law can provide sociology of law with a concept of the jural mode of experience that is dynamic (i.e. never fixed or closed in an *a priori* fashion). In such an analysis the jural aspect will turn out to be identifiable but inseparable from all other aspects of our horizon of experience, both in its fundamental *irreducibility* and in its unbreakable *coherence*. Gurvitch too quickly rejects every transcendental "definition of law" and places it on equal footing with various "metaphysical, normative, psychological, utilitarian and sociological" definitions as "arbitrary and dogmatic constructions."[1] Too quickly, because on the one hand he is only acquainted with a transcendental method of defining the concept of law in neo-Kantian, so-called "critical-idealistic" conceptions, and on the other hand because he assigns to the concept of the general jural mode of experience the impossible task of providing criteria for the demarcation of a specifically juridical reality. We saw that such a reality in a purely jural sense does not exist, and that even as "construction of reason" it remains meaningless.

As far as the first point is concerned, I would like to point out that in my so-called "Philosophy of the Cosmonomic Idea" I have developed a new method for a modal analysis of the structure of the transcendental *modes* or *modal aspects* of our experience. This method has nothing to do with what Gurvitch calls rationalistic dogmatism, working with "fixed and mummified categories," as can justly be said of, say, Rudolph Stammler's critical-idealistic concept of law. Our jural mode of experience is not, as Stammler thinks, constituted by some complex of so-called transcendental logical forms of thought or categories in which we are supposed to order an "experiential matter" of psychical desires, nor is the jural mode of experience *identical* with the epistemological concept of the latter.

And exactly because of its transcendental character, this jural mode cannot be determined *per genus proximum et differentias specificas*, as Stammler still holds, since a genuine transcendental experiential mode is by its very nature of an ultimate generic character. Its modal structure is a dynamic meaning-structure, in which the center is the structural nuclear moment which I call the "modal meaning-nucleus" of the juridical aspect of experience. It guarantees the irreducibility of this modality with respect to others. But this nuclear moment can only reveal its own

---

1 Cf. *Sociology of Law*, p. 40, and more extensively in his *Experience Juridique et la Philosophie Pluraliste du Droit* (1935) pp.19 ff.

dynamic character of meaning in indissoluble coherence with a series of "analogical" meaning-moments that respectively refer back to, or forward to all those modal aspects that occupy either earlier or later positions in the transcendental-temporal order of our experience. These analogical moments of meaning (which I further define as being either retrocipatory or anticipatory) assure the unbreakable meaning-bond between the juridical and other modes of experience, *viz*. those of numerical quantity, space, (extensive) movement, energy, those of the biotic, the sensitive, the analytical, the cultural-historical, the symbolic, and those of social intercourse, the economic, the aesthetic, the moral and the pistical (the latter being the experiential mode of faith). But their modal meaning here is *qualified* by the modal meaning-nucleus of the jural mode of experience and may, therefore, never be confused with the modal meaning of the correlate modal structural moments of non-juridical modalities. In this way the modal structure of the juridical aspect reflects the entire order and inter-modal meaning-coherence of the transcendental modes of experience, as is also the case in the modal structure of all the other aspects of experience.

Quite distinct from these are the transcendental structural principles that determine the typical inner character of the various social areas. They are, as mentioned earlier, principles of individuality-structures. Potentially they embrace *all* modal aspects of our experiential horizon. Although they do not affect the general inter-modal *order* of the experiential aspects, they do bind the various modal functions of the societal spheres within these aspects into the structural-typical coherence of an individual whole. As far as the structural principles of *differentiated* social life-areas functioning in a highly developed, opened-up society are concerned, this occurs in the first place because one of their modal aspects takes on a central, qualifying role in the typical structural whole. For within that structural whole, the social collectivity concerned, in accordance with its inner character, finds its *internal qualifying function* distinguished carefully from the objective and subjective purposes which it serves, or can be made to serve, because such purposes presuppose the internal-transcendental structural principle of that social sphere, and can, therefore, never be part of it.

Marriage as institution, for example, is, in accordance with the creational order, undoubtedly able to serve procreation of the human race, and one can therefore consider forming a family and rearing children as *objective* purposes of marriage. But such a *telos* cannot possibly determine the intrinsic structure of marriage. The reason is that a family in its narrowest sense, as natural community of two parents with adolescent children whether born in wedlock or legitimized, is in its inner nature something different from the communal bond of marriage between husband and wife. This remains the case, regardless of how closely the children, when they are born, are actually tied in with the family. A childless marriage too retains its internal character, i.e. that of the communal bond.

As a final point, procreation can occur also by sexual intercourse outside the matrimonial community. Clearly, therefore, the so-called objective goal of procreation lies beyond that of the inner nature of the communal bond.

It is the typical leading function, or in other words (always understood from the modal point of view) the directional function of its inner structural principle, which in the Philosophy of the Cosmonomic Idea is called its *internal qualifying function*, that enables us to distinguish the connubial bond that is genetically founded in it.

In this connection it should be noted that the internal structural principles of the various societal spheres, which determine their typical essential nature, necessarily have the character of typical structural norm-principles. They must receive positive content through human form-giving in accordance with the cultural-historical situation of a society. A human society is not regulated and maintained by invariable instinctive social drives, as in the case of the animal world. The societal life-spheres functioning in human society have intrinsic structural principles of a normative character, and their actualization, therefore, implies a task for those who are charged with concretizing them. In our sinful world this actualization is only possible in an imperfect way, and these defectively positivized structural norms can be violated by the factual behavior of those who are subject to these norms in a given societal sphere.

The example I used, marriage, is, as I have extensively tried to show in other writings, intrinsically qualified as a moral community of love for the duration of the common life span of two persons of different sex. Within the boundaries of the general modal structure of the moral aspect this love relationship shows an individuality type that does not have an original character within the aspect, but finally refers back to an original individuality type within the organic life aspect of the conjugal relation, namely the lasting sexual biotic bond between husband and wife. In view of its original character the Philosophy of the Cosmonomic Idea calls this the nuclear type of the individuality of the internal connubial community. The moral individuality type of the conjugal love community is typically founded in the sexual-biotic function of marriage, and by means of this coheres in a structural-typical way with this biotic individuality type. Thus the inner structural principle of the institution of marriage, which determines the irreducible typical inner nature of this community, is characterized by two structural functions, the so-called "*radical functions*." The first (the moral conjugal love relation) is the leading, or internal qualifying function; the second (the sexual-biotic) is the foundational function.

The leading function ought to open up all the modal functions preceding it in the inter-modal aspectual order of the internal structural whole of the marriage community, and should direct them to the intrinsic qualifying and leading function of that community as moral conjugal love community. The modal structure of its pre-moral aspects makes this possible, because their anticipatory meaning-moments – those that point to later aspects – typicalized by the internal structural principle of this community, can open themselves up under the guidance of the intrinsic qualifying function. This holds in the first place for the typical foundational function of the conjugal community, the durable sexual-biotic bond between husband and wife, which under direction of the moral conjugal bond of love is radically different from the periodic instinctive mating drive found in the sexual biotic functioning of animals.

Thus the internal structural principle of marriage can express itself in every one of its modal aspects.[1]

In this way the structural principles also determine its intrinsically typical jural sphere, which should be distinguished carefully from the spheres of civil law and ecclesiastic law, or (in a still-undifferentiated society) the primitive tribal law, in which the matrimonial relations have only an external function because of their intertwinements respectively with state and church, or with the undifferentiated tribal community. All intrinsic juridical relations between husband and wife are, according to the normative structural principle of marriage, qualified in a typically moral way by the conjugal love relation, which in turn is typically founded biotically. Hence the internal juridical rights and duties of the marriage partners in relation to each other can never, as civil rights do, be sanctioned by the compulsive legal power of the state. This does not detract from their modal juridical character, since this does not depend on the typical structural principle of the private and public law of the state. They can, however, have some juridical consequences in the sphere of civil law, insofar as typically morally qualified jural duties are acknowledged as natural obligations.[2]

The internal juridical spheres of the other social areas of life as they function in a differentiated society ought to be theoretically delimited in

---

1 In its faith-aspect, insofar as it has been opened up by the gospel of Jesus Christ and the Holy Spirit, it refers beyond the temporal conjugal love-bond to the religious fullness of the love bond between Christ and his *"spiritual body,"* the church (Ephesians 5:25-33).

2 The Dutch *Supreme Court* has accepted this kind of natural obligation since its famous judgment of March 12, 1926 (N.J. 1927, 777). In a judgment of Nov.30, 1946, the *Supreme Court* decided that, if a husband performs his moral duty to make provision for his wife after his death, this is not to be considered a gift but meeting a natural obligation.

accordance with the same structural-typological method briefly sketched above.[1]

Transcendental categories of our social experience

The actual structural-typological investigation of societal relationships, however, is necessarily founded upon a number of preliminary distinctions which form the basis for the horizontal systematic classification of these relations, and overarch their vertical structurally-typical divergence. These basic distinctions may not be arbitrary either. They ought to rest upon the *transcendental categories of our social experience*, as they are called in the Philosophy of the Cosmonomic Idea, because they constitute the basis for all structurally-typical distinctions of the societal relationships, and thus make them possible.

1. The most fundamental of these categorial distinctions between societal relations is that of communal and coordinational (inter-individual and inter-communal) relations. By the first I mean all those social relationships wherein people function as members of a whole. The second are those in which individuals or the communities do not together function as members of a whole, but in co-ordination; either in cooperation or in a mutually neutral position; either in sympathetic or in antagonistic relations (competition, war, etc.). All structurally-typical distinctions in the communal and inter-individual or inter-communal relations presuppose this categorial distinction. It is a distinction that at the same time implies correlativity. For, viewed externally, every communal relation has its necessary correlate in inter-individual or inter-communal ones and vice versa. In the jural mode of experience this categorial relation expresses itself in the mutual relation between communal and inter-individual or inter-communal jural relations that cannot be reduced to each other.

2. The communal relations are categorially divided into natural ones, and those that characteristically depend on organization. The first (marriage, domestic family, the cognate-family in a broader sense) are inherently unorganized and can, because of their natural character, actualize themselves at all times, be it in extremely variable societal forms. The arising of communities of the second type, however, is dependent upon certain historical conditions. Organization lends them continuity, regardless of the life span of the members or the duration of their membership. In line with current German sociological terminology we can call these organized communities *sociale Verbande* and their internal juridical order *Verbandsrecht*. In

---

[1] The third volume of my *A New Critique of Theoretical Thought* (Amsterdam and Philadelphia, 1957), contains an extensive structural-typological analysis of societal relationships.

every one of the *sociale Verbande* we necessarily meet with authority and subordination. Among the natural communities the wider cognate family lacks an inherently characteristic authority-subordination relation. Inter-individual and inter-communal relations lack it *per se*. In their case there is great diversity of gifts, of possession, of power, so that in social intercourse with others, certain individuals or communities gain a position of leadership, but intrinsic authority and duty of obedience do not exist here, nor does durable organization.

3. A further categorical distinction is that between institutional and non-institutional communities. Institutional communities are those that, according to their nature, embrace their members either for their entire life (as in the case of natural kinship), or during part of it, irrespective of their own will. Besides the natural communities, the state and the church (*if it has baptismal members*) are also of this character. In an undifferentiated society the undifferentiated sibs, tribes and brotherhoods are of this character as well. But non-institutional organizations characteristically rest upon the principle of voluntary membership, implying freedom to join and to leave. The typical originating forms of such societal relationships are free association or one-sided establishment, both taken in the sense of founding-acts, in which, unlike the originating forms of institutional communities, the determination of *ends* and *means* is a necessary or constitutive element.

4. Finally, the social relationships are categorically to be divided in connection with their historical level of development into differentiated and undifferentiated.
Undifferentiated organized communities in particular present general sociology, sociology of law, and the science of legal history with a special structural-typological problem. This is because in these cases the most diverse typical structural principles may be interwoven in one organizational form. Structural principles as different, for instance, as those of a unilateral and partially fictional family-bond, of a political defense, and of peace, organization, a cult-community, an economic enterprise – all together make for a bound unity of a typical structural whole. How is this possible?
This socio-philosophical problem is completely eliminated when, as in the case of Gurvitch, the distinct types of social relations that are interwoven in undifferentiated organizations are simply identified with each other and when such organizations, together with differentiated ones, are classified after a functional criterion which proves to be useless here. Take for example the patrilineally or matrilineally organized clans or sibs, which function in various primitive

peoples (although certainly not in all) as truly institutional communities. Is the clan here identical with the political group, with the cult-community, etc. as Gurvitch claims it is? This cannot possibly be maintained.

The clan is an organized community that cuts across the natural family and the cognate kinship relation and therefore never quite absorbs them. And the clan is not identical with its function as political, or religious, or agricultural community. It can unite the characteristics of all these types, but this undifferentiated social unit can only become a typical structural whole because the family principle fulfils a central, leading function in it, so that the organization of the entire community depends upon an artificial, unilateral and partly fictional system of blood-relation. This also explains the rule of sib-exogamy, in virtue of which sib or clan members are not allowed to marry each other, even where the blood-relation rests on a fictional, mystic foundation. It can be said, therefore, that the undifferentiated structure of the clan or sib-community is typically *qualified* by the family or kinship principle, and that this qualification expresses itself in every type of its internal organized communal relationships, which therefore remain enclosed within an undifferentiated whole. Still, this social totality-structure is not typically biotically founded as is the natural cognate family (limited by fixed degrees of genetic blood-relation). It has a typically cultural-historical foundation in an undifferentiated power-organization which receives, by way of artificial systems of ancestry, an exceptional cohesiveness and intensity, reinforced by factors of magic and religious power.

Hence, the sib, along with other undifferentiated communities, is doomed to disappear as soon as the process of differentiation in the cultural-historical development of human society begins. And it is also clear why it is not yet present in weakly organized primitive communities, as for instance the well-known American ethnologist Lowie, in his *Primitive Society*, has pointed out as an objection against evolutionistic reconstruction of this process of development.

Conclusion

In conclusion, I will make a few brief remarks concerning the fundamental significance of the transcendental structural typology of differentiated societal spheres and their typical intrinsic juridical areas for determination of their mutual relation in the usually extremely complex *structural interlacing*, in which they in their variable societal forms are necessarily involved. The problem of this mutual relation cannot be evaded, and the question as to how it is conceived determines the total view a student of differential sociology of law will have concerning jural life in an all-inclusive society.

In the Philosophy of the Cosmonomic Idea inter-structural intertwinement between societal relations of radically different inner nature is called *enkapsis*.[1]

Enkapsis should not be confused with the relation of a social whole and its parts, as is present for instance in the case of the state of the Netherlands with its subdivisions into provinces and municipalities. The part-whole relation can only occur within the internal sphere of one and the same typical structural whole, and is determined by the latter's intrinsic structural principle. Accordingly, in a differentiated society, the natural communities of marriage and family, a church denomination, an economic enterprise, a university or a labour union, can never be part of the state, although they are established within its territory. Their typical inner structural principle is simply radically different from that of the state. Their interrelation with the latter is rather that of a territorial enkapsis – an enkapsis that only concerns the external relations between them and the state, but which cannot encompass their inner communal sphere determined by their internal structural principle. This holds even when the enkapsis takes on a very closely bound character, so that we could speak of a "union" between political and non-political relationships. In this way enkaptic structures originate such as of a state-church or a church-state, a state-university, state-industry, a partisan-state, etc.

The particular "variability-type" that state, church, university, etc., display in such cases are not due to the intrinsic structural principles of these societal relationships but to the variable societal forms in which they are actualized.

All types of societal relationship, according to their categorial correlation of communal and inter-individual or inter-communal relations, become involved in enkaptic structural intertwinements by way of the societal forms in which they are realized. Within these societal forms they take on variability types, distinct from their inner structural types.

This distinction between internal structural types and variability types of communal and inter-individual or inter-communal societal relations is of fundamental significance for the structural typology of the various legal spheres in a differentiated human society. Delimitation of the internal juridical spheres of the distinct social life-areas is possible only

---

[1] This term, introduced by the Swiss biologist Heidenhain, was given a general philosophical sense by the German thinker Theodor L. Haering in his small but important book *Ueber Individualität in Natur- und Geisteswelt* (Tübner, Leipzig und Berlin, 1926). He used it, in a sense quite different from that explained in the text, to indicate the relation between an individual whole and its individual and relatively autonomous parts.

on the basis of the typical internal structural principles of the latter, which are the condition for their different variability types. These intrinsic structural principles also determine, in principle, the original (i.e. not juridically deduced) spheres of competence in the area of formation of positive law.

On the other hand, the juridical originating forms of positive legal rules, and of positive subjective legal relations in the various legal spheres (civil private law and internal public law of the state; international law, supra-national law; internal church-law, internal industrial law, etc.) are veritable knots of enkaptic intertwinements between the distinct juridical spheres. Without philosophical insight into the internal structural types of these different jural spheres a proper analysis of their enkaptic intertwinement is simply not possible.

The relation of the individual and community from a legal philosophical perspective[1]

AN AGE OVERESTIMATING the individual is necessarily followed by one overestimating the community. This is also true of legal life and the philosophy of law.

Post-medieval legal philosophy, in its first period, is characterized by the modern humanistic doctrine of natural law as it was founded by Grotius. In reaction to this phase the second period emerged as the Historical School of Law and became the dominant trend in modern sociology.

Individualistic and Universalistic conceptions of Law

Theoretically seen, the individualistic doctrine of natural law is strongly influenced by the modern humanistic natural science-ideal. This ideal sets out to *control* reality by reducing complex phenomena to their simplest elements. Its aim is to analyze these elements with the aid of exact mathematical concepts in order to unveil the laws determining reality fully. The methods of mathematics and occasionally that of mathematical physics (Hobbes) serve as model in this regard. The modern doctrine of natural law similarly attempts to explain the organized communities of human society in terms of their elements, the *individuals*. It performs this jural construction on the basis of the social contract theory.

The Historical School and to some extent also the sociological doctrine of law are positioned against this *individualistic* and constructing approach in its advocacy of a *universalistic* view proceeding from the *totality* in order to understand its *parts*. This, however, is not done in a consistent way. The Historical School, for example, does not get beyond the *people* comprising the "totality of the national culture." From the individual folk nature of the latter, it asserts, the unique legal order, language, mores, art, etc. of that people flow as products of history.

With this the idea of an order of natural law itself, fitting all times and peoples, is rejected.

---
1 This article appeared in the "Algemeen Nederlands Tijdschrift voor Wijsbegeerte en Psychologie," Year 39, Number 1, October 1946, pp.5-11 – under the title: *De verhouding van individu en gemeenschap rechtswijsgeerig bezien* (The relation of the individual and community from a legal philosophical perspective). *Translator:* D.F.M. Strauss; *Editor:* Alan M. Cameron.

The relation of the individual and community from a legal philosophical perspective

The struggle between these two main trends occupies a prominent place in the divergent evaluation of the Roman *ius gentium* (world law).

The Germanistic wing of the Historical School viewed the reception of the *ius gentium* in Germanic countries of the continent as a forging of the "Germanic conception of law." The latter was supposed to be permeated to a great degree by a "social spirit." It viewed all law as displaying in principle the same character.

Roman law, by contrast, breathes the spirit of Cain, that of an unbridled individualism, and proceeds from a sharp separation between public law and private law. It causes the individual and the state to stand irreconcilably over against each other. The same concern is expressed in the dominant sociological doctrine of law. This approach still uses the (now outdated) depiction of the "spirit of Roman law" as a "spirit of disciplined egoism" in the way that it was put forward dramatically by von Jhering.

On the other hand, from its outset, the doctrine of natural law of the 17th and 18th century viewed the Roman *ius gentium* as the *ratio scripta* and as the *residue* of the true natural law.

One can follow this struggle in the divergent assessments of the modern codifications of civil law which, as an effect of the Enlightenment, were introduced in Prussia, France, Austria and presently also in The Netherlands.

The currently all-powerful historicistic and sociological views of law claim to recognize in these codifications the continual influence of the individualistic spirit of Roman law and a desire for a radical transformation of the "social spirit" which is, according to this view, already in the process of emerging. The call for a *droit social* as substitute for the *droit individuel* has become universal. Various national-socialistic jurists have already spoken about a "farewell to the Civil Code."

Within the idea of the *droit social,* seen as a communal demand permeating legal life in its entirety, an overestimation of the community-idea manifests itself, similar to the fashion in which the idea of a *droit naturel* managed to push the pendulum to the other extreme of an overestimation of individual freedom in the 18th century. For legal philosophy and for legal life the struggle between these two trends is a matter of serious concern.

If one looks at the humanistic doctrine of natural law only as an aprioristic construction, designed in a rigid way, as a legal system to fit all people and times and deduced by applying a mathematical method, then one views it too one-sidedly according to its theoretical and legal philosophic pretensions. For in this sense both its foundation and its method are no longer defensible.

But the doctrine of natural law also had a prominent *practical* tendency – something modern criticisms often have not recognized. This practical tendency is even present in the work of an author such as Grotius who had the intention of developing his doctrine of natural law fully independent of political issues, similar to the mathematician who constructs his figures entirely divorced from "matter."

Civil Law and the idea of the State

Essentially this has initiated the quest of pursuing the basic principles of *civil private law* and the *modern idea of the state*. However, both these ideals were lost again during the medieval period since it came into conflict with indigenous Germanic legal practices that were still primitive in many ways. It also clashed with the feudal system, a whole complex of royal rights, privileges, and a diversity of property relationships reflecting differences in social rank (old farmer serfs, landlord serfs, church serfs and so on), all of which still strongly reflected the stamp of an undifferentiated society.

On the other hand, when the Roman world law was seen as *ratio scripta* and as a positive expression of natural law, then this view was fully consistent with the classical Roman jurists, for these latter maintained a close connection between the *ius naturale* and the *ius gentium* – so intimately that it sometimes was identified incorrectly.

The *ius gentium* was the first realization of a truly *civil law* within the Roman world imperium. It fundamentally differs from the older primitive *ius civile*, i.e. the Roman folk law. The latter can at best be compared with the primitive Germanic folk laws, as they were described in the *leges barbarorum* during the Frankian period.

This kind of folk law still belongs to an *undifferentiated* condition of society – a phase in which all law still displays only one character because as yet society did not know differentiated spheres such as that of the church, the state, commerce and business firms, free associational organizations, and so on.

Undifferentiated spheres of life, such as that of the *familia*, neighborhood, guilds (in the sense of brotherhoods or fraternities), the communal life of the Roman people and the tribe, still encompassed human life totally, with respect to all spheres of life. These spheres take on all tasks that, at a deepened level of cultural development, are performed by independent differentiated societal collectivities. The undifferentiated sphere of power of these collectivities, often strongly rooted in a pagan religion of life, is *absolute* and *exclusive*. The entire legal status of a human being, as a consequence, is completely dependent upon membership in these primitive collectivities. Whoever finds himself outside this bond is *hostis, exlex*, i.e. without any rights or peace. The undifferentiated community absorbs the individual according to that person's entire legal status.

This is also valid with regard to the old Roman *familia* where the head, the *pater familias*, had an undifferentiated power over all members, rooted religiously in the exclusive power of the house and hearth gods. This power was an absolute and exclusive *dominium* simultaneously incorporating authority and the competence to dispose of property rights. This undifferentiated concept of property was not close to an individualistic spirit at all, as was suggested by von Jhering. Much rather, it is an expression of the totalitarian primitive conception of community.

Civil private law is totally different from primitive folk law. It is the product of a long developmental process, giving birth to a *differentiation* of society. As soon as the undifferentiated spheres of life are transcended, it becomes possible for the differentiated societal collectivities to manifest themselves. Then, according to their inner nature, no single one of them can any longer encompass the human being with respect to *all* spheres of life. Thus it becomes possible to acknowledge the *rights of the individual human being as such*, apart from all particular communal ties such as gender, race, nation, church orientation, social rank and status.

The human being *as such* now witnesses the allocation of an individual sphere of freedom that embodies the *private autonomy* of that person.

By virtue of its particular nature civil law does not accept a difference in principle between human beings on the basis of race, social status or rank – they all enjoy *civil legal freedom* and *equality*.

The classical Roman jurists understood this in terms of their idea of the *ius naturale*. This idea, because it is rooted in the intrinsic nature of civil law, brought to expression, in a pregnant way, the *constant basic principles* of civil law. In doing that, it sharply distinguishes itself from the Aristotelian idea of natural law which also comprises communal ties evincing inequality in position. These classical Roman jurists were justified in positing this essentially *civil legal ius naturale* as the basis of the Roman *ius gentium*. We have seen that they often even presented the two as being identical.

However, this identification is not valid, since the *ius gentium* continued to accept the institute of slavery and, therefore, in this respects deviated from the *ius naturale*. Furthermore, it only gave a completely *historically* determined *positive* form to the former.

The modern humanistic doctrine of natural law advocated this notion of the *ius naturale* to an increasing degree. During the Enlightenment it crystallized in the doctrine of *innate and inalienable human rights*.

Within modern differentiated legal life, civil law constitutes only one of the distinct spheres of private law. As such it is closely connected with the state.

The multiple spheres of private law are fully determined according to the differentiated structural principles of human society. For example, the sphere of internal ecclesiastical law, in its internal jural character and original sphere of competence, is delimited by the peculiar structural principle of the church-institute as institutional community of

Christian believers within the organized service of the Word and the Sacraments. Ecclesiastical law unmistakenly evinces a private communal character and its own irreducible nature. It can never be delineated merely on the basis of its juridical genetic form (ecclesiastical rules of procedure), since within this genetic form ecclesiastical law may be interlaced with legal spheres of a different nature.

Similarly, there also exists the internal legal sphere of a modern factory, which, according to its internal character, is delimited by the structural principle of the firm as one that is qualified by the economic entrepreneurial organization of capital and labor.

This piece of private law, originating from the juridical form of the rules of procedure of the factory, also bears a specific *communal* character, though it lacks the typical *institutional* feature of ecclesiastical law since it completely rests on a voluntary basis.[1]

The same applies to the domain of law related to the sphere of interaction in trade and commerce. This domain is also economically qualified though it does not share a communal character. It exhibits a coordinational nature since individuals participating in this legal relationship are coordinated with each other and are not bound together into a durable unity.

We may consider in this regard the so-called "standard clauses" regularly incorporated in separate agreements reached within the different branches of trade and business. In spite of the fact that, as "generally accepted stipulations," they are *acknowledged* by civil law, these "standard clauses" have an internal nature different from civil law.

Each one of the different societal institutions has its own internal law (consider a social club, a philanthropic association, a trade organization, etc., etc.). All of them stand in service of, and are qualified by, the particular qualifying function of the societal spheres to which they belong. In that way they have a specifically organized communal character since the members of a corporation are organized into a unity.

Civil private law is not a *specific* law in this sense. In other words, it is not fit to serve, and qualified by, a typical internal guiding function which itself lies *outside* the jural aspect. It is a *ius commune*, a common *law*, as it is called by the British. By itself it has no other destination than to bring to expression the requirements of the *ius naturale*, of *natu*-

---

1 *Translator's note:* Dooyeweerd distinguishes between *institutional* and *voluntary* societal collectivities. Communities "destined to encompass their members to an intensive degree, continuously or at least for a considerable part of their life, and as such in a way independent of their will," are called *institutional* (*A New Critique of Theoretical Thought*, 1957, Vol.III:187).

ral justice in the classical sense of the word,[1] as we have explained above.

According to its internal nature it is built upon the basis of individual human rights of freedom and equality. This character prevents it from having a communal nature. Therefore it has to be distinguished from the domain of what is known as *social labor rights* – a domain with its own unique constitution and destination.

The attempt to *transform* it into a communal law, according to the model of the modern idea of the *droit social,* inevitably cancels its civil legal nature. For the *intrinsic nature* of the different legal spheres is not something *made* by human beings, since, to every person forming law, it is a *given*, based upon the order and structure of reality.

Civil private law, in its nature, constitutes the juridical asylum of the human personality, the stronghold of individual freedom and as such it is destined to provide a beneficial counter balance against the excessive pressure of communal demands within legal life.

In our modern era, due to the reign of historicism and a naturalistic sociologism, this is hardly understood any longer. Both these spiritual trends are united in their historicistic view of human society, according to which everything is caught up in continual development and in a flowing transition. They do not have an eye for the *constant structural principles* that determine the nature of the different spheres of life and that themselves make all historical development possible in the first place.

The Historical School, in a dangerous fashion, starts to link civil law to the individual character and spirit of a people (*Volksgeist*) and in doing so it attempts to eliminate fundamental difference between civil law and primitive folk law. The attempt is accompanied by a serious attack on the classical Roman and the modern humanistic doctrine of the *ius naturale*. All forms of law are seen as the historical product of the peculiar disposition of a people (*volk*) which, therefore, in principle is *communal* law, bearing a typical "folk" character.

> The Romanistic wing did not pursue the consequences entailed in this approach. It continued to adore the Roman world law in its classical phase of development as "ratio scripta," although it rejected the doctrine of the *ius naturale*.

But in the Germanistic wing the basic thesis of the Historical School initiated an assault against the "individualistic" ius gentium of the Romans. And modern sociology, disseminated from France, launched an attack against the "abstract metaphysics" of the ideas of freedom and equality.

---

1 *Editorial note* (AC): "Natural justice" in this context has to be distinguished from the same expression when it is applied in administrative law.

It is remarkable that the attack against the foundations of civil law is always accompanied by an assault in principle on the *modern idea of the state*, which rests upon a sharp distinction of public and private law and on the principle of the *salus publica* in its clear separation from all group interest.

Leon Duguit, the French scholar in constitutional law, who required a "transformation du droit civil"[1] according to the spirit of a *droit social*, simultaneously proclaimed the statement *l'état est mort*.[2] But already in the case of Count St. Simon (with Auguste Comte the founder of positivistic sociology), we can see to what an extent the battle against the "metaphysical" doctrine of human rights is accompanied by an attack on the state, which, as the instrument of class domination, is destined to "die away."

We need not be surprised by this intimate connection in the fight against civil law and the state, since the internal law of the state, as *ius publicum*, shares with *civil private law* the absence of a qualification outside the jural guiding function. The state is, just as the church, an *institutional* community, though, through its structural principle, the state radically differs from the church. According to this structural principle the state is characterized as a *public legal community* of government and subjects on the basis of a monopolistic territorial organization of the power of the sword. The internal "destinational" function of the state is given in the creation of a *public legal community*, which stands in an indissoluble structural coherence with a typical historical foundation in a monopolistic organization of the power of the sword. The *salus publica* as fundamental principle of the public institutional law of the state essentially has to be conceived of as an idea of *public law*.

This presupposes in the first place that the state cannot assume an absolute sovereignty over the other societal spheres that differ in principle from the state.

Every form of *legal* power, that of the state also, is structurally delimited by the inner nature of the sphere of life within which it is exercised. For law finds its symbol in the scales of Themis. It requires, according to its nature, *delimitation* and *counter-balance* of every competence by another one.

As soon as one ascribes an *absolute* sovereignty to the state, one has abandoned the *boundaries of law* and collapses into state absolutism, based upon a deification of the state. Then also the idea of the *salus publica* degenerates into a lever for an unhampered state absolutism, echoing the frightening sound of the Leviathan, the "Behemoth."

---

1 A "transformation of civil law."
2 "The state is dead."

The inner delimitation of the legal power of the state is given by the internal structural principle of this societal institution. The *ius publicum*, constitutive of the internal law of the state as public legal institution, does not permit service to group interests external to the jural qualifying function of the state.

Therefore, the nature of the state is irreconcilable with the allocation of *privileges* to specific persons or groups. Similarly, no individual or group may withdraw from the public legal power of the government within the *sphere of life of the state*.

The State as Public Legal Institution

For that reason the state had to commence its entry into the world scene by starting to do away with the undifferentiated spheres of authority of private lords and societal collectivities which withdrew their subjects from the legal power of the state.

In order to achieve this aim the *public legal principle* of *freedom* and *equality* has to be pursued. It also forms the basis upon which *civil legal* private freedom and equality are to be attained. As long as it is possible for private lords and for private societal collectivities, to exercise an exclusive and undifferentiated power over their subjects, there is no room for a truly *ius publicum* and for a truly *civil ius privatum*.

It is only the *state*, on the basis of its public legal power, that can open up to the individual person a *civil legal* sphere of freedom, providing that person with a guarantee against the overexertion of power by specific private communities and also against an overexertion of the public legal power itself, as long as the public office bearers keep alive an awareness of the inner limits of their competence.

The state, in view of the inner nature of the *ius publicum*, does not have the competence to bind the exercise of civil private rights to a specific social-economic destination, simply because the *ius publicum* intrinsically lacks any specific *economic qualification*.

It lacks this competence also because civil law leaves it to private autonomy, in the exercise of civil private rights, to determine its own specific destination. Therefore, the modern sociological doctrine concerning legal abuse in civil private law, employing as a criterion the use of a subjective right contradicting the social-economic destination for which it was given (compare article 1 of the so-called Civil Codes of the Soviet Republics), cannot be reconciled with the foundations of civil law. It is a cautionary example of the undermining influence that the idea of *droit social*, in its overextension, exerts on civil private law.

III

ESSAYS IN POLITICAL PHILOSOPHY

The contest over the concept of sovereignty[1]

Introduction

IN THE EVOLUTION of Jurisprudence and Political Science in the second half of the last century many tenets that used to be taken for unassailable truths, were cast into the melting pot of criticism. But among these none was of such signal importance as the concept of sovereignty.

Notably, since the two World Wars the idea that the dogma of sovereignty ought to be consigned to the scrap heap, both from a scientific and from a practical point of view, has increasingly taken hold in the democratic countries.

Undeniably the attack has been especially focused now on the consequences of the dogma in the area of international law, because international relations have more and more become the center of interest.

But in the theory of constitutional law and in the general theory of the state the opposition against this dogma had already begun to arise in the second half of the last century.

As early as 1888 the German doctor of constitutional law Hugo Preusz thought that the elimination of the concept of sovereignty from the dogmas of constitutional law would only be a small step forward on the road this science has in fact long since taken.[2]

Since then sociology of law has asserted itself as a participant in the controversy and several of its prominent exponents have pointed out that the important metamorphosis of the social-economic structure of Western society has increasingly ousted the state from its central position, which formerly seemed to be the basis of the doctrine of sovereign power.

Lastly, one of the well-known proponents of neo-Scholastic philosophy, Jacques Maritain, has also made his stand against this dogma. In a recent article, "The Concept of Sovereignty," he declared: "The two

---
1 Rectorial address, delivered on the occasion of the 70th anniversary of the Free University on 20 October 1950. This oration – considerably enlarged – was published in Dutch by J. H. Paris, Amsterdam: *De Strijd om het souvereiniteitsbegrip in de moderne Rechts- en Staatsleer* (The contest over the concept of sovereignty in modern Jurisprudence and Political Science) (62 pp.).
2 *Gemeinde, Staat, Reich als Gebietskörpershaften*, p.135.

concepts of sovereignty and absolutism have been forged together on the same anvil. They must be scrapped together."[1]

That, in spite of these combined attacks, the concept of sovereignty had by no means been eliminated from jurisprudence and political science became evident from the forcible plea Herman Heller made for its complete rehabilitation (1927), a plea that became a fierce arraignment of the tendencies aimed at the undermining of this fundamental concept.[2] Also, the Viennese professor Alfred Verdrosz, once an adherent of Kelsen's *Reine Rechtslehre* (pure doctrine of law) and, as such, a fierce opponent of the traditional conception of the authoritative sovereign state, accepted the latter in his book on international law (published in 1937) as the necessary foundation of the law of nations.

On the whole it may be said that in dogmatic jurisprudence the doctrine of sovereignty still predominates, even though there is a tendency to avoid its extreme consequences in international relations.

Before the tribunal of science, one would certainly not be justified in taking a stand in this topical contest before realizing the many-sided part that the traditional concept of sovereignty has played in jurisprudence and political science since the 16th century, and the problems that would present themselves if it were eliminated.

In the second place it is an undeniable duty of both science and politics to inquire whether the currents that are asserted to oppose the doctrine of sovereignty have indeed disengaged themselves from it or only tend to enforce it again on science and practice in another form. As so often happens in controversies on normative concepts, terminological misunderstandings and obscurities may cloud scientific discussion.

Finally, for those who in studying science take their stand on the basis of the fundamentals of our University it is of paramount importance to ponder whether they can accept the way the problem is presented in the modern contest about the traditional concept of sovereignty, or whether those who start from the principles of the Reformation must follow essentially different lines of thought.

It does not seem out of place on this 70th anniversary of our University to draw your attention to these fundamental questions. In doing so I shall first of all review the original content and the further evolution of the doctrine of sovereignty since the 16th century when it made its entry into jurisprudence and political science.

---

1   *The American Political Science Review*, vol. XLIV (1950), no 2 p.343.
2   H. Heller, *Die Souveranität* (1927).

The History of the Dogma

Bodin's concept of sovereignty and the humanistic doctrine of natural law

Five years after the massacre of St Bartholomew, when Jean Bodin published his famous work *Six livres de la Republique*, in which he founded his conception of the state on the concept of sovereignty, he made an impact which became of revolutionary importance both for political science and positive law.

Although he made use of the Romanized train of thought of early and late-mediaeval legists and although in the further elaboration of his concept of sovereignty he had a near precursor in AENEAS SYLVIUS, the counsellor of the Emperor FREDEDRICK III, none before him had declared sovereignty to be the essential characteristic of every state. The central idea of this concept of sovereignty was not contained in its definition in the Latin edition of Bodin's book: *summa in cives ac subditos legibusque soluta potestas* (supreme power over the citizens and subjects which is not bound by state law). This formula is often misunderstood on account of insufficient study of Bodin's theory from the original source. Bodin by no means maintained that the sovereign head of state was above all laws. He considered the sovereign, in explicit contradiction to Macchiavelli, to be subject to natural and divine law. He considered him, like any of his subjects, to be bound by treaties (contracts), which he, as opposed to medieval German conception, distinguished from laws as authoritative ordinances.

And although in his time there could not yet be any question of positive international law, as the concept of state had hardly dawned, it was certainly not in accordance with Bodin's doctrine of sovereignty to deny that the state was bound to treaties it had entered into. Only subjection to a *higher worldly power* is, according to him, incompatible with state-concept. Bodin did not even mean to raise the sovereign head of the state above the so-called *lois fondamentales* of absolute monarchy. According to him the French king is subjected to these fundamental laws in so far as they are inherent in the possession of the crown, notably to the Salic law of succession. The adage *Princeps legibus solutus est* (the Prince is above the law) was, as we all know, derived from the commentary on the *lex Julia et Papia* (I, iii, 31) by the Roman legist Ulpianus and was in late-Imperial times explained in terms of absolutism. It was commonly accepted in the post-glossarist school and the rising humanistic legal school of Alciat, Budé and Zasius. And, in opposition to the extreme absolutist conception, we find it, for example, defended in the legal school of Toulouse in the reign of Francis I. It was Zasius who started the (qualified) ethical conception, as it was afterwards defended by Bodin and by Calvin. So in this respect Bodin's concept of sovereignty was nothing new.

On the other hand the way in which he elaborated the concept of "supreme power" was epoch-making. According to him the unity and indivisibility of sovereignty does not allow for any restriction of its mandate, either in power or in task or in time. The Emperor of the Holy Roman Empire, whose sovereign power was much curtailed by the well-known *Wahlkapitulationen*, was therefore – greatly to the vexation of the German legists – denied the title of sovereign and consequently that of supreme head of state. The French king is not subordinate either to him or to the Pope. Mixed forms of government are inexorably rejected as being incompatible with the concept of sovereignty. But above all, this latter implies, according to Bodin, the *absolute and only original competence for the creation of law within the territory of the state*. The legislative power as the first and most important consequence of sovereignty does not allow for any other original authority for the creation of law. The validity of custom is made absolutely dependent on direct or indirect recognition by statute law, and the same holds, by implication, for all direct creation of laws in different spheres of life that are contained within the territory of the state. The monopoly in the domain of the creation of law, which the Roman Emperors had not claimed before absolutist Byzantine times, is here proclaimed, as the natural outcome of sovereignty, to be the essential characteristic of any state whatsoever.

In its general application to the growing absolute state, this theory was to become a practical programme and dominate the whole concept of positive law for the next few centuries. Science was pressed into the service of politics, which aimed at complete demolition of medieval society.

On the collapse of the Carlovingian state, society in the Germanic countries had relapsed into a split-up undifferentiated condition, in which only the hierarchy of the organized church could bring about unity and coordination. Society presented a secular infra-structure and an ecclesiastical supra-structure, which in their mutual relation corresponded to the fundamental religious motive of Roman Catholicism (the predominating cultural power down to the 14th century): the nature-grace motive.

The secular infra-structure presented a variegated aspect of social corporations, which were cut on two patterns: the guild-pattern and the pattern of the *mundium*-relation, with many crossovers in between.

The guild-pattern was an artificial imitation of the primitive old-Germanic sib whilst the *mundium*-relation was a somewhat weakened imitation of the old-Germanic absolute domestic power: the *mundium*.

The first pattern was evolved in the medieval cities with their trade-guilds, and in the country in the free villages and *Markgenossenschaf-*

ten. The second took effect, more or less markedly, in all medieval relations and gradations of authority (*Herrschaft*), i.e. in the higher, medial and lower lordships (*seigniories*), the feudal relations, the *Grundherrschaften*, etc.

Governmental power could be traded in. In other words, it was a *res in commercio*, not a public office in the service of a *res publica*. The sovereign lords could freely dispose of it. Once in the hands of private persons or corporations it had become their inviolable right. Hence medieval autonomy always implied the exercise of governmental power on one's own authority, which did not change even with the rise of political estates. In this undifferentiated condition of society, in which the guilds covered all spheres of human life, a real state could not evolve.

The idea of the *res publica* only continued in the theory of the legists versed in Roman law and in Aristotelian-Thomistic philosophy. But it was not founded on contemporary social reality. In this state of affairs it is to be understood that Bodin, in his concept of sovereignty, claimed the exclusive control of the creation of law for the sovereign head of state. Medieval autonomy in the creation of law was indeed incompatible with the state-concept for the very reason that it was undifferentiated. In this situation every autonomous law-sphere that claimed an original competence-sphere did at the same time claim governmental power of its own, which turned against the idea of the res publica, as it did not recognize any limitation of the public interest.

But Bodin's doctrine of sovereignty, which was favorable to the policy of bureaucratic centralization of absolute monarchy, defeated its own objective, namely the monopolization of governmental power. As soon as the process of differentiation of society is carried through and the state has monopolized all governmental power, it turns out that at the same time the evolution of law is passing through a differentiation as well, which cannot possibly be pressed into the framework of the law-sphere of the state. The doctrine that all positive law finds its legal source in the will of the sovereign law-giver then proves to be a political dogma in the fullest sense of the word, a dogma that is at complete variance both with the general meaning of all law and with the rich structural variety of society.

It is the everlasting credit of the Calvinistic jurist Johannes Althusius that at a time which was scientifically quite ripe for this absolutist conception of state-law, he expounded a theory of the structure of society, founded on the recognition of a divine world-order, and the intrinsic character of the social orbits of life, in which it was pointed out that each of the latter has its *lex propria* and its own legal sphere, which cannot be derived from any other. It may be true that this doctrine of the "symbiosis" lacked the scientific apparatus for a deeper analysis of these social structures, i.e. that, in its legal construction of every form of human society from some sort of contract, it followed the uniform schematic methods of natural law and that it was not yet quite free from the hierarchical-universalistic views of medieval theories. But, whatever the case may be, it had emancipated itself from the Aristotelian-Scholastic theory, which only bestowed the autonomous competency for the creation of law on the so-called *societates perfectae*, namely the state and the church. And for that reason it could not resist Bodin's doctrine of sovereignty in the domain of secular law on principle.

Meanwhile, the future apparently lay with the latter. Science – legal theory and the theory of the state included – was increasingly affected by the modern humanistic philosophy with its religious root-principle of *nature* and *freedom*, the domination of the realities of nature by science, and the absolute autonomy of the free human personality in the domain of science, morals and religion.

The domination-motive gave rise to the classic-humanistic ideal of science, which proclaimed the methods of mathematics and natural science – the latter having been founded by Galileo and Newton – to be the universal mode of thought, on which a new theoretical picture of reality was designed, and which left no room for structural and natural differences founded on the order of creation.

It had been called into existence by the new motive of freedom but was, if carried through consistently, bound to collide with the latter. In a construction of reality modeled on the concepts of natural science no room was left for autonomy and freedom of the human personality.

Even in Bodin's political philosophy this scientific ideal – not yet consolidated in his time – began to make its influence felt. Science was pressed into the service of a policy that wanted to build up the state as a rational institution for the purpose of domination, after the demolition of the undifferentiated society of the Middle Ages.

This being the object, Bodin, in his political theory, wanted to develop the means to this end in a rigorously methodical, mathematical way.

It starts with a definition: "The state is the lawful government of several households and what they have in common, it having sovereign power."

And then Bodin declares: "We premise this definition, because in all things one must trace the principal object first, and only afterwards the means to attain it. Well then, the definition is nothing but the object of the matter under discussion; and if it is not well-founded, everything that is built on it, will collapse soon after."

But his definition was by no means the result of a conscientious inquiry into the inner nature and structure of the state-organism and of the other social spheres of life. It had been dictated by a political objective that ignored the divine world-order from which Althusius started, and only aimed at the complete domination of society by the instrument of the state.

Within the framework that had thus been determined by his political objective, Bodin's concept of sovereignty performed the following various functions, which we ought to remember in their mutual relation in order to be able to assess correctly their several pros and cons:

1. drawing the boundary lines between the state and all other political and non-political social spheres of life;
2. defining the concept of positive law as the certified will of the lawgiver;
3. defining the relation between the different orbits of competence in the creation of law, all of which are to be dependent on the only original competence, i.e. that of the sovereign state by virtue of its legislative power.

The humanistic doctrine of natural law, founded by Hugo Grotius, accepted Bodin's concept of sovereignty. It was also pressed into the service of the policy of demolition and renovation. *More geometrico*, by the analysis of society as it presents itself into its "elements," i.e. the individuals, and by the synthetic construction of the desired new society from these social elements with the help of a juridical social contract, it wanted to build up a new social and legal order. In order to make Bodin's concept of sovereignty acceptable to the humanistic ideas of liberty and autonomy, the humanistic doctrine of natural law constructed the state from a social contract between naturally free and equal individuals, mostly complemented by an authority- and subjection-contract, and in Pufendorf even by a third contract about the form of government. In Hobbes' *Leviathan* and in Rousseau's so-called infallible and all-powerful *volonté général* the concept of sovereignty got its most consistently absolutist elaboration.

Like Bodin's concept of sovereignty, his conception of the relation between legislation and custom was also accepted. The indigenous customary law had under the test of the classic-Roman tradition of the *ius naturale et gentium* become a *ius iniquum*, a bulwark of feudal society, which was doomed to ruin.

In the new order no other law was permitted besides civil law and the *ius publicum*, that is to say the two frameworks of state-law. For that purpose positive law was to be elaborated in exhaustive codes.

It was not until the British philosopher John Locke appeared on the scene that there arose in the doctrine of natural law a reaction against the absolutist concept of sovereignty, i.e. from the angle of the humanistic concept of freedom.

The liberal idea of the constitutional state, developed by Locke, led to a rigorous distinction between state and society while the theory of the division of power, which was presently to get its definite shape in Montesquieu's doctrine of the *trias politica*, was also bound to result in the inner decay of the dogma of sovereignty.

The historical interpretation of the concept of sovereignty and the doctrine of state-sovereignty

At the time of the Restoration (i.e. after the destruction of the Napoleonic empire), the doctrine of sovereignty takes quite a new turn, because it now joins up with the principle of legitimacy and the so-called monarchical principle, and fundamentally denies every contractual construction as propounded by the doctrine of natural law.

Whereas in the preceding period the problem of sovereign power had been tackled from the viewpoint of natural law, quite detached from the historical past, and whereas only a formulation in accordance with that point of view had been applied to the absolutist or to the more liberal-constitutional tendencies of the time, now, in accordance with the conservative historical mode of thought of the Restoration movement, full stress is laid on the real or imaginary historical rights of the dynasties that had been dethroned by the revolution. The pre-revolutionary position of the Bourbons in France served as a model. In the introduction to the chapter on Louis XVIII, which preamble was drafted by Beugnot, the latter provided the standard formula that passed into the constitutions of several German states and was proclaimed to be the unassailable dogmatic starting-point for the deduction of the constitutional status of the princes in art.57 of the Final Treaty of Vienna.

In this formulation the sovereignty of the king was not based on the constitution, but inversely the constitution was granted as a charter by the sovereign prince by virtue of his supposed fullness of power, which was considered to be founded on historical rights. And the required co-operation of the estates or the parliament for the exercise of legislative power rested on the voluntary self-restriction of sovereign power.

On the one hand the concept of sovereignty – for that matter in accordance with Hobbes's and Rousseau's conceptions – was thus tightened up even from that of Bodin's conception. Bodin considered royal sovereignty legally bound to the *lois fondamentales* of the realm, which were independent of that sovereignty. However, on the other hand the historical views of Restoration times struck the first blow to the principle of Bodin's doctrine as regards the monopoly of the sovereign law-giver in the domain of the creation of the law. This came about under the influence of an irrationalistic and universalistic turn in the humanistic freedom motive as it was elaborated in post-Kantian idealism (notably in Schelling's transcendental idealism).

The absolute value of *individuality* was turned against the overstrained notions of *uniform generality*; and in opposition to the apotheosis of the *individual* in the individualistic mode of thought of the exponents of natural law, the *community* was now enthroned.

Society was no longer considered an aggregate of free and equal individuals, but an organic whole with parts, and the free and autonomous individual personality of a person was looked on in the light of that person's membership in an equally individual natural community, on which a collective personality was conferred.

This new conception of the humanistic freedom motive also asserted itself in science. The standard mode of thought borrowed from physical science was ousted everywhere by a historical way of approach, which aimed at understanding the individual in its individual-historical relations in accordance with modes of thought in the spiritual branches of science. Over against the rationalistic belief that one could construct political and legal order on an unalterable model which would be in accordance with the doctrine of natural law and ready-made for all times and all peoples, independent of the historical past, all stress was now laid on the organic character of the historical development of a culture that has its true source in the individual national character or *Volksgeist*. Thus a new ideal of science arose, which, by making the historical aspect of society absolute, led to an exaggerated historical vision (or *"historicistic"* vision, if you like) of reality.

And this historical mode of thought was, of course, bound to turn against the traditional conception of positive law as a product of the sovereign will of the law-giver.

The *Historical School of law*, founded by Fr. Carl von Savigny, who proclaimed law to be a phenomenon of historical evolution that originally springs organically (i.e. without being intentionally created) from the individual spirit or conviction of the people, totally broke with the former rationalistic conception of the relation between statute law and customary law.

Over against the doctrine of *natural law* was placed that of folk-law (*Volksrecht*) in its historical evolution. That folk-law, they held, did not spring from the will of the sovereign law-giver but from the historical law-mindedness of the people.

Folk-law at first reveals itself in the *Uebung* as customary law but when social relations are becoming more complicated, it gets a technical organ in the class of lawyers, and its technical form in the *Juristenrecht*. In relation to this, legislation has only a secondary task. If this train of thought were consistently carried through, the traditional concept of sovereignty would have to be discarded as a necessary element in the definition of positive law.

However, it was not the *Romanistic*, but the *Germanistic* wing of the Historical School, led by its two principal exponents Georg Beseler and

Otto Gierke, which began to draw conclusions from the doctrine of folk-law that turned out to be fatal for the traditional concept of sovereignty. If all law is, as von Savigny taught, a historical product of the individual *Volksgeist* the reception of the Roman law in the Germanic countries must be considered as a denaturation of the healthy development of the Germanic legal institutions. The spirit of Roman civil law, stigmatized as being individualistic, was, just as the absolutist concept of government of the Roman imperium, quite antagonistic to the "social, corporative" foundations of Germanic law. The study of the Germanic corporate system led to a more sociological view of jurisprudence and the Germanists proclaimed, in diametrical opposition to the Romanist Puchta, the autonomy of corporations to be a formal original source of law. They discovered internal corporate law as being *Sozialrecht*, which was unknown to classical tradition.

At first, under the influence of the historical mode of thought, this Germanistic rush threatened to undermine completely the foundations of civil law and of the state-concept. But Gierke saw the danger in time and compromised with the idea of natural law. The doctrine of the rights of individuals (in the classic tradition of the *ius naturale et gentium* the foundation of civil law) could not be sacrificed to the Germanic concept of folk-law which bound the whole legal status of the individual to the undifferentiated social corporations. The *Individual-recht* was to be maintained as an independent sphere of law beside the newly discovered *Sozialrecht* of the corporations. The classic concept of the state as a sovereign *res publica* could also not be allowed to succumb to the undifferentiated corporative principle of Germanic law.

However, Gierke wanted to replace the conception of the bureaucratic sovereign state, derived from the idea of the Roman Empire, which conception was pregnantly expressed in Bodin's identification of the *res publica* with the government, by an "organic" idea of the state, in which the government was to be recognized as an essential organ of an organization of the state that comprised both the government and the people.

This organized state is, according to him, just as any other social corporate sphere, a real "spiritual organism" with a personality of its own. But it is a *gegliederte Gemeinschaft*, in which both the legal subjectivity of the individual citizens and that of the narrower corporate spheres, integrated into the whole of the state, remain untouched. The Germanic *Genossenschaftsprinzip* could in this way successfully *impact* the modern idea of a constitutional state.

Sovereignty in its fullest sense then could not belong to the government or to the people, but only to the state as a whole. The government can only exercise sovereign power as an organ of the essentially corporate state.

Thus the doctrine of the *sovereignty of the state* was born, which in the form propounded by Gierke was in many respects of a higher conception than those of Gerber, Laband and Jellinek, who are generally considered the typical representatives of this doctrine. And it was notably superior to Bodin's doctrine of sovereignty, which was not based on a truly corporate conception of the state.

Meanwhile, the new doctrine of the sovereignty of the state, in so far as it was really in accordance with the thought of the Historical School, held all the germs which were destined to completely undermine the traditional humanistic concept of sovereignty.

Since the theory of folk-law had led to the doctrine of the autonomous creation of law in the different social spheres, the concept of sovereignty, when elaborated consistently, could no longer have the characteristic quality of being the only original competency for the creation of positive law.

So the question was bound to arise as to what role it could still play in the definition of the *state*.

Gierke himself still stuck to Bodin's conception that sovereignty was to be considered an essential quality of any state. The latter, in his opinion, is distinguished from all other social spheres of life as a "sovereign organization of power," which is not to be taken in the sense of *Genossenschaft*, but of *Gebietskörperschaft*, because the first concept applied in his system only to the non-political spheres.

Thus the concept of sovereignty had unmistakably been transferred from the *legal sphere* to the *historical-political* sphere of power and had become a historical category instead of one that belonged to the domain of natural law.

This conclusion had been emphatically drawn by Gerber, Laband and Jellinek from the rupture with the conception of the doctrine of natural law. And from this it further followed that they, in contradistinction to Gierke, no longer considered sovereignty an essential characteristic of the state, but also acknowledged the existence of non-sovereign states.

As soon, however, as the concept of sovereignty was transferred from the sphere of natural law to the historical sphere of power, a problem presented itself for which the doctrine of the sovereignty of the state could not offer a satisfactory solution, namely the question about the relation of the sovereign power of the state to "law."

The problem, in this form, had been put in a decidedly uncritical way. For "state" and "law" are not to be compared in this way. The sphere of law is, among many others, only a modal *aspect* of human society. The state, on the other hand, is a real corporate sphere of social life, which in this capacity functions in *all* aspects, so necessarily also in its juridical aspect. And the typical structures of the differentiated spheres of social life (state, church, trade, family, etc.) introduce into the juridical aspect that typical variety which makes it impossible to speak of "law" as such, without further social qualification.

Thus public law and civil law are the two characteristic legal spheres of the state, which differ fundamentally from the internal ecclesiastical law, the internal law of trades and industries, etc., and can never be placed *in opposition to* the state.

Gierke, however, went wrong in stating the problem, so that he could not offer a sound solution.

According to him "state" and "law" are "two autonomous and specifically different sides of communal life. The former manifests itself in the powerful pursuance of chosen communal goals and culminates in political *action* while the latter reveals itself in the delimitation of action-spheres appropriate for the will bound by these spheres and reaches its peak in legal acknowledgement (when it is accepted as law)."[1]

This untenable juxtaposition of state and law showed the inner conflict between the concept of sovereignty rooted in the humanistic power- or domination-motive and the folk-law theory of the Historical School, which was based on the humanistic freedom motive and was only prepared to acknowledge law as the free and autonomous expression of the "conviction of the people."

In other words, the problem was born of the humanistic basic motive of nature and freedom itself and Gierke only tried in a dialectical way to unite the two antagonistic motives of domination and freedom; because giving a positive form to law, according to him, needs the sovereign state. Conversely, the sovereign power of the state, in order not to degenerate into despotism, is in need of law for its foundation.

However, it could not be denied that the concept of sovereignty clashed with Gierke's doctrine of the social corporate spheres and their autonomous creation of law. Gierke's disciple, Hugo Preusz, starting from this doctrine and the folk-law theory of the Historical School, was the first to eliminate on principle the concept of sovereignty. The latter is according to him the necessary correlate of the individualistic concept of personality with both originating from Roman law. In contrast to the absolutist state, the modern constitutional state has developed from the Germanic legal principle of the autonomous *Genossenschaft*. And the concept of sovereignty does not suit this constitutional state any longer.

---

1 *Die Grundbegriffe des Staatsrechts und die neuesten Staatsrechtstheorien* (Tübingen, Mohr, 1915), p.105: "zwei selbständige und spezifisch verschiedene Seiten des Gemeinlebens. Jenes manifestiert sich in der machtvollen Durchführung gewollter Gemeinzwecke und kulminirt in der politischen *That*, dieses offenbart sich in der Absteckung von Handlungssphären für die von ihm gebundenen Willen und gipfelt im rechtlichen *Erkennen* (für Recht erkennen)."

If the state is, as Gierke has expounded, an organic corporate person among a series of organic corporate persons, which can be integrated as members into more comprehensive "persons" of that kind, the problem of the composing parts of the Germanic federal state and of the insertion of that state into the organization of the nations on the basis of international law can also be solved. Everywhere the concept of sovereignty stood in the way of the right insight into this matter.

But this concept of sovereignty is not so easily done away with. From the outset it had played a far more varied role than how it came across in Preusz' speculations. The Germanistic wing of the Historical School had posited the autonomy of the corporate social spheres as an original formal source of law but had failed to mention a material criterion for the demarcation of the original orbits of competency of the state and the other spheres of life in the domain of the creation of law. Which of them would have to give way in case of conflict?

The doctrine of sovereignty had at least given an unequivocal answer. And Gierke himself did not know how to replace it by another. He too contended that no autonomous corporation law could assert itself against the sovereign will of the state.

The concept of sovereignty cannot be eliminated unless another solution can be offered for the problem concerning the mutual relation of the original orbits of competency in the domain of the creation of law.

And the paramount question in this matter is whether one considers this an intrinsic problem of *law* or a historical question of *power*.

The traditional doctrine of sovereignty had essentially always put it as a question of *power*, for the construction of the sovereign power of the government from a voluntary contract – as the doctrine of natural law had proposed – had likewise been nothing but a juridical mask for the humanistic power- and domination- motive.

This had created a conflict between *might* and *right* that could not be allayed either in Gierke's "dialectical" way or by Jellinek's well-known doctrine of the voluntary self-restriction of the will of the state by law.

The doctrine of the sovereignty of law (Rechtssouveranität) and its presumed victory over the traditional dogma of sovereignty

This conflict seemed to be avoided by the doctrine of the *sovereignty of law*, which in three variants, namely the *psychological* one of Krabbe, the *norm-logical* one of Kelsen and the *legal-sociological* one of Duguit and Gurvitch, turned against the traditional concept of sovereignty, no matter whether it presented itself in the form of the sovereignty of government, of the people, or of the state.

In reality, however, the doctrine of the sovereignty of law has not in any way overcome the antimonies of the traditional concept of sovereignty. It wants us to believe that the problems for which the latter seemed to give a solution, would vanish in thin air, if only, instead of the state or the people or the government, impersonal legal order were proclaimed sovereign. But legal order is only the law- or norm-facet of the juridical aspect of human society, and the great variety in structure which characterizes our modern, much differentiated society, is, as we observed before, also bound to be expressed in its juridical aspect.

So the doctrine of sovereignty of law cannot escape a definition of the mutual relation of the competency of the state and that of the other social spheres of life. For which of the variants of law could rightfully claim sovereignty? Constitutional law, international law, the internal laws of trades and industries, ecclesiastical law?

Whatever one's choice may be, one will always be obliged to endow one of the social spheres of life with an absolute competency and sovereignty. But an absolute competency can never be a real legal power, as it does not allow for any real demarcation by law.

Thus the doctrine of the sovereignty of law in its turn collides with the general character of all law and is obliged in the end to resolve the problem of juridical competency into a historical question of power.

And yet this doctrine owed its very origin to the attempt to save the independence of the law over against power!

Recently, Gurvitch (*Sociology of Law*, 1947) tried to escape the difficulty by attributing absolute sovereignty to the unorganized "supra-functional" community of the nation and the international community of peoples which he calls the all-embracing infra-structures of society. These would in an absolutely variable way demarcate the orbits of competence of all differentiated "functional" communities like state, church, industrial organizations, etc.

The supra-functional sovereign communities are here thought of as being "undifferentiated." In them the idea of "law" would be embodied "in all its ways," whereas in the "functional" communities only special aspects of this law-idea would be expressed.

But there are no unorganized communities with a supra-functional character. The undifferentiated spheres of primitive society are always *organized* and they are doomed to disappear when the process of differentiation sets in. Hence Gurvitch is compelled again to proclaim a differentiated corporate sphere to be the exclusive representative and binding interpreter of the absolutely sovereign legal order of the all-embracive "supra-functional communities."

In these periods of state-absolutism in which personal liberty and the liberty of other spheres of life run the greatest danger, that representative, according to Gurvitch, must be the state itself, which now, for its usurping interference with the original orbits of competency of the other spheres of life, even receives the sanction of "sovereign law"!

Thus in this theory of the sovereignty of law too, sovereignty swallows up law so that the power-motive predominates over the freedom motive.

The traditional concept of sovereignty and the doctrine of sovereignty in its proper orbit

Surveying once more the evolution of the concept of sovereignty in humanistic legal and political science, I think I may state the following: in all its manifestations, including also in the doctrine of the sovereignty of law, the concept of sovereignty implied the denial of the existence of original, materially and juridically defined orbits of competence of the state and the other spheres of life.

Original spheres of competence in this material and juridical sense can never be based on an order of positive law, because any formation of positive law as such presupposes the original competence or jural power to this end. Only derived competency can be based on positive law and consequently have a necessarily variable foundation.

Irrespective of how far one ascends in any possible hierarchy of derived competencies formed according to the rules of positive law, in the end one will arrive at the original competency from which the said hierarchy itself has been derived. What then is the basis of this original jural power as the presupposition of all positive law?

This jural power can only be founded on and be materially defined by the inner nature, by the internal structural principle of the social sphere within which it is executed, which principle is independent of any human discretion. As an *original* jural power – not derived from another temporal sphere of life – it may be called *sovereign*, provided this concept of sovereignty is immediately circumscribed by "in its proper orbit." And then at the same time it becomes the radical opposite of the concept of sovereignty construed by humanistic theories. For, in spite of all attempts to provide the latter concept with a juridical basis or at least some legal demarcation, it broke theoretically with inner necessity through the boundaries of the original social spheres of competency, and at the same time through the modal confines of the law.

"Sovereignty in its proper orbit" is not some vague political slogan, the cry of a special Christian political party. It is deeply rooted in the whole real order of things, and is not to be ignored with impunity. For it is the expression of the sovereign divine will and wisdom of the Creator, who created all things after their own kind and set their constant structural boundaries in the order of temporal reality. And it is he who maintained this temporal order of reality even after the fall of humankind, to reveal it in the redemption by Jesus Christ in all its religious fullness of meaning: the focussing of all temporal reality on the loving service of the glorification of God.

In other words, sovereignty in its proper orbit is a universal ontological principle, which gets its special *legal* expression only in the juridical aspect of reality. It reveals two different givens in the structure of reality: (i) the mutual irreducibility of the different aspects of reality; (ii) their indissoluble intertwinement and connection in the temporal order of reality.

For only in their indissoluble connectedness can they reveal their irreducible uniqueness.

This holds both for the structures of *the different modal aspects of reality*,[1] which in general structure the unique coherence of the latter, and the *typical structures of individual totalities* in which these modal aspects are united in their integral connectedness and are grouped and individualized into an individual whole in characteristically different ways.

All jural relations – in whatever typical social structure of totality (that of the state, the church, trade, international relations, etc.) they may present themselves – are as *jural* relations determined by the general modal structure of the juridical aspect of reality.

In this modal structure the whole order and connectedness of the different aspects are expressed in an irreducible *modus*. As I set out and argued in detail in my *De Wijsbegeerte der Wetsidee* , *Vol.II*, it is built up from a *nuclear moment*, which warrants the irreducibility of the aspect, and from a series of other structural moments, some of which (the so-called analogies) maintain the inner coherence of the jural aspect with all those modalities occupying an earlier position in the order of aspects, while others (the so-called anticipations) maintain connection with those positioned later in the order of aspects although all of them are qualified by the nuclear moment of the jural aspect.[2]

Among the analogical moments in the modal structure of this aspect, the juridical competency or jural power takes an essential place. It is the prerequisite for all human molding of the principles of law into concrete

---

1   In my work *De Wijsbegeerte der Wetsidee* (The Philosophy of the Law-Idea) the following modal aspects of empirical reality are distinguished: The aspect of quantity (number), the space-aspect, the aspect of motion, [this aspect was only introduced in 1950 – DFMS] the energetic (physico-chemical) aspect, the biotic aspect, the psychical aspect of feeling, the logical or analytical aspect, the historical aspect, the symbolic or linguistic aspect, the aspect of social intercourse, the economic aspect, the aesthetic aspect, the jural aspect, the moral aspect and the faith aspect.

2   *Editorial note* (DFMS): As mentioned earlier in the third note on page 55, Dooyeweerd later on explained the inter-modal coherence between the different aspects by grouping both *retrocipations* and *anticipations* together as *analogical structural moments*. Systematically one should therefore distinguish between retrocipatory and anticipatory *analogies* (cf. *A New Critique of Theoretical Thought*, Vol.II, p.75).

form, through which these principles are elaborated into positive norms of law.

Competency is *jural* power, and in this strong term (i.e. jural power) the indissoluble connection between the *juridical* and the *historical* aspect of reality is expressed. For *power* (or *control*) is the modal nuclear moment of the historical aspect which is the aspect pertaining to cultural development.

Jural power is not power in the original sense of history. It is only a historical analogy in the modal structure of law, which is always qualified by the modal nuclear moment of the juridical aspect. But it is *founded* in historical relations of power, and can never be independent of the latter.

Essentially this juridical competency is never absolute or exclusive. It is premised on a number of original orbits of competency that exist in jural relations of mutual circumscription and balance. For as in all fundamental concepts of jurisprudence, there is to be found in the concept of competency also a *numerical* analogy, in which the inner coherence between the juridical and the quantitative aspect is expressed. Jural life in which only one jural subject would function is no more possible than true jural life in which only one original orbit of competency for the formation of law would be given. Even in a still undifferentiated society this is impossible.

From this it is once again evident that the traditional concept of sovereignty must necessarily collide with the modal sovereignty-in-its-orbit of the juridical aspect of social reality.

Because in the theoretical conception of reality, from which this notion of sovereignty started, there was not even any room for the modal structures of the different aspects of social reality, it could *a fortiori* have no place for the typical structures of the different social spheres since the latter cannot be understood without being based on the former. So the concept of sovereignty was proclaimed the essential characteristic of the state, because the internal structural principle of the latter (and with it its inner *nature*) had been eliminated.

Well, it is exactly these structures of the social spheres of life that lend to each of the original spheres of competency their *typical* material content and delimitation.

In the order of reality they are founded as structural *principles*, but they can only be realized by being *molded into concrete form* by humankind.

The results of this fashioning human activity are the *social forms*, which always have a historical foundation and vary throughout with the historical evolution of society.

The typical structural *principles* of the social spheres of life, on the other hand, have a constant and invariable character, because they determine the *inner* nature of these spheres. The *inner nature* of the state or of the church-institute do not change in the course of time, but only the *social forms* in which these social institutions are realized. These social forms are the nodal points of the intertwinement of the orbits of life, which are so entirely different from each other in their internal structure and nature.

But as each of the modal structures of the aspects in their mutual connectedness retains its modal sovereignty in its proper orbit, so each of the typical structures of the differentiated social spheres in their mutual intertwinement maintains its typical sovereignty in its proper orbit and thus, for example in the juridical aspect it maintains its original sphere of competency in the domain of the creation of law.

The state has no exceptional position in this respect. It has only sovereignty in its proper orbit. However, this does not do away with the fact that its original jural power is of quite a different kind.

In conformity with its internal structure, the state must be characterized as a territorial and institutional corporation of public law, a public juridical community of government and subjects on the historical basis of a monopolistic organization of the power of the sword. For, as with any differentiated social structure, that of the state is also *typified* by two modal functions acting in different modal aspects, the first of which is called the typical "qualifying function" or "directive function," the second the "typical basic function."

The internal structural principle is also expressed in the other aspects of the life of the state: the moral, the economic, the symbolic, the sensory, the biotic aspect, etc.

The directive function of the state – in contrast to all other spheres of life – has its place in the *juridical* aspect of social reality. This means that the state, acting as such in the domain of the creation of law, has no original competency for the creation of law that will serve some non-juridical destination.

All law is specific law, i.e. *ius specificum*, if, in in conformity with the internal societal structure within which it obtains, it typically serves a meta-juridical destination, such as the economically qualified internal law of trades, or for example, the internal ecclesiastical law, which is qualified by its faith-destination.

The law, framed by the state, on the other hand, is by its very nature *ius commune*.

In accordance with its special modal structure, law shows a correlation of what we call coordinational and communal relations, because in any social relation, whatever its typical structure may be, this correlation is inherent.

In the partner-relation, the subjects do not act as members of a whole, but are juxtaposed, *next to* or even *over against* each other. In the communal relation, on the other hand, they are united as members of a whole that comprises all of them.

In typical state-law we therefore meet with the correlation of two typical spheres, namely *civil law* and *public law*, the first being a state-law regulating the civil coordinational relations of individuals as such, the latter being an inner social law of the state as a public community.

These are the two original spheres of competency of the state in the domain of the creation of law, which are materially demarcated by their inner structure and uniqueness.

In accordance with their typical constitution, *internal* trade law or *internal* ecclesiastical law cannot assume the character of public law or civil law.

Non-state law, it is true, will, as *ius specificum*, be subjected to a typical *binding* in civil and public law, and therefore it would seem as if the state had absolute sovereignty as to the creation of law. These deceptive appearances become even stronger when the internal structural principles of the social spheres and their typical legal spheres are not recognized while the juridical forms in which positive law is laid down, such as acts, ordinances, contracts, statutes, jurisdiction, etc. receive all the attention exclusively.

For just as social forms proved to be the nodal points of the mutual intertwinement of social orbits, so in the juridical aspect the formal sources of law are the nodal points of the mutual intertwinement of the original orbits of competency. But even in the closest intertwinements each of these spheres maintains its sovereignty in its own proper orbit.

This is neither the time or the place to elaborate further on all this here. Allow me, therefore, to conclude my reflections on the concept of sovereignty with a final word.

In the course of my argument the fundamental objections I have set forth against this concept in its traditional interpretation have a deeper background, i.e. in the total theoretical conception of reality from which it was born.

The theoretical conception of reality from which the different branches of science take their starting point is never neutral towards religion but is intrinsically dominated by the religious basic-motive through which scientific thought-activity gets its central driving force.

Here lies the inner and necessary point of contact between religion and science.

As our University expands, the inner reformation of our theoretical view of reality becomes more and more urgent.

For it is not steeds and horsemen that will lead us to victory in the effort to realize the ideal of our institution's founder, but it is only and finally the inner motive-power of the Scriptural basic-motive of the Reformation: that of the creation, the fall of humankind and our redemption by Jesus Christ, which must also radically change our theoretical vision of reality, if we want to aim at a science that is not merely *scholastically accommodated*, but really *re-formed* in an intrinsic Christian sense.

The Christian Idea of The State[1]

TO SPEAK OF "the" Christian idea[2] of the state in the face of the current disparity of thought amongst Christians might seem an audacious undertaking. This may perhaps have been possible during the Middle Ages under the supremacy of the Roman Catholic Church, but surely today's countless schisms within the church and the many different Christian political groups make it seem rather presumptuous, if not far-fetched, to conjecture about one overall Christian Idea of the state.

Emil Brunner rejects the Christian idea of the state

Even Protestants themselves consider – and always did consider – the idea of a Christian state to be a Roman Catholic fallacy. Emil Brunner, one of the leading figures of the so-called Swiss Theology founded by Barth, made the following cutting statement in his well-known book *Das Gebot und die Ordnungen*[3] (1932): "The Christian state never existed, and it never will." According to him it was precisely one of the fundamental concepts of the Reformation that the state, instituted because of the fall, does not belong to the "Kingdom of Christ," but rather to the natural, secular ordinances. He claims that a Christian state is no more possible than a Christian culture, Christian learning, economy, art, or Christian social action. Brunner views all life in the temporal world, permeated as it is by sin, as belonging to the area of nature. Here "worldly ordinances" are valid. It is the realm of law as loveless rule, from which Christians have been liberated in their inner life of grace, so that they can act in accordance with Christ's command of love of the moment. *Nature* (the realm of temporal world-life outside faith, subject to inflexible "ordinances") and *grace* (the faith-realm of the supra-

---

1 "The Christian Idea of The State." (*De Christelijke Staatsidee*) Presented at a day for Anti-Revolutionary youth on October 3, 1936 (Apeldoorn, Rotterdam-Utrecht, Libertas-Drukkerijen).
Translator: John Kraay; *Editor:* D.F.M. Strauss.

2 *Editorial note* (DFMS): It may be well to explain the meaning of the term "idea," as it is used by Dooyeweerd. An *idea* represents a way of knowing transcending *conceptual knowledge*. It points beyond a conceptual diversity towards the totality, unity and origin of creation. Ideas explore the anticipatory direction of modal aspects (also called the transcendental direction of time). Cf. *A New Critique of Theoretical Thought*, Vol.II, pp.186 ff.

3 *Translator's note:* English translation: *The Divine Imperative* (1937).

temporal kingdom of God, subject to the commandment of love which, in the Christian believer, has broken with law and has put it aside [as no longer conceived of] as a universally valid rule), are for Brunner unbridgeably separated. The Roman Catholic Church, he maintains, erred when it propagated the idea of a "Christian world-life" and thus also that of a "Christian state." Such a view, he claims, is only possible if a temporal church hierarchy can be accepted as ruler of both state and other secular societal relationships – a type of government that the Reformation rejected outright.

National-Socialism and Fascism and the idea of the Christian state

If we now turn to look at the recently evolved use of the term "Christian state" by National-Socialism and Fascism, the picture of spiritual chaos is complete. For these two bring together in a tempting way both the pagan notion of a total state, embracing all life-spheres, and the Christian concept of solidarity and love to one's neighbor.

Indeed, never did the idea of the Christian state seem more problematic than today!

Add to this that the spiritual chaos of our restless times penetrates alarmingly into our own ranks so that many hardly comprehend what positive power of attraction Calvinistic political principles can have,[1] and one can understand the only partially veiled indifference with which many Christians speak of the "Christian idea of the State."

The ever new, inspiring idea of the Christian state and the causes of its decline

And yet the idea of the Christian state will not be sidelined as an abstract notion that has "outlived its usefulness," and now belongs to a dead tradition. Rather, it is still a spiritual treasure, ever new, ever living and inspiring, touching the very heart of one's Christian life – a treasure which we must keep at all costs.

The fundamental cause of the inner weakening of Christian political thought, yes, of the entire Christian mode of life among many Christians in our day, lies not so much in external factors but in inner decay, threatening Christianity from the beginning in its positive endeavor regarding culture, learning, political life and social movement. This was also the danger of which Joshua, called by God, warned the Israelites when they had arrived in the promised land, namely, integration with heathen peoples and the search for a compromise between the service of Jehovah and the worship of idols.

As soon as Christianity began to compromise education, culture, and political life with pagan and humanistic philosophy, with its view of

---

1 *Translator's note:* References to Dutch historical events are omitted in this translation.

state and culture, Christianity's inner strength was broken. At that moment the process of "becoming like unto the world" began, repeatedly arrested through the grace of God by a spiritual *reveil*, a reformation.

Synthesis and Antithesis

Time and time again such a reformation had to affirm the uncompromising antithesis against the weakening synthesis, the spirit of compromise with the world.

Is it possible that after the latest (Calvinistic) *reveil* under the inspiring Kuyper[1] this process has again repeated itself? Did the spirit of synthesis perhaps infiltrate almost unnoticed also in our own circles? Is it true that Calvinism as a cultural and political movement has lost its sharp edges? Did it become fashionable and acceptable to the world because gradually it became identified with liberalism carrying a Christian stamp?

If so, surely it is high time that once again we realize the radical antithesis that separates the Christian idea of the state from all pagan and humanistic views.

Actually, there is but one radical and Scriptural idea of the Christian state

It is not true that the Christian view of the state is divided into as many interpretations as there are Christian political groups or movements. Rather, these differences are the fruit of the perilous marriage of Christianity with the movements of the age, which arise from the spirit of this world.

The genuinely Christian idea of the state is rooted in the radical, Scriptural view regarding the relationship between the kingdom of God in Christ Jesus and the temporal societal structures, in which God's general or common grace arrests the dry-rot caused by sin. What then, is this view?

The contrast of "nature" and "grace" is non-Scriptural. Scripture posits the heart as the religious center of human existence

God's Word does not teach us a contrast between "nature" and "grace," that is, between the nature of God's creation and the redemption in Christ Jesus. It teaches only and exclusively the radical, uncompromising antithesis of sin and redemption, of the realm of darkness and the kingdom of God in Christ.

God created humankind in His image. In the heart of humankind, the religious root, the center of its being, God concentrated all of creation toward His service; here He laid the supra-temporal root of all temporal

---

[1] *Translator's note*: Abraham Kuyper, (1837-1920), Christian statesman, founder of the Anti-Revolutionary Party in the Netherlands, founder of the Free University of Amsterdam, and prolific author.

creatures. This human heart, from which according to Scriptures flow the wellsprings of life, transcends all things temporal in the service of God. The whole religious sense (meaning) of God's creation lies in our heart, our entire ego, our complete self. This heart, in which according to the Word eternity has been laid, is the true supra-temporal center of human existence. At the same time it is the creaturely center of all of God's creation. The apostasy of this heart, of this root of creation, necessarily swept with it all temporal creation. In Adam not only all humankind fell, but also that entire temporal cosmos of which humankind was the crowned head. And in Christ, the Word become flesh, the second Covenant Head, God gave the new root of His redeemed creation, in Whom true humanity was implanted through self-surrender, through surrender of the center of existence, the heart.

The pagan view that "reason" is the supra-temporal center of a person's being

Pagan philosophy, however, taught that the nature of a person, and in it the nature of all temporal things, finds its supra-temporal center in "reason." But this "reason" is in reality nothing other than a composite of temporal functions of consciousness, functions of our self, aspects of our heart in the full scriptural sense. Temporal organic-biotic life, feeling, sense of beauty, our function in historical development, in language, in jural and economic life, etc. – all these are also functions of the heart in this sense.

The kingship of humankind in God's undefiled creation did not lie in the "rational-moral" nature of human beings, but in this great mystery: that God concentrated all of His creation in the heart of humankind, in the whole self of a person, and brought creation together in this deeper unity.

The fall, the fundamental separation from God, consisted in this: the human heart rebelled against its divine Origin; humankind thought itself to be something by virtue of itself; humankind sought itself and with that, God, in temporality. This was the idolatry in the apostasy from the true God, as He had revealed Himself in the heart of humankind through His Word.

A manifestation of this apostasy was also the pagan view that natural human existence has its origin in reason as *supposed* supra-temporal center, and that God Himself is the Absolute, that is *idolized*, *Reason* (Aristotle). Sad to say Christian thought has largely taken this over in the area of so-called "natural" knowledge.

The effects of compromise of Christian and pagan views. The scheme of "nature" and "grace" as a result of this compromise

As soon as Christian thought had compromised with this pagan philosophy, the truly Scriptural relationship between life in the temporal world and the kingdom of God was no longer understood and false philosophical constructions began to obscure the profound clear truth of God's revelation.

The heart was no longer understood in the Scriptural sense because people no longer understood themselves; and they no longer understood themselves because they had obscured the true knowledge of God with an impossible compromise with apostate philosophical speculations. The "heart" became identified with the temporal psychical function, which was considered the stimulant of the will. That is why men of the Middle Ages began to argue the question which in "human" and in "divine" nature has priority: the intellect (reason) or the will, which according to Greek philosophy arises out of the function of feeling. Thus they also construed a false contrast between "nature" and "grace" because "nature" was considered to be the God-created structure of reality as seen in the light of Greek philosophy, and "grace" the supra-temporal revelation of God, including all Christ's redemptive work.

Thomas Aquinas on human nature. "Nature" as portal of "grace"

Christ, the Word become flesh, was now no longer seen as the New Root of the order of creation, as the Rectifier of true nature. "Nature," concentrated in "reason," was declared self-sufficient and autonomous in her own area, the temporal world-order. Thomas Aquinas, prince of Roman Catholic Scholasticism, made natural reason independent of the revelation of God in Christ Jesus. Learning, morality, political life, and "natural theology" were then, as autonomous areas of natural reason, practiced in a pagan-Aristotelian manner. But in addition to this intrinsically pagan idea of "nature," a "supra-temporal" area of grace was construed which transcends natural reason and can only be apprehended by the light of God's revelation. "Nature" was made a lower autonomous portal of "grace," and the latter would merely bring the former to "higher perfection."

The Christian view of the fall now had to be accommodated to this pagan conception of "nature" as well. The Scriptural view of a center of human nature in the heart, the religious root, had been abandoned in favor of the Aristotelian concept viewing "reason" as the origin of human nature. Thus it could no longer be admitted that human nature is depraved in its very root because of the falling away of the heart from God. Instead, it was taught that "nature" was not completely spoiled by sin, but merely "wounded," that is, the supra-natural gift of grace had been lost.

Aristotle: the pagan idea of the state. The state as the highest bond of human society, of which all other societal relationships are but dependent parts

What did this mean in terms of the idea of the state? The state was counted with the so-called "natural realm" and the pagan, Aristotelian view was taken over. This view came down to this: The state is the highest form of the community. All other societal relationships, such as marriage, family, blood relation, vocational and industrial groupings, all these are merely lower components which serve the higher. According to Aristotle, the state is grounded in the "rational-moral" nature of humankind. One cannot realize one's natural perfection in isolation, but only within the community. Nurture of marriage and family are the first, "lower" necessities of life, the "next higher" are fulfilled by the village community. But these lower societal relationships are not autonomous; only the state can, as perfectly autonomous community, provide a person with all that which serves the perfection of that person's "rational-moral" nature.

Thus the relation between the state and other temporal societal relationships is constructed according to the scheme of *the whole and its parts* and of the *goal and the means,* from the *"lower" to the "higher."* The "lower" relationships as different kinds of parts of the state have no goal in themselves, but all must serve the state. By nature the human being is state-oriented, for already in the forming of marriage, family, and blood-relations the natural compulsion to form the state is germinating. By nature the state precedes the individual. The state is implicit in the rational-moral nature, as the mature form of a plant in its seed, or the full-grown body of an animal in its embryo.

The pagan totalitarian idea of the state and its revival in National-Socialism and Fascism

This Aristotelian idea of the state was the philosophical expression of the ancient Greek popular conviction. People really saw the state as the highest rung of humankind's moral development, as the highest and most perfect body to which the free citizen had to subject all areas of life. It was very much like the idea of the totalitarian state as recently taken up by Fascism and National-Socialism, although there the idea is no longer based on a so-called "metaphysical" order of reason, but is oriented irrationally to the community feeling of the people (*das Volk*).

Originally this pagan view of the state was grounded in the doctrine that human existence is rooted in a "rational moral" nature, that from this spring the directions of life, and that reason is the supra-temporal center, the deeper unity of human existence. As we have seen, this view is directly opposed to God's Word-revelation in Jesus Christ. It originated from an idolatrous, apostate conception concerning the center of a person's being, from a lack of self-knowledge caused by an idolatrous conception of God (making "reason" divine).

The truly Christian view of the state takes its stance in the supra-temporal root-community of redeemed humanity in Christ Jesus

Christian religion had laid the axe to the religious root of this pagan idea of the state, and with that to the root of the whole pagan conception of temporal society. It revealed the true supra-temporal root of all temporal human societal structures grounded in the God-created world-order, that is, the religious root-community of humankind in the kingdom of God, which must reign in the heart of a person.

That deepest root-unity of humankind had fallen to the kingdom of Satan through Adam, but through Christ it has been redeemed and renewed.

Thus the "Church of Christ" – not in temporal diffused form, but in the supra-temporal unity in Christ – is the true root of all temporal societal relationships as required by God in His creation plan, just as all the temporal functions of human existence – physical movement, biotic life, feeling, thought, justice, morality and faith – must stem from the heart, the religious center.[1]

All temporal societal relationships ought to be manifestations of the supra-temporal, invisible church of Christ

In other words, all temporal societal relationships, including state and organized church-institute, are, in accordance with their God-willed structure, merely temporal manifestations, temporal expressions of the one and only true supra-temporal root-community of renewed humankind in the "body of Christ," the "invisible church" of which Christ is the only Head.

The kingdom of God as the all-embracing rule of God

We see here that Christianity proclaims a total rule of God, opposed to the pagan idea of the total state as light is opposed to darkness. Paganism, unable to transcend time, seeks a last and highest temporal bond of which all other societal relationships can be no more than dependent

---

1   *Editorial note* (DFMS): Dooyeweerd *first* realized that the human selfhood transcends the diversity of modal aspects and individuality-structures and *then* developed his philosophy of time in which he restricts time to the modal aspects and the dimension of individuality-structures. Consequently, since the human selfhood was considered to be supra-modal and supra-structural, the central religious dimension to which it belongs was considered to be supra-temporal.

parts. Christianity does not place a temporal church-institute above the state as an ultimate bond, but in Christ it looks beyond time toward the total theocracy, the invisible church of Christ. Here all temporal societal relationships are rooted and grounded, and each of these, after its own divine structure and God-given law, must be an expression, be it an imperfect one, of that invisible kingdom of God.

This basic Christian idea[1] of the kingdom of God is the only possible ground for the Christian idea of the state.

The Christian idea[2] of sphere-sovereignty over against the pagan view that the state is related to the other societal structures as the whole to its parts

This idea of the kingdom of God is directly opposed to the apostate view of temporal society, that is, the self-willed, rational view which construes the mutual relation and deeper unity of temporal societal bonds as one of part and whole; one total state and the other societal relationships its parts. But neither marriage, nor family, nor blood-relation, nor the free types of social existence, whether they are organized or not, can be considered as part of an all-embracing state. Every societal relationship has received from God its own structure and law of life, sovereign in its own sphere.

The Christian world- and life-view, illumined by the revealed Word of God, posits sphere-sovereignty of the temporal life-spheres over against the pagan totality-idea.

However, if this idea of sphere-sovereignty is typified as peculiarly Calvinistic, we must protest. We must protest also when other views, which reject this sphere-sovereignty because they themselves have compromised with pagan philosophy, are considered as at least comparable Christian views. There is only *one* Christian view concerning human relationships which indeed takes seriously, without compromise, the Scriptural principle[3] of the kingdom of God.

The Roman Catholic view of the Christian state – Thomas Aquinas – is a falling away from the Scriptural conception

Roman Catholic thought concerning human society fell away from this Scriptural basis when it compromised with Aristotelian philosophy. It accepts the Aristotelian idea of the state for the area of "nature" and believes it can accommodate this to the Christian idea of the total rule of

---

1 *Translator's note*: Dutch *grondgedachte* (I shall occasionally note the Dutch for this word and similar ones.)
2 *Translator's note*: Dutch: *idee*.
3 *Translator's note*: Dutch: *grondgedachte*.

God by building another level, the realm of "grace," above the pagan edifice of nature.

But this departure from Scripture also penetrated views concerning the grace of the "Civitas Dei."

Infiltration of the pagan totality-idea in the Roman Catholic concept of the church

It was not foreseen that the pagan totality-idea, which seeks in temporal society an "ultimate bond" of which all else can only be parts, would influence the Roman Catholic *view of the church*.

The state was seen in pagan manner as the totality of all temporal societal relationships in the *natural* (rational-moral) area. Now in turn it is looked upon as a lower serving part of the temporal church-institute. The church was now considered to be the total bond of all Christendom, the rule of the realm of grace in its temporal manifestation. In other words, the temporal church-institute with its papal hierarchy came to be identified with the so-called "invisible church," the supra-temporal kingdom of God in the body of Christ.

A false view of the Christian state: the state is subject to the temporal church-institute

This immediately had a fateful influence upon Thomas' idea of the Christian state. Its Christian character was not Scripturally sought in the expression of Christ's Kingdom within the inner structure of the state itself. Rather, Roman Catholicism continued to see the inner structure of the state in the old pagan way as the total bond of all natural society, and continued to deduce the principles for political life by "natural reason," detached from revelation.

The state can participate in the realm of grace, not from within but, since it is itself strictly natural, can do this only by enlisting in the service of the temporal church-institute. This service consists of the eradication of heresy and paganism, and the subjection of the state to church leadership in all things that the church judges to touch the welfare of souls. In that view such and only such a state can be called Christian.

Penetration of this view in modern denominational political parties

This Roman Catholic error continues even today in all those semi-Christian political conceptions that consider the Christian character of the state to consist of its ties to a given church-institute (thus in general every denominational grouping in politics).[1]

---

1 *Translator's note*: Dooyeweerd mentions some Dutch political parties in this connection, which are omitted here.

The notion that the Christian state must recognize a certain denomination as "state-church," or at least as the only true church, or that the Christian state must bend to a certain creed, as being the "only true one," the status of official legal authority, essentially stems from this old conception of Roman-Scholasticism which ascribes the totality of all temporal revelation of the body of Christ to just such a temporal church-institute.

The Reformation over against the Roman Catholic view of Christian society

From the very start the Reformation has protested vehemently against this basic error. For its starting-point it returned to the invisible church, the supra-temporal body of Christ. It placed itself squarely over against the Roman Catholic *identification* of this invisible church (the total rule of God) with the temporal church-institute. The Reformation broke with the Roman Catholic view concerning the relation of nature and grace, at least theologically. It rejected the Church's teaching that the fall has not corrupted the root of 'natural existence', but has only caused a "supra-temporal gift of grace" to be lost. Consequently, the Reformation condemned the Roman Catholic doctrine of "natural merit of good works" and proclaimed again with power the good message of justification by faith alone.

And yet, this Scriptural, radically Christian foundation did not, especially in Luther, consistently penetrate the Reformation's view of temporal human society and its conception of the Christian state.

Nominalism in Late-Scholasticism

Already in the late Middle Ages (14th century), a line of thought had turned itself in opposition to the compromise that Thomas Aquinas had sought to effect between Christian faith and Aristotelian philosophy. This line of thought was to become of world-wide importance, and is known by the name "Late-Scholastic Nominalism." The father of this movement was the English Franciscan William of Occam. What did this movement want? As we saw above, the whole Aristotelian-Thomist view of the "realm of nature" (as distinguished from the "realm of grace") was rooted in an absolutization of rational functions. In the Being of God intellect was also held to be predominant. This idea had come out most strongly in Thomas's thesis: The good is not good because God commands it, but God *had to* command the good, since it was good. That is, it was grounded in the general *concept* of good because it agrees with the "rational-moral" nature of a person. This was in flagrant disagreement with the Scriptural teaching of God's sovereign will. The Creator, far above all human measure, is not Himself subject to a law, for He is the Origin of all law, the Origin also of the norm of good and evil.

The nominalistic conception of the law as subjective arbitrariness and the Thomistic idea of the law as rational order

The nominalist movement wished to reassert God's sovereignty as Creator over against Thomas's deification of reason in the realm of nature. But how did it go about this? Instead of positing truly Scriptural thought over against Thomas it explained God's holy, sovereign Creator's will as despotic voluntarism. Nominalism spoke of *Deus exlex,* that is to say, a God whose laws are grounded purely upon disposition. God, Occam thought, could just as well have willed an egotistical moral law instead of the Ten Commandments.

Of course, Nominalism, distorting the Christian teaching of God as sovereign Creator into a tyrannical voluntarism divorced from the holiness of God, overthrew Thomism, which had championed a doctrine of a rational moral nature, and of a natural moral law grounded in reason. The law as general rule rooted in reason, loses, in this nominalism, the lofty position Thomas had accorded it in his rationalistic world of thought. The law is pulled down to a lower level. God Himself is not bound by law. But even Christians are elevated above the law, at least in their inner life of grace. Law is merely the positive ordering of temporal world-life, where sin reigns. And even when the Church and Scripture posit laws for external society, Christians have no longer anything to do with these ordinances in their inner life. They must subject themselves to this utterly incomprehensible positive command of the will of God, but only externally, and only as long as they move in the temporal world. From the inner life of grace the law has been removed.

The nominalist dualism of nature and grace

This nominalistic view of law radically destroyed the artificial compromise that Thomas Aquinas had attempted to construct between the pagan-Aristotelian conception of "nature" and the Christian understanding of "grace."

Thomas had taught: "nature" (understood in the rationalistic sense of Aristotle) is the lower, serving portal of "grace," the lower "matter" which, through divine grace of which the Church is the dispensary, is brought to "higher form" and higher perfection.

This line of thought became unacceptable to nominalism. "Nature" continued to be understood in all its manifestations in education, statesmanship, family life, etc. as the lower realm subject to law. But the natural order could no longer be considered as the portal to the order of grace. "Nature" as realm of law had come into implacable opposition to "grace" as area of Christian freedom (nominalistically understood). Now it was but one more step to identify the ordinances of "natural life" with the "sinful world," where harsh and inexorable law serves only to curb the wantonness of humankind.

There is really no place in such nominalistic thought for Christian learning, Christian political theory, or Christian organizational life. All of these belong in this view to the "kingdom of this world," to "sinful (human) nature," to the area of law, from which Christians have been freed in their inner life through grace in Christ. In no sense did created nature become any more Christian than it had in Thomas' thinking. On the contrary, it was completely cut off from the church, put on its own feet, and left to its own laws, as an autonomous area over against that of grace. Thus it was that nominalism, in bitter opposition to the hierarchical view of Thomas and his followers, began everywhere to resist the supremacy that the church-institute had exercised over education, economic life, etc. during the era of the 10th to the 13th centuries – "nature" and "grace" were separated, unbridgeably so.

This dualism was perpetuated in Luther's law-gospel polarity
Luther had been brought up in this nominalistic line of thought before he made his appearance as Reformer. His own testimony is: "Ich bin von Ockham's Schule." Although Luther's life and mighty faith broke radically with Roman-Scholasticism in theology and church-life, and thus opened the way for the further development of the Reformation, he still retained in his world- and life-view the old nominalistic dualism of nature and grace, now as the polarity of *law* and evangelical *freedom*.

Melanchthon's synthesis
Melanchthon[1] was soon able to search once more for a synthesis between Luther's reformational view of Scripture, classical philosophy, *and* the contemporary humanistic way of thinking which continued the nominalistic strain in the realm of nature and proclaimed human personality as sovereign ruler of the cosmos.

Brunner continues Luther's dualism
In contemporary thought this dualism has been consistently carried through in Karl Barth and Emil Brunner. Hence their fundamental rejection of the idea of Christian culture, Christian learning, and Christian political life.

Brunner, in his *Das Gebot und die Ordnungen,* teaches the autonomy of the whole natural realm of ordinances (the area of law) over against the grace-realm of the Christian faith which is not subjected to the law (ordinances), but acts in freedom in accordance with the evangelical command of love. The latter does not posit a general rule for action, but is, according to Brunner, nothing other than the voice of a calling God

---

1 *Editorial note* (DFMS): Melanchthon initially supported Luther, subsequently showed sympathy with the Calvinistic doctrine of the Lord's supper and finally reverted to a more humanistic position which rejects the radical fall of humankind – reminiscent of the admiration he had in his youth for the great leaders of the humanistic movement: Agricola, Erasmus and Pirkheimer.

who places us at every turn before the responsibility of a single, concrete decision, never to return in the same form. Christian love, in his view, never acts in accordance with principles. It is in the full sense of the word *unprincipled*. The Christian statesman, as politician, must never reach for the impossible ideal of a Christian political theory according to Christian principles. The command of love, says Brunner, heard in faith, certainly calls that statesman to political activity, but for the fulfillment of his task it points to the "natural ordinances," to political life with its "law unto itself" – a law which is in effect in contradiction with Christian love. The Christian need never rationalize this contradiction; the whole sinful world, according to Brunner, is full of it.

However, when certain existing laws do not allow Christians the freedom to fulfill their task of love toward their neighbors, then they must strive for a better ordinance, also politically. But here again, it is not faith that decides, but only natural reason, which the Christian has in common with all humankind. Therefore, no Christian political parties, but rather the greatest possible cooperation of all concerned, regardless of their life-view or their religion. According to Brunner, such a cooperative group can, in a realistic manner, work towards a given political improvement, for example in his case, to do away with today's mammon-inspired capitalist system. Christians may not always find the necessary support of the existing parties for their program. Or, perhaps these parties are possessed of such a demonic spirit that Christians cannot possibly become involved with them. If that is the case, Christians may decide to form a temporary group of their own, Brunner suggests, but at no time do they have the right to call such a party "Christian."

Calvin breaks with the dualistic nature-grace scheme

The truly radical break with the nature-grace scheme, inaugurated during the Middle Ages, really began with Calvin. With that radical break the way was finally and truly opened up toward building the Christian world- and life-view in the Scriptural sense, without compromise with paganistic and humanistic lines of thought.

In Calvin we no longer find law placed over against nominalistic evangelical *freedom*. Paul's message of the Christian's freedom from the curse of the law and his rejection of Pharisaic self-justification go hand in hand with the Scriptural view that each creature is subject to God's ordinances, completely and universally. An ordinance of creation is not to be viewed, as nominalism taught, as a divinely despotic command only valid for the lower area of "nature" and to be obeyed only externally, but as a holy, wise, and perfectly good ordinance of the Highest Majesty, without Whom the created cosmos would fall apart in utter chaos.

Calvin's Scriptural view of law

Thomas Aquinas, following Aristotle, taught that the temporal ordinances of God find their deeper unity in a rational idea of God. But for Calvin the deeper unity lies in the religious fulness of God's law: service toward God with the whole heart. Created human nature is, whenever Calvin allows Scripture to speak, no longer concentrated in the rational-moral functions, but in the heart, the supra-temporal religious root of human existence. Thus Scripture could be understood again. Christ, the New Root of reborn humanity, is the Fulfiller of the law, that is, He has fulfilled the law of God in the religious fulness and unity of its meaning.

This radically Christian beginning of Calvin's world- and life-view *had* to become of far-reaching significance for the whole Calvinistic conception of the relation between temporal cosmos and supra-temporal kingdom of God in Christ Jesus.

The law as boundary between God and creature

Calvin sees the law as the actual boundary between the sovereign God and His creature, and takes this law as divine ordinance in its deepest meaning to be *directed to the heart* as center, not to "reason." Only God is not subject to this law, not because His will would be despotic, but because His holy, wise, and perfectly good will is the Origin of all norms for good and evil. God gave every temporal sphere of life its own law in accordance with His will.

Calvin's view of the divine creation-order contrasted with Thomas Aquinas

Calvin chose his starting-point in the supra-temporal religious root-unity of the divine law as revealed by Christ Jesus and fulfilled by Him. Therefore, with respect to the temporal fulness and diversity of ordinances which God has laid down in temporal life, the insight had to follow that none of these temporal spheres can be derived from or valued lower than any other.

Aristotle and Thomas, as we saw earlier, did think that the spheres could indeed be derived and valued in that manner. But then their conception did not spring from the Scriptural view of the true supra-temporal root-unity and Origin of divine law, but from self-willed human rational constructs. It sprang from the autonomy of reason and considered the rational-moral functions the actual supra-temporal and "immortal" center of human existence. Thus, this view also claimed the divine world-order to be an order originating in reason, where all spheres of life are ordered in an ascending scale from lower to higher, from means to end. In the realm of natural society the state became the highest bond – all other relationships were considered its serving parts.

But from a truly Scripturally Christian standpoint such a view of the divine world-order, which is essentially pagan, cannot but be radically rejected. For only then do we begin with the true Root of creation, Christ Jesus as fulfillment of divine Word Revelation. From here the root, the supra-temporal unity, the deeper unity of all creation, is seen in Christ, Whose Kingdom has been established in people's hearts. From this standpoint the true Origin of all temporal ordinances is not seen deified in "reason," but in the holy will of God, the sovereign Creator.

The principle[1] of sphere-sovereignty: Calvin and Althusius

From this truly supra-temporal Christian religious standpoint the relationship among the temporal ordinances can only be understood as sphere-sovereignty. This basic, cosmic principle Calvin grasped in essence, and worked out with great clarity in his teaching regarding the temporal church-institute maintaining its inner independence from the state.

In the 17th century a Calvinistic German jurist, Johannes Althusius, oriented his social teaching to this principle.[2]

The greater influence of Melanchthon's synthesis predominates

But this Scriptural line of thought could not immediately develop unhindered. The predominant influence of Melanchthon's synthesis program – another compromise between Christian and pagan thought – held sway in Protestant universities and from there took over leadership in practical life, particularly in political life. Calvin had not been able to free himself completely from Greco-Roman political theory, but Melanchthon once again sought his footing there!

Under these circumstances the Christian idea of the state relapsed into medieval Scholastic patterns: the state, part of the realm of "nature," could only receive its Christian stamp through serving the temporal church-community; except that, instead of a Roman Catholic church-institute, it was now the state-church. Again the basic motive of the Reformation was caught in an intrinsically impossible synthesis with pagan philosophy. No wonder that the ensuing ages have witnessed a gradual decline of the principles of the Reformation.

A new life- and world-view began to triumph in modern Western culture. Humanism, utterly oriented to this temporal life, placed sovereignty of the human personality at the center. Originally it had joined

---

1 *Translator's note*: Sphere-sovereignty is often referred to as a *"grondprincipe"* = *basic principle*.
2 *Translator's note*: Cf. *The Politics of Johannes Althusius*, Abridged and translated by Frederick S. Catney, with a Preface by Carl J. Friedrich, Boston: Beacon Press, 1964.

the Reformation, struggling to overthrow the rule of the church-institute over all natural life, but now it pushed its former ally into a corner.

The rise of the modern humanistic world- and life-view

Humanism secularized the message of Christian freedom and of creation, fall, and redemption. Scripture's revelation of creation by God was gradually displaced by the idea of the creative power of science. Christian freedom was metamorphosed into sovereign freedom of the human personality. The humanistic world- and life-view was concentrated in two ground-motives: the humanistic ideal of personality and the new science-ideal. The first meant to teach absolute autonomy, self-sufficient "ethical determination." The second was intent upon a construction of the temporal world coherence, based on the "autonomy of scientific thought."

The overpowering influence of the new mathematical science-ideal upon modern culture

Very quickly this new world- and life-view assumed a leading role in the shaping of modern culture. Leadership of science (*Wissenschaft*) was in humanistic hands. The new humanistic science-idea was inspired by a motive of dominance, a striving for power – the whole world was to be subjected to the sovereign human personality. Very quickly it oriented itself to the mathematical natural science which arose in the 16th century.

The new humanistic science-ideal received a dominant importance in the humanistic world-view and with its individualistic and rationalistic consequence it was simply impossible to combine it with a recognition of the Christian principle of sphere-sovereignty, because in the latter is posited a rich diversity of the temporal cosmos in inner indissoluble coherence of its differentiated aspects. Instead of God's sovereign will as Creator, creative mathematical thought was declared to be the origin of all laws that regulate temporal life. And since mathematical thought seeks to construct all complex figures from the simplest elements, humanistic philosophy tried to do the same with the complex whole (oneness) of the temporal world. Insofar as it was able to be consistent in its application of the new science-ideal, humanism tried to deduce all temporal order from one single, simple, natural-scientific law. Thus the British philosopher Thomas Hobbes (17th century) tried to construe the temporal cosmos theoretically from a mechanistic principle of attraction and repulsion.

The other pole, the humanistic personality-ideal with its idea of freedom did not become predominant in humanistic philosophy until later.

The humanistic ideal of science continues in the modern individualistic idea of the state

When applied to temporal society, this new science-ideal led to the view that all societal relationships from family to state and church must be constructed from their "simplest mathematical components," here meaning individuals, abstract units. It was held that these individuals must be thought of as originally in a "state of nature" where perfect equality and freedom reigned. But now, in a so-called "social contract" they have given up more or less of this freedom to the state, the *body* of citizens.

It is obvious that this view was permeated with remnants of nominalism: positive ordinances that hold within the societal bonds were understood in terms of the arbitrary will of individuals united in a social contract. The constitution was then the *"volonté générale"* (general will). No individual can complain of injustice for in the social contract (Rousseau: *contrat social*) that person agreed to all laws the state might impose.

Relativizing character of modern individualism in its view of society

This individualistic view of society, fruit of the new humanistic ideal of science, erased all the limits or borders that God in His wisdom had set in His temporal world-order. For every societal relationship (family, state, church, etc.) God has posited its own law of life; He created in each of them an inner structure, in its own sovereign sphere. But on the strength of its entire scheme humanistic rationalism had come in conflict with such a creed. All societal relationships were explained in terms of a uniform abstract scheme of social contract.

Humanistic natural law over against its Aristotelian-Thomistic counterpart

The school of humanistic natural law (from Hugo Grotius to Rousseau, Kant and Fichte) defended this individualistic theory of society.

We are here dealing with a doctrine that differs in principle from that of the Aristotelian-Thomistic line. True, the latter also started with natural right, that is, the rational principles of justice and morality that are created part and parcel of human nature. But here an individual human being was not considered to be self-sufficient by nature, but was a member of the social community, the state. Aristotle and Thomas had taught that by nature the state preceded the individual. Thus they in principle rejected any individualistic conception of a natural state without societal relationships. They did not want to construct a state arising from the individual, like humanistic natural law, but rather the other way around – the individual from the state.

Two mainstreams in humanistic natural law and the idea of the *Rechtsstaat* in its first phase of development[1]

We can distinguish two main streams in the development of humanistic natural law (1) *state-absolutism* (Grotius, Hobbes, Pufendorff, Rousseau, and others), where all freedom of the individual is lost to the state, and (2) *anti-state absolutism* (Locke, Kant, and others), which starts from inviolate absolute constitutional rights of the individual over against the state, and thus seeks to limit the state task to organized safeguarding of these rights.

From the latter came the *old-liberal theory of the Rechtsstaat* with its doctrine of the inviolate constitutional rights of the individual (such as freedom of the press, free enterprise, free association, etc.), and with its teaching of the separation of powers (separate legislative, executive and judicial powers). In practice, this theory has become a powerful co-influence in the modern idea of the state, but in its individualistic-humanistic basic conception it was in a sense Christian in origin. That basic conception underlies the old-liberal *"laissez faire"* program that rejects any "encroachment" of the state on economic life, particularly in industry.

The old-liberal view of the *Rechtsstaat* and the separation of Church and State

That basic conception also underlies the humanistic idea of tolerance in the old-liberal sense, which seeks complete separation of church and state, and constructs the temporal church-institute as a private organization, again with the help of a uniform social contract – an organization where the individual is the sovereign authority (collegial or congregational type of church government). There is no room for a truly Christian idea of the state. The Christian religion has been relegated to the inner chamber.

Tolerance in State-absolutism

In opposition to this main stream, however, the other movement in humanistic natural law, State-absolutism, taught the absolute sovereignty of state over church, and denied the church any internally independent law-sphere (this is so-called territorial church-government: the state has to maintain tolerance within the church; it opposes any doctrinal discipline). Such were the tenets of Hugo Grotius and the Arminians, and in Germany particularly Thomasius.

---

1 *Translator's note:* There is no English equivalent for the Dutch (and German) term *Rechtsstaat*. The term can be applied to a state in which a constitutional or accepted law and order is maintained, e.g. in sentences like: The *Magna Carta* safe-guarding the English *Rechtsstaat;* Hitler abolished the German *Rechtsstaat* and replaced it with his dictatorial National-Socialist *regime*. Elsewhere, Dooyeweerd also uses "rule of law."

The natural law idea of the state in Anti-state-absolutism with its own particular view of the *Rechtsstaat* has been linked unjustly with Calvinism. Liberalism (Otto Gierke in Germany, Eigeman in the Netherlands) was always intent on presenting the Calvinistic idea of sphere-sovereignty as derived from the liberal natural law view of the state. Even a Calvin scholar, the well-known Frenchman Doumergue, saw in Calvin the fore-runner of the ideas of freedom of the French Revolution. It is true that the Calvinistic idea of the state has been infiltrated at times with humanistic natural law; but, insofar as that is the case, it must be seen as nothing less than a falling away in principle from the Scriptural, Christian view of the state.

The Calvinistic view of sphere-sovereignty has nothing in common with the humanistic freedom-idea of natural law

After all, humanistic natural law begins with a supposed sovereignty of the human personality and that taken individualistically. Calvinism begins with God's sovereignty, revealed in religious fulness in the supra-temporal kingdom of Christ, and intended to shine forth from this root-community in all temporal societal forms. Humanistic natural law recognizes only "constitutional rights" of the individual, but it misjudges and levels the genuine societal structures as they have been embedded in the temporal world-order through God's sovereign will as Creator. That is why humanism, when it comes to the relation between state and other societal structures, can only base this relation on the natural (i.e., born-into) rights of the individual.

Again, Calvinism takes its starting-point from the Scriptural message of solidarity, from the religious root-community of humankind in creation, fall, and redemption. From this supra-temporal religious structural complex we behold the richly diversified panorama of temporal societal structures. In this God's sovereign will holds for all people. Therefore, these structures cannot be constructed after a scheme of a whole and its parts or a relativized individualistic social contract: they can be understood in their mutual relation only by way of the principle of sphere-sovereignty.

By the same token, whoever rejects this Scriptural principle *cannot* understand the idea of the Christian state in its truly Scriptural sense. For, as we saw, the genuine idea of the Christian state begins with the religious ground-idea of a supra-temporal Christian church, which reveals itself temporally in all societal structures equally. Denial of sphere-sovereignty is the immediate consequence whenever one chooses a starting-point for a world- and life-view in temporal reality. Such a starting-point within temporal reality has occasioned the absolutization of reason by some thinkers; others made too much of a certain temporal societal relationship – church or state; still others overestimated the abstract, mathematical component that the individual was held to be, and consequently constructed and relativized all societal structures after the uniform scheme of social contract.

The truly Christian idea of the state cannot be separated from a recognition of sphere-sovereignty

Since it appears that the truly Christian idea of the state stands in indissoluble coherence with the recognition of sphere-sovereignty, this principle must first be investigated more closely. The more so since its true sense is often no longer understood, even in our own circles. It is for this reason that "sphere-sovereignty" is constantly identified with the political principle of *autonomy*. This shows clearly that relativizing ideas are infiltrating our Calvinistic view of the state.

The radical difference between sphere-sovereignty and autonomy

The principle of autonomy makes sense only when speaking of the relation of a given whole to its parts. One can speak of municipal and provincial autonomy within the state.[1] Municipalities and provinces are indeed parts of the state and have no other structure. But family, state, church, school and industry differ radically in their respective structure. They can never be related to each other as parts to a whole. Hence, from a Christian point of view it is meaningless to speak of an autonomy of family, church, school and industry within the state. The inter-relation can only be sphere-sovereignty. In the final analysis autonomy, as relative independence of the parts within the whole, depends upon the requirements of the whole. Only the government can decide how far the limits of municipal and provincial autonomy can reach in terms of a well-functioning state. And the power, i.e. the jurisdiction, of autonomous parts can never be original or un-derived from the whole.

Autonomy is proper only to parts of a whole; sphere-sovereignty does not allow for such a relation

It is quite different with sphere-sovereignty. It rests solely and completely upon the structures that are in place for the societal relationships and that are founded in the temporal world-order by God's sovereign will. Societal relationships whose structures are irreducible, such as family, state, church, etc., always have an *original* sphere of competence, in principle limited with respect to each other. The boundaries of sphere-sovereignty therefore can never be set one-sidedly by one party in a certain societal relationship such as a state or a church. These boundaries are placed in the divine world-order and do not depend on human arbitrariness. In the fullest sense they exist "by the grace of God."

What then are these structural principles by which temporal societal relationships are instrinsically differentiated and through which is given the divine guarantee for their sphere-sovereignty?

---

1 Compare the "autonomy of local churches" with that of a larger church organization.

A proper answer to this question is a prerequisite for the right insight into the Christian idea of the state. For how can we gain this insight if we construe the state as totality of all societal relationships, or derived from the individual, mathematically conceived? How can we gain insight into the state if its inner, God-ordered law-structure is negated? The various structures of temporal society and their sphere-sovereignty can be viewed only from society's deeper root-community which is the kingdom of God in Christ Jesus' invisible church.

Sphere-sovereignty and antithesis go hand in hand in Kuyper

Dr. A. Kuyper (1837-1920), called by God to lead the Calvinistic *Reveil* after Groen Van Prinsterer's death (1876), repeatedly emphasized the laws that apply to the life of societal relationships. In spite of liberalistic scorn he persistently posited an antithesis against the deadening synthesis of his time, and recognized sphere-sovereignty as fundamental cosmic principle. This connection between antithesis and sphere-sovereignty was not by chance. It is exactly the search for synthesis of scriptural and pagan or humanistic views of society that muddles the insight into the law-structure of societal relationships and sphere-sovereignty. Synthesis caused this in the past and causes it today.

Kuyper broke with nature-grace and distinguished between church as institute and as organism

Kuyper, following Calvin, broke radically with the Scholastic and Lutheran nature-grace dualism. In his view of the relation between the kingdom of God and temporal societal relationships Scripture broke through powerfully, and caused him to see a distinction between the church as temporal institute and as organism. He saw that the Christian idea of the state could not be Scripturally understood as long as its Christian character was considered to have been proven if and when the boundaries between church and state are diluted. Hence his objection to article 36 of the Belgic Confession. The invisible, supra-temporal church of Christ is the center for him that must be revealed, not only in the temporal church-institute, but equally in all societal structures: in the Christian family, the Christian scientific community, etc. The church as an organism is the hypostasis (foundation), the revelation of the invisible, supra-temporal church in all societal structures equally.

This great conception opened the way for a truly Scripturally Christian view of society. In recent years it has been worked out further in deeper investigation of the various structural principles underlying the bonds of temporal society.[1]

---

1 Cf. Dooyeweerd's *A New Critique of Theoretical Thought,* especially Vol.III.
  [Editorial note (DFMS): As mentioned this work forms part of the A-Series of

Elaboration of Kuyper's views the first meaning of sphere-sovereignty, the sovereign law-spheres

If insight into these structural principles is to be gained, it is first of all necessary to obtain insight into the rich diversity of aspects manifest in temporal reality. These aspects become clearest to us when we compare our theoretical and our non-theoretical, everyday experience of things. In daily life we view a blossoming apple tree as a complete unity, an individual thing. For the various sciences however, this one thing can be considered from a particular point of view or in terms of a certain aspect. For mathematics only the aspects of numerality and space; for physics only the aspect of motion; for biology, organic life; for psychology only under the aspect of being a sense-object; for logic as objective coherence of logical characteristics that we subjectively combine in the concept of a tree; for historians only as an object of human culture; for linguistics as receiving a name; for economics as object of appraisal; sociology considers the tree as object in human social functioning; aesthetically a tree is considered as an object of artistic harmony; jurally as an object of right of ownership, etc.; ethically as an object of love or hate; and theologically as an object of faith. (We believe that the tree is created by God and is not a fortuitous product of blind forces of nature.)

Temporal aspects of reality in distinct law-spheres

Temporal reality functions in all of these aspects: in number, space, motion, organic life, feeling, logical analysis, historical form-giving, symbolic meaning (language), social manners, economic value, artistic harmony, justice, love, and faith. Furthermore, the full reality of a thing does not allow itself to be enclosed in any one of these aspects. For example, when a person says, in conformity with a materialist stance, that a tree is no more than a mass of moving matter, that person speaks nonsense since, by saying so, such a person forms a sense-perception and a logical concept of this thing, and gives it symbolic meaning in words. Implicitly therefore, that person recognizes that the numerical, spatial, and physical aspects are only certain sides of the real tree, and that these cannot be experienced without psychical feeling, logical understanding or language. These aspects of temporal reality cannot be reduced to each other either. Each has its own law-sphere, and is embraced in that law-sphere. Here the fundamental principle of sphere-sovereignty reveals itself in its primary sense.

Dooyeweerd's Collected Works (volumes A1, A2, A3, and A4) – currently being published by The Edwin Mellen Press.]

The religious root-unity of the law-spheres

The deeper unity of all temporal reality aspects within their own spheres of divine ordinances (law-spheres) cannot be found in any one of these aspects themselves. It is of a supra-temporal, religious character. The fulness of number, the spatial omnipresence, the fulness of force, of life, of feeling, of knowledge, of historical power, of communion, of beauty, of justice, of love, and of faith is in Christ Jesus, the Root of the reborn cosmos! In Him all these aspects of temporal reality find their true fulfillment of meaning, their deeper root-unity in the concentration upon service of God with the whole heart.

As sunlight diffuses itself in prismatic beauty . . .

As sunlight breaks into a marvelous diversity of rainbow hues, and as all these pure pastel colors find union in unbroken, shimmering white, so also do all temporal reality aspects find their supra-temporal unity in Christ Jesus, in Whom God has given us everything. All temporal aspects of created reality are in Christ Jesus, the true Root of creation, concentrated into the religious supra-temporal fulness of meaning. That is why, as Kuyper says, there is indeed no area of this life of which Christ does not say: Mine! There is no autonomous area of "nature" existing independently of Christ, above which His kingdom, a supposed "area of grace," looms as a superstructure.

Common grace and the grace of rebirth (*palingenesis*): no dualistic doctrine

Nor is there a "realm of common grace" independent from a "realm" of "special grace" in Christ Jesus. The fall turned the heart, the root of creation, away from God. Creation therefore had to be reborn in its root through Christ. Special or saving grace can accordingly not be a "separate realm." It touches, as did the fall, the supra-temporal core, the heart, the root of all temporal creation. "Common grace" does not touch this supra-temporal root, but only the temporal ordinances of life: God halts the decomposition caused by sin. But this common, merely temporal grace of God has no other root than Christ Jesus. The grace of rebirth, given to us by God in Him, is the true hidden root of common grace which must be made evident in the "church as organism," that is, in Christian unfolding of life within all temporal structures of reality. When, by God's common grace in this sinful temporal life, culture, learning, art, family and political life, etc., are still possible, the inescapable call comes to the Christian to make Christ, as true Root of creation and as King of all temporal life, visibly manifest. For the Christian this task makes political life also a sacred Christian calling. It is true that under the rule of common grace Christ's kingdom cannot come to unbroken realization, for the power of sin continues to turn itself against this kingdom until the last day, but fundamentally in the root of Creation the victory has been won by the Lamb of God, and creation, in all its structures, has been maintained, saved, redeemed!

Sphere-universality of the law-spheres

If we find in all temporal aspects of our cosmos, as they are enclosed in their sovereign law-spheres, their supra-temporal unity and religious fulfillment of meaning in Christ Jesus, then this deeper unity must come to expression in each of these law-spheres. The theory of the law-spheres has indeed shown that every aspect of temporal reality expresses itself in coherence with every other. This phenomenon is called sphere-universality, the complement of sphere-sovereignty.

Here too, the analogy of the prism holds true, for in the seven colors of the spectrum every color is such that all others are mirrored in its particular tone. And as these seven colors are not indiscriminately mixed, but follow one another in a set order of wave lengths so also do the various aspects of temporal reality. They exhibit a set order of succession, from earlier to later.

Succession of the law-spheres and the organic character of sphere-sovereignty

It can be shown that in the temporal world-order number precedes the aspect of spatiality. The latter in turn precedes motion, then, respectively, organic life, feeling, logical thought, historical development, language, economy, art and justice while, finally, the aspect for love precedes that of faith. No single aspect of reality and thus no single sphere of temporal divine ordinances can be considered as being independent from the others or purely by itself. Here the deeper unity of the law of God comes to rich expression. Whoever violates God's law in one temporal law-sphere does in reality violate the entire coherence of divine ordinances and in a deeper sense the religious root-unity of divine law as revealed to us through Jesus Christ. God's law is so rich and deep that in none of its temporal spheres does it permit only partial fulfillment. God's juridical ordinances cannot be repudiated without violating at the same time the norms for love, harmony, etc. The temporal world-order is a radically organic coherence even while it maintains sphere-sovereignty of the individual law-spheres.

This coherence is already guaranteed in the sphere-universality of which we spoke earlier. Let us take as example the aspect of feeling, investigated by the science of psychology. In this aspect, first of all, the bond with the aspects of number, space, and motion, which precede feeling in the temporal world-order, is maintained. Furthermore, this bond with spatiality is mirrored in a sense of spaciousness and a sensory space-screen; in emotion we see the bond of feeling with the physical motion aspect of reality; in the sensuous or the sensory aspect the bond with the organs of a living body. This connection with the earlier, preceding aspects of reality can be shown not only in human life, but also in animal life. In an animal, however, this life of feeling is limited to sensory feeling, tied to number, space, motion, and biotic organism. Human sense-life, on the other hand, displays a deepening and disclosure as compared to animal life, since here the psychical aspect reveals itself as connected also with the subsequent aspects of reality. A person also has a logical, historical, lingual, economic, and esthetic sense, a jural and moral sense, and a feeling of faith. Thus the meaning of number is disclosed and deepened in its coherence with the spatial and physical aspects of reality. And sense-life bound rigidly to the psychical, when opened up to the mental feeling of logic, justice, beauty, etc., is always directed by these later aspects upon which the disclosed psychical life anticipates.

Disclosure and deepening of the meaning of a law-sphere

What we found with respect to feeling in temporal reality actually holds for all aspects of that reality in its order of sovereign spheres. Logical thought deepens itself from being strictly bound to sense-perception to theoretical, scientific thinking. Such opening up reveals a logical harmony of system, etc., in anticipation of the historical, the lingual, the economic and the aesthetic aspects of reality. So also the meaning of retribution of the juridical aspect opens up in anticipation of the ethical. One need only compare primitive retribution, where punishment was measured in terms of external result, with the modern retribution where, under influence of Christianity, punishment is determined in accordance with the measure of guilt and responsibility!

The second meaning of sphere-sovereignty: individuality-structures in things and in societal relationships

The preceding brief summary of the main points of the theory of law-spheres, where the principles of sphere-sovereignty and sphere-universality are investigated, was necessary for an insight into the structural principles of the temporal societal relationships, such as the state, church, etc., in which the second meaning of sphere-sovereignty reveals itself.

In the normal experience of everyday life we never take hold of these aspects of reality in an articulated way; we do not distinguish them theoretically. Rather, these aspects are experienced implicitly in concrete things, events, relationships etc. Only science distinguishes and analyzes these law-spheres. But concrete things, events, and societal forms, immediately experienced, are based upon concrete, divine structural principles, in which the various aspects of reality are grouped in their individual way. Every concrete thing, be it a tree, a horse, a table, or a chair, functions in all aspects of reality. However, when we look more closely at the peculiar structural law of these things it becomes apparent that the various aspects are grouped in a different way in each of these structures.

Concrete things function in all law-spheres indiscriminately. The significance of the typical qualifying function

For example, a tree undoubtedly functions in the aspects (law-spheres) of number, space and motion; in the first law sphere as a unity of the plurality of its roots, trunk, branches, leaves, etc.; in the second as a certain spatial figure; in the third as a moving mass of matter. But as long as we merely look at these aspects of a tree it is as yet senseless to speak of a tree. Mathematics, physics and chemistry do indeed eliminate the individual thing and investigate only the external relations in number, space, or motion. For them the peculiar inner structure of the thing functioning in them is not important. The physical law of gravity is valid for a tree just as it holds for a falling stone or planetary motion in the universe.

But when we shift our attention to the aspect of organic life things appear in a different light. For biologists, who study this reality-aspect, it makes eminent sense to speak of a tree. The organic life function, therefore, must take a very special place in the structure of a tree. This is the last aspect of reality in which the tree still functions as subject. In all later reality aspects it functions only objectively, as object. The tree lives as subject, but cannot sense psychically, can only be sensed as object. The tree does not think subjectively, but can be grasped as object in a concept. It is not a jural subject, but only an object of legal possession, etc.

However, the organic function has yet another role in the inner structure of the tree. For in this inner structure all the functions of the tree in earlier aspects of reality are typically directed toward their goal. Undoubtedly, the tree is subject to the general laws of mathematics and physics in its aspects of number, space, and motion. But in the inner structure of this thing, its functions in the three preceding law-spheres typically disclose and point to the destination of existence of the individual thing. In this inner structure no motion is purposeless. Chemical catalytic motions are typically pointed to the goal of tree-life. They are individually directed by the organic life-function.

The first meaning of sphere-sovereignty (law-spheres) is not voided in the individuality-structure of things. The thing as individual totality

Hence we name this last function the typical end function of a tree, which finally qualifies the thing as a tree. Sphere-sovereignty of the various aspects has not been superseded with this. In the inner structure of the tree also, spatial relations do not become motions, nor do they become organic life processes. Thus the laws proper to these aspects of reality are not broken. But within this framework of sovereign aspects, the individuality-structure of the tree becomes apparent as individual whole. Here the various aspects are grouped in such a way that the organic life function has the role of guiding or qualifying function. The structural principle, the inner structural law, cannot, therefore, be placed on equal footing with the divine laws of a given law-sphere such as number or space. It is rather a divine ordinance that overarches the distinct aspects of reality, and groups the individual totality of a thing in a particular way, in such a manner that a certain aspect, in this case the biotic, receives the role of leading function.

The basic error of humanistic science: the attempt to dissolve the individuality-structure of a thing in a pattern of lawful relations within one aspect of reality

The primary error made by humanistic science (*Wissenschaft*) was the belief that the structural principle of things could be resolved in the laws of a single law-sphere. Thus it was thought that a living tree could analytically be construed completely as a complex of mechanical, material motion. The individual thing was theoretically resolved within one of its aspects (here mechanical motion), and the actual structural principle was left out of consideration.

Now, not only do the things of nature, such as a tree, or a mountain, or an animal, have their divine structural principles, but things formed by human skill (technics) have them too. In actuality temporal reality never exists without such individuality-structures. This in turn also holds for the various forms of society.

The individuality-structure of societal relationships

Societal bonds such as family, church, school, state, etc., are therefore also individual totalities with their own inner structure. They too, cannot be reduced to or resolved into a single aspect of reality e.g., the economic or the juridical; in principle they function in all aspects of reality. They are radically distinguished from each other, however, in their inner structural principle for this determines the typical end function of a societal bond. This qualifying function gives the typical direction to all the functions of a societal structure in the prior aspects. It gives this structure its distinctive stamp, its particular qualification.

Thus an industrial unit is typically qualified as economic, that is, it has an inner structural principle whereby the various aspects of its reality are grouped in such a way that the economic aspect typically leads and directs all earlier functions. So also with the temporal church-institute: it is qualified as Christian community of faith based upon a common creed. That is to say, the inner structural principle of the church points to the faith-function as the typical qualifying function of this relationship, which typically leads and directs all earlier functions. Likewise the family: on the strength of its divine structural principle it is qualified as a typically ethical community of love between parents and children. And finally, the state is, in accordance with its inner structural principle, a societal relationship where the role of the qualifying function is fulfilled by the typically juridical community of rulers and subjects.

The typical founding function

But the qualifying function alone does not yet determine the inner structure of societal relationships. In all these relationships this qualifying function points back to another aspect of reality, wherein the entire structure of a given relationship is typically based or founded. Consider the qualifying function of the family: the typical (ethical) parent-children love community. It is immediately clear that the expression of love between parents and children finds its actual basis in the natural blood-ties, in the natural genetic relationship. Now, this genetic relationship has its temporal foundation in the aspect of organic life, the biotic aspect of reality. And the typical community of love that has the role of qualifying function is thus founded in this biotic, genetic relationship – the natural blood-ties. This communion of love is not the same as the comradeship that one might expect in a labor-community. It is not the same as general neighborly love, or love among compatriots. Rather, it has its own unique structure based upon a genetic relationship.

The distinctive structure of the family relationship then is determined by the indissoluble coherence of (1) the ethical end function (the communion of love between parents and children) and (2) the biotic function of the genetic or blood-ties on which it is founded. This latter one we will call the founding function of this societal relationship.

In this way all societal relationships have their own qualifying function and their own founding function, both determined as such by the inner structural principle.

The structural principle of the state. The state an institution required because of sin. This Scriptural view not maintained by Thomas Aquinas

What then is the structural principle of the state? The state as societal relationship is not like the family, founded in natural blood-ties. Rather its typical founding function is given in the historical aspect of reality – in a historical power formation, the monopolistic organization of the power of the sword over a given territory. Wherever this foundation is lacking we cannot speak of a state.

This typical founding function of the state reveals immediately that it is a divine institution required because of sin. Thomas Aquinas, and Roman Catholic political theory following him taught that the state as such is not instituted or required because of sin. Only the power of the sword is. The state is grounded in the nature of the human being and is the totality-bond of natural society. In other words, the power of the sword is, in the Roman Catholic view, not an essential part of the structure of the state. This is a falling away from the Scriptural view of the state as still strongly defended by the church-fathers, notably Augustine. This falling away is explicable in terms of the synthesis mentioned earlier – a synthesis of Christian doctrine and pagan Aristotelian theory. For, as we saw, the latter taught that the state is grounded in the "rational-moral nature," and as such is the total bond of which all "lower" relationships are never more than dependent parts.

One-sided action for national disarmament is a neglect of the structural principle of the state

Whenever one denies the organization of the powers of the sword as typical founding function of the state's structure, one denies the structural principle proper to this societal relationship. It is then impossible to gain insight into the sphere-sovereignty of the societal structures. Thus it is clear that all action for one-sided national disarmament results from a denial of the divine structural law for the state. Anarchistic action against the state is then the (unwanted) outcome rooted in a misunderstanding of sin. The state is typically a divine institution of "common grace," i.e., the temporal, preserving (behoudende) grace of God. The power of the sword is not an end unto itself as modern imperialism teaches.

The indissoluble coherence of the typical foundational function and the typical qualifying function of the state

In the divine structural principle of this societal relationship the power of the sword is unbreakably bound up with the typical qualifying function of the state, that is, the maintenance of a public jural community of rulers and subjects. All the intrinsic matters of state ought to be directed by this juridical nucleus, on the strength of the inner structural law. A state where the power of the sword becomes an end in itself degenerates into an organized band of highwaymen, as Augustine and Calvin have remarked.

A public community of law which, as qualifying function, qualifies the state, is utterly different from the internal jural community of other societal relationships, such as family, school, or church. In all of these the internal jural community is directed by the particular qualifying function of the relationship concerned. Internal church-order, for instance, coheres inseparably with the typical qualifying function of the temporal church bond as community of believers, united by a common creed, founded upon a historical organization of office. Think of church discipline, by which the purity of life and doctrine is maintained.

Only in the case of the state does the jural community itself operate as qualifying function, but always founded upon territorial organization of the power of the sword. The internal community of law of the state is a community of jural government, where the government, as servant of God, does not carry the sword inappropriately. The government may, in accordance with the state's inner law of life, never allow itself to be led by any other point of reference than that of justice. But there is no question of a private community of law, as in the other societal relationships, but a public one, subject to the jural principle of the common good. And precisely here, in the understanding of the principle of the common good, does the difference between Christian and pagan or humanistic ideas of the state become clearly evident.

The "common good" (public welfare) as jural principle and as absolutistic principle of power

For, insofar as pagan or humanistic political theory is absolutistic, it views the principle of the common good from the idea that the state is the total bond of all temporal society. Of such a state then, all other societal relationships are no more than dependent parts. From this point of view it is impossible to see "common good" as a truly jural principle.

As long as the relation between state and other social structures is understood as a whole-parts relation, justice cannot prevail in the face of the "common good." And thus it is that out of necessity the state is granted, at least juridically, absolute jurisdiction and absolute competence. But absolute competence of authority cannot exist side by side with the very meaning of justice, for justice demands a balanced delimitation and harmonizing of jurisdiction. Yet, when the state is given absolute competence, it is assumed that the state as the wellspring of positive justice is itself above the law. Thus the teaching of the well-known sixteenth century Frenchman Jean Bodin: *Princeps legibus solutus est* – the government stands above legislated law.

The modern message of the citizen without rights in relation to the state as proclaimed by National-Socialism and Fascism, is but a consequence of such thought.

The old-liberal idea of the *Rechtsstaat* proves powerless to control the absolutism of "common good"

The liberal idea of the *Rechtsstaat* proved inadequate and powerless over against the absolutism of common good. In its classical, individualistic dress of natural law it attempted to control absolutization by means of external restriction of the task of the state. The social contract that had supposedly inaugurated the state was intended to give the state no other task than the organized safe-guarding of natural, constitutional rights of the individual – life, property, and freedom.

The humanistic idea of the *Rechtsstaat* in its second, formalistic phase

However, when historical developments confronted the state with a far broader task, and forced it to become involved with social and economic life, in culture, education, etc., this old-liberal idea too, became obsolete. Hence, it was now modified; the state is no longer limited in its task only to the protection of the rights of the individual. Many other "goals" may be striven for: furthering of culture, stimulation of economy, etc. But, the idea was that the state may only do this when remaining formally subject to administrative legislation. This new and fundamentally modified conception gave the citizen only formal protection against the absolutism of the so-called "common good." For after all, this protection lay only in the provision that the "executive" was formally subject to the law. But the law-giver as such was not curbed in any way by this formal idea of the *Rechtsstaat*. The juridical sovereignty of the law-giver was accepted unreservedly. With that the latter was placed above and beyond the law. Only the executive branch of government was subordinated to the legislative power.

Only the Christian idea of the state, rooted in the principle of sphere-sovereignty, is the true idea of the *Rechtsstaat*

The radically Christian idea of the state, the idea that has fundamentally broken with any absolutization of either state or individual, is the proper idea of the *Rechtsstaat*. It alone can grasp the principle of the common good as a truly jural principle of public law, because it is grounded in the confession of a supra-temporal root-community of humanity in the kingdom of Christ Jesus, and because it accepts therefore the principle of sphere-sovereignty for the temporal societal bonds.

But to see the principle of sphere-sovereignty in the correct light, we must remember that it does not impose external boundaries on the task of the state. The old-liberal idea of the *Rechtsstaat* did this with its demand that the government refrain completely from any involvement with social and economic life. However, we have seen that every societal relationship – and therefore also in the state – in principle functions in all aspects of reality (law-spheres). It was the basic error of humanistic thought concerning the *Rechtsstaat* in its old-liberal, individualistic form that it maintained that the state could be understood as an abstract community of law, or rather as a simple juridical social contract, and nothing more. But the truth is that the inner structural principle of the state ought to express itself in all aspects of temporal reality equally. For the state is not merely a community of law, but also a spatial community (the country and its boundaries), a community of life, of feeling, of thought, of historical cultural form, and of social and moral dimensions (think of patriotism). And the Christian idea of the state demands that the structure of the state expresses itself also in a Christian community of faith, embracing both governors and those governed.

The task of the state cannot be limited externally by excluding the state from certain aspects of reality

But imposing limitations on the task of the state in all these areas of life is an intrinsic limitation, determined by the inner structural principle of the state. The internal economy of the state relationship cannot, as such, express itself like the structure of a private business. Neither can the internal social community within the state relationship (for instance, national festivities, public ceremony, etc.) take on the form of the social community of a clan, or a family, or an association.

The public justice of the state finds its boundaries in the internal private communities of law of the other societal relationships. Thus also, the Christian state as such can reveal itself in the area of faith only within the boundaries of its own inner structural principle, and may not assume the structure of a church-institute. For the state is not, like the temporal church community, qualified as a community of believers in Christ. That is to say, neither the state, nor any other non-ecclesiastical societal relationship has as its typical goal the area of faith and confession.

The state, with its function as political faith-community, may not be subjected to an ecclesiastical creed

For that reason the state may not be tied to a certain ecclesiastical creed, as was long the rule. Nor may the demand be made that offices in the state be held by candidates of a certain denomination, or group of denominations (e.g., Protestant or Roman Catholic). A confession concerning the task of a Christian government, such as the old article 36 in the Belgic Confession, does not belong in an ecclesiastical creed. And in the same way the Christian state as community of faith should not tie itself to a confessional creed concerning the sacraments and the preaching of the Word. The creedal basis of the Christian state in its function as community of faith can only be the confession of God's sovereignty revealed in the reign of Jesus Christ, the Governor of all governments on earth. But this political creed entails for all of state-life the recognition of the truly Scriptural basis for political life. And the heart of it all remains the confession of God's sovereignty in Christ Jesus in which is included the recognition of sphere-sovereignty of the various societal relationships.

Christian faith deepens the typically political principles of justice. The Roman and the Christian idea of justice

These jural principles of the structure of the state, opened up and deepened by Christ's universally redemptive work, ought to take the leading role in the Christian state. Undoubtedly, in a pagan state God's common grace maintains the inner structural principle, but in that type of state political life in its faith-function is without its direction towards the kingdom of God in Christ Jesus. The true Root of common grace, Christ as supreme Governor, remains hidden in the pagan idea of the state – there is no visible manifestation.

For instance, classical Roman law, in spite of its admirable technical development, remained rigidly bound to an egotistical imperialistic idea of power and was without any disclosure and enrichment in the sense of a Christian idea of solidarity, in which power, love, and justice are caught up in the full sense of their religious root-unity, a unity majestically revealed to us in the cross of Christ.[1] Thus we find no trace of Christian social legislation in pagan Roman public law. The jural sphere of the pater familias (head of the Roman household), egotistically absolutized, is there in unrelenting opposition to the absolute imperialism of the Res Publica Romana. Over against this absolute imperialism the Roman citizen had no rights, for the state was thought of in a totalitarian sense as the whole of society. In private life, on the other hand, the egotistic spirit of Cain ruled: Am I my brother's keeper?

The liberal-humanistic and the Fascist views of justice

In the modern humanistic view of justice one can rediscover this isolating Roman dualism of public and private law.

Old-liberal politics with its principle of exclusion raised private advantage to the highest directive of private life. And in the recent reaction against this liberalism by Fascism and National-Socialism it is true that great emphasis is placed upon common good and upon the requirements of the community of the people, also in the sphere of private law, but nevertheless, all this is at the cost of sphere-sovereignty and individual freedom. For here too, the old pagan idea of the state dominates an idea that teaches that the state is the totality-bond of which all others can only be dependent parts.

Only the radically Christian idea of sphere-sovereignty can keep the absolutism of "common good" in check. No other view allows us to see the true harmony among the various spheres of life, as willed by God in

---

[1] Translator's note: By "disclosure" (*ontsluiting*) and "enrichment" (*verdieping*) Dooyeweerd calls attention respectively to the unfolding expression of the retrocipatory moments, and the anticipatory moments, in this case within the jural sphere.

His creation-order. Hence it alone can reveal the truly Christian idea of the *Rechtsstaat*.

All non-Christian theories of the state are essentially theories of power (Machtsstaatstheorieen)[1]

For the Christian idea of the Rechtsstaat, sphere-sovereignty is the cornerstone. In the final analysis all pagan and humanistic views of politics are invariably theories of a Machtsstaat, because at best they can give arbitrary, but never true boundaries to the task of the state. It can be understood, therefore, that modern National-Socialistic and Fascist theories of the Machtsstaat deny the individualistic liberal idea the right to name itself with the proud title of idea of the Rechtsstaat.

The true relation of state and church: not a mechanical division, but sphere-sovereignty

The radical difference between Christian and liberal humanistic political doctrine is nowhere clearer than in their respective views of the mutual relation between state and church.

Insofar as liberalism wished to safe-guard the freedom of church-life over against the state it could not do otherwise than (1) effect a watertight division between state and church, and (2) introduce the "religionless state," where faith is completely excluded. The freedom of the church was then derived from the absolute constitutional rights of the "religous individual." The church became a private association, and in it the "general will" of the members was declared sovereign.

Scriptural Christianity, on the other hand, can never take over this liberalistic slogan of separation of church and state without spiritual suicide. Sphere-sovereignty does not yield a watertight compartment or mechanical division among the areas of life. It is, as we have seen, an organically most deeply cohering principle, for it begins with the religious root-unity of the life-spheres.

---

1 Translator's note: The term *Machtsstaat* is to be taken as the exact opposite of *Rechtsstaat*. In humanism, and already in Greek thought each represents a horn of the same (false) dilemma. Broadly, the idea of the *Machtsstaat* is a view of the state as characterized historically by power (the view of the sophist Kallikles, Machiavelli, Nietzsche, Hegel, etc.), while the idea of the *Rechtsstaat* views the state as characterized by natural justice, conceived apostatically as based on natural law, inborn right, absolute standards, etc. (Plato is a good example here.) In contemporary political theory these are in dialectical opposition to each other, and are often unsuccessfully forced together. This is what Dooyeweerd sees as the crisis in humanistic political theory. For a fuller explanation of this crucial point see *A New Critique of Theoretical Thought*, Vol.III, Part II, chapter 3, and *De Crisis in de Humanistische Staatsleer* (The Crisis in the Humanistic Theory of the State – N.V. Boekhandel H. TEN HAVE, Amsterdam, 1931, 209pp.).

The inseparable, interwoven texture of the various structures of society

The various social structures by which sphere-sovereignty is internally guaranteed do not stand alongside each other in isolation. In temporal life they are intertwined and interwoven. All other societal relationships also have a function within the state, just as, conversely, the state functions in all other societal relationships. But in the final analysis all these structural interplays remain of an external character with respect to sphere-sovereignty. Members of a family, a congregation, or a business enterprise are at the same time citizens. And conversely, the state is always dealing with families, churches, and business enterprises. But the competence, the sphere of jurisdiction of the state can never be expanded into the internal, structurally determined concerns that are proper to these societal relationships without thereby violating in a revolutionary way the cosmic constitution of sphere-sovereignty. Chaos rather than order and harmony is then the inevitable result.

The prophetic task of Christianity in these times

Thus the Christian idea of the state in its only possible, that is radical Scriptural, sense remains the liberating message – also, yes especially, in our volatile times. And it is to us, kindred in spirit, to take hold of this incomparably rich idea, to make it our own, to possess it spiritually as the heritage of our fathers. That we may carry it everywhere – for the benefit of the entire community, now so drastically tortured, as the only balm for its wounds.

Glossary

[The following glossary of Dooyeweerd's technical terms and neologisms is reproduced and edited by Daniël F. M. Strauss, with the permission of its author, Albert M. Wolters, from C. T. McIntire, ed., The Legacy of Herman Dooyeweerd: Reflections on Critical Philosophy in the Christian Tradition (Lanham MD, 1985), pp. 167-171.]

THIS GLOSSARY OF HERMAN DOOYEWEERD'S terms is an adapted version of the one published in L. Kalsbeek, Contours of a Christian Philosophy (Toronto: Wedge, 1975). It does not provide exhaustive technical definitions but gives hints and pointers for a better understanding. Entries marked with an asterisk are those terms which are used by Dooyeweerd in a way which is unusual in English-speaking philosophical contexts and are, therefore, a potential source of misunderstanding. Words or phrases in small caps and beginning with a capital letter refer to other entries in this glossary.

* Analogy (see LAW-SPHERE) – Collective name for a RETROCIPATION or an ANTICIPATION.

* Anticipation – An ANALOGY within one MODALITY referring to a later modality. An example is "efficiency," a meaning-moment which is found within the historical modality, but which points forward to the later economic modality. Contrast with RETROCIPATION.

* Antinomy – Literally "conflict of laws" (from Greek anti, "against," and nomos, "law"). A logical contradiction arising out of a failure to distinguish the different kinds of law valid in different MODALITIES. Since ontic laws do not conflict (Principium Exclusae Antinomiae), an antinomy is always a logical sign of ontological reductionism.

* Antithesis – Used by Dooyeweerd (following Abraham Kuyper) in a specifically religious sense to refer to the fundamental spiritual opposition between the kingdom of God and the kingdom of darkness. See Galatians 5:17. Since this is an opposition between regimes, not realms, it runs through every department of human life and culture, including philosophy and the academic enterprise as a whole, and through the heart of every believer as he or she struggles to live a life of undivided allegiance to God.

Aspect – A synonym for MODALITY.

Cosmonomic idea – Dooyeweerd's own English rendering of the Dutch term wetsidee. Occasionally equivalents are "transcendental ground idea" or "transcendental basic idea". The intention of this new term is to bring to expression that there exists an unbreakable coherence between God's law (nomos) and created reality (cosmos) factually subjected to God's law.

Dialectic – In Dooyeweerd's usage: an unresolvable tension, within a system or line of thought, between two logically irreconcilable polar positions. Such a dialectical tension is characteristic of each of the three non-Christian GROUND-MOTIVES which Dooyeweerd sees as having dominated Western thought.

*Enkapsis (enkaptic) – A neologism borrowed by Dooyeweerd from the Swiss biologist Heidenhain, and derived from the Greek enkaptein, "to swallow up." The term refers to the structural interlacements which can exist between things, plants, animals, and societal structures which have their own internal structural principle and independent qualifying function. As such, enkapsis is to be clearly distinguished from the part-whole relation, in which there is a common internal structure and qualifying function.

Factual Side – General designation of whatever is subjected to the LAW-SIDE of creation (see SUBJECT-SIDE).

Founding function – The earliest of the two modalities which characterize certain types of structural wholes. The other is called the GUIDING FUNCTION. For example, the founding function of the family is the biotic modality.

* Gegenstand – A German word for "object," used by Dooyeweerd as a technical term for a modality when abstracted from the coherence of time and opposed to the analytical function in the theoretical attitude of thought, thereby establishing the Gegenstand relation. Gegenstand is therefore the technically precise word for the object of SCIENCE, while "object" itself is reserved for the objects of NAIVE EXPERIENCE.

Ground-motive – The Dutch term grondmotief, used by Dooyeweerd in the sense of fundamental motivation, driving force. He distinguished four basic ground-motives in the history of Western civilization:
(1) form and matter, which dominated pagan Greek philosophy; (2) nature and grace, which underlay medieval Christian synthesis thought (3) nature and freedom, which has shaped the philosophies of modern times; and (4) creation, fall, and redemption, which lies at the root of a radical and integrally scriptural philosophy.

Guiding function – The highest subject function of a structural whole (e.g. stone, animal, business enterprise, or state). Except in the case of humans, this function is also said to QUALIFY the structural whole. It is called the guiding function because it "guides" or "leads" its earlier functions. For example, the guiding function of a plant is the biotic. The physical function of a plant (as studied, e.g. by biochemistry) is different from physical functioning elsewhere because of its being "guided" by the biotic. Also called "leading function".

* Heart – The concentration point of human existence; the supratemporal focus of all human temporal functions; the religious root unity of humans. Dooyeweerd says that it was his rediscovery of the biblical idea of the heart as the central religious depth dimension of human multifaceted life which enabled him to wrestle free from neo-Kantianism and phenomenology. The Scriptures speak of this focal point also as "soul," "spirit," and "inner man." Philiosophical equivalents are Ego, I, I-ness, and Selfhood. It is the heart in this sense which survives death, and it is by the religious redirection of the heart in regeneration that all human temporal functions are renewed.

* Immanence Philosophy – A name for all non-Christian philosophy, which tries to find the ground and integration of reality within the created order. Unlike Christianity, which acknowledges a transcendent Creator above all things, immanence philosophy of necessity absolutizes some feature or aspect of creation itself.

* Individuality-structure – This term represents arguably one of the most difficult concepts in Dooyeweerd's philosophy. Coined in both Dutch and English by Dooyeweerd himself it has led sometimes to serious misunderstandings amongst scholars. Over the years there have been various attempts to come up with an alternate term, some of which are described below, but in the absence of a consensus it was decided to leave the term the way it is.

It is the general name or the characteristic law (order) of concrete things, as given by virtue of creation. Individuality-structures belong to the law-side of reality. Dooyeweerd uses the term individuality-structure to indicate the applicability of a structural order for the existence of individual entities. Thus the structural laws for the state, for marriage, for works of art, for mosquitoes, for sodium chloride, and so forth are called individuality-structures. The idea of an individual whole is determined by an individuality-structure which precedes the theoretical analysis of its modal functions. The identity of an individual whole is a relative unity in a multiplicity of functions. (See MODALITY.) Van Riessen prefers to call this law for entities an identity-structure, since as such it guarantees the persistent identity of all entities (Wijsbegeerte, Kampen 1970, p.158). In his work (Alive, An Enquiry into the Origin and Meaning of Life, 1984, Ross House Books, Vallecito, California), M. Verbrugge introduces his own distinct systematic account concerning the nature of (what he calls) functors, a word first introduced by Hendrik Hart for the dimension of individuality-structures (cf. Hart: Understanding Our World, Towards an Integral Ontology, New York 1984, cf.pp.445-446). As a substitute for the notion of an individuality-structure, Verbrugge advances the term: idionomy (cf. Alive, pp.42, 81ff., 91ff.). Of course this term may also cause misunderstanding if it is taken to mean that each individual creature (subject) has its own unique law. What is intended is that every type of law (nomos) is meant to delimit and determine unique subjects. In other words, however specified the universality of the law may be, it can never, in its bearing upon unique individual creatures, itself become something uniquely individual. Another way of grasping the meaning of Dooyeweerd's notion of an individuality-structure is, in following an oral suggestion by Roy Clouser (Zeist, August 1986), to call it a type-law (from Greek: typonomy). This simply means that all entities of a certain type conform to this law. The following perspective given by M.D. Stafleu elucidates this terminology in a systematic way (Time and Again, A Systematic Analysis of the Foundations of Physics, Wedge Publishing Foundation, Toronto 1980, p.6, 11): typical laws (type-laws/typonomies, such as the Coulomb law – applicable only to charged entities and the Pauli principle – applicable only to fermions) are special laws which apply to a limited class of entities only, whereas modal laws hold universally for all possible entities. D.F.M. Strauss ('Inleiding tot die Kosmologie', SACUM, Bloemfontein 1980) introduces the expression entity structures. The term entity comprises both the individuality and the identity of the thing concerned – therefore it accounts for the respective emphases found in Dooyeweerd's notion of individuality-structures and in Van Riessen's notion of identity structures. The following words of Dooyeweerd show that both the individuality and identity of an entity is determined by its 'individuality-structure': "In general we can establish that the factual temporal duration of a thing as an individual and identical whole is dependent on the preservation of its structure of individuality" (A New Critique of Theoretical Thought, Vol.III:79).

Irreducibility (irreducible) – Incapability of theoretical reduction. This is the negative way of referring to the unique distinctiveness of things and aspects which we find everywhere in creation and which theoretical thought must respect. Insofar as everything has its own peculiar created nature and character, it cannot be understood in terms of categories foreign to itself.

* Law – The notion of creational law is central to Dooyeweerd's philosophy. Everything in creation is subject to God's law for it, and accordingly law is the boundary between God and creation. Scriptural synonyms for law are "ordinance," "decree," "commandment," "word," and so on. Dooyeweerd stresses that law is not in opposition to but the condition for true freedom. See also NORM and LAW-SIDE.

Law-Side – The created cosmos, for Dooyeweerd, has two correlative "sides": a law-side and a factual side (initially called: SUBJECT-SIDE). The former is simply the coherence of God's laws or ordinances for creation; the latter is the totality of created reality which is subject to those laws. It is important to note that the law-side always holds universally.

Law-Sphere (see MODAL STRUCTURE and MODALITY) – The circle of laws qualified by a unique, irreducible and indefinable meaning-nucleus is known as a law-sphere. Within every law-sphere temporal reality has a modal function and in this function is subjected (French: sujet) to the laws of the modal spheres. Therefore every law-sphere has a law-side and a subject-side that are given only in unbreakable correlation with each other. (See DIAGRAM on p.165.)

* Meaning – Dooyeweerd uses the word "meaning" in an unusual sense. By it he means the referential, non-self-sufficient character of created reality in that it points beyond itself to God as Origin. Dooyeweerd stresses that reality is meaning in this sense and that, therefore, it does not have meaning. "Meaning" is the Christian alternative to the metaphysical substance of immanence philosphy. "Meaning" becomes almost a synonym for "reality." Note the many compounds formed from it: meaning-nucleus, meaning-side, meaning-moment, meaning-fullness.

* Meaning-nucleus – The indefinable core meaning of a MODALITY.

Modality (See MODAL STRUCTURE and LAW-SPHERE) – One of the fifteen fundamental ways of being distinguished by Dooyeweerd. As modes of being, they are sharply distinguished from the concrete things which function within them. Initially Dooyeweerd distinguished fourteen aspects only, but since 1950 he introduced the kinematical aspect of uniform movement between the spatial and the physical aspects. Modalities are also known as "modal functions," "modal aspects," or as "facets" of created reality. (See DIAGRAM on p.165.)

Modal Structure (see MODALITY and LAW-SPHERE) – The peculiar constellation, in any given modality, of its meaning-moments (anticipatory, retrocipatory, nuclear). Contrast INDIVIDUALITY-STRUCTURE.

* Naive experience – Human experience insofar as it is not "theoretical" in Dooyeweerd's precise sense."Naive" does not mean unsophisticated. Sometimes called "ordinary" or "everyday" experience. Dooyeweerd takes pains to emphasize that theory is embedded in this everyday experience and must not violate it.

Norm (normative) – Postpsychical laws, that is, modal laws for the analytical through pistical law-spheres (see LAW-SPHERE and DIAGRAM on p.165). These laws are norms because they need to be positivized (see POSITIVIZE) and can be violated, in distinction from the "natural laws" of the pre-analytical spheres which are obeyed involuntarily (e.g., in a digestive process).

* Nuclear-moment – A synonym for MEANING-NUCLEUS and LAW-SPHERE, used to designate the indefinable core meaning of a MODALITY or aspect of created reality.
* Object – Something qualified by an object function and thus correlated to a subject function. A work of art, for instance, is qualified by its correlation to the human subjective function of aesthetic appreciation. Similarly, the elements of a sacrament are pistical objects.

Opening process – The process by which latent modal anticipations are "opened" or actualized. The modal meaning is then said to be "deepened." It is this process which makes possible the cultural development (differentiation) of society from a primitive ("closed," undifferentiated) stage. For example, by the opening or disclosure of the ethical anticipation in the juridical aspect, the modal meaning of the legal aspect is deepened and society can move from the principle of "an eye for an eye" to the consideration of extenuating circumstances in the administration of justice.

* Philosophy – In Dooyeweerd's precise systematic terminology, philosophy is the encyclopedic science, that is, its proper task is the theoretical investigation of the overall systematic integration of the various scientific disciplines and their fields of inquiry. Dooyeweerd also uses the term in a more inclusive sense, especially when he points out that all philosophy is rooted in a pretheoretical religious commitment and that some philosophical conception, in turn, lies at the root of all scientific scholarship.

Positivize – A word coined to translate the Dutch word positiveren, which means to make positive in the sense of being actually valid in a given time or place. For example, positive law is the legislation which is in force in a given country at a particular time; it is contrasted with the legal principles which lawmakers must positivize as legislation. In a general sense, it refers to the responsible implementation of all normative principles in human life as embodied, for example, in state legislation, economic policy, ethical guidelines, and so on.

Qualify – The GUIDING FUNCTION of a thing is said to qualify it in the sense of characterizing it. In this sense a plant is said to be qualified by the biotic and a state by the juridical [aspects].

* Radical – Dooyeweerd frequently uses this term with an implicit reference to the Greek meaning of radix = root. This usage must not be confused with the political connotation of the term radical in English. In other works Dooyeweerd sometimes paraphrases his use of the term radical with the phrase: penetrating to the root of created reality.

* Religion (religious) – For Dooyeweerd, religion is not an area or sphere of life but the all-encompassing and direction-giving root of it. It is service of God (or a substitute no-god) in every domain of human endeavor. As such,

Glossary

it is to be sharply distinguished from religious faith, which is but one of the many acts and attitudes of human existence. Religion is an affair of the HEART and so directs all human functions. Dooyeweerd says religion is "the innate impulse of the human selfhood to direct itself toward the true or toward a pretended absolute Origin of all temporal diversity of meaning" (A New Critique of Theoretical Thought, Vol.I, 1953, p.57).

* Retrocipation – A feature in one MODALITY which refers to, is reminiscent of, an earlier one, yet retaining the modal qualification of the aspect in which it is found. The "extension" of a concept, for example, is a kind of logical space: it is a strictly logical affair, and yet it harks back to the spatial modality in its original sense. See ANTICIPATION.

* Science – Two things are noted about Dooyeweerd's use of the term "science". In the first place, as a translation of the Dutch word wetenschap (analogous to the German word Wissenschaft), it embraces all scholarly study – not only the natural sciences but also the social sciences and the humanities, including theology and philosophy. In the second place, science is always, strictly speaking, a matter of modal abstraction, that is, of analytically lifting an aspect out of the temporal coherence in which it is found and examining it in the Gegenstand relation. But in this investigation it does not focus its theoretical attention upon the modal structure of such an aspect itself; rather, it focuses on the coherence of the actual phenomena which function within that structure. Modal abstraction as such must be distinguished from NAIVE EXPERIENCE. In the first sense, therefore, "science" has a wider application in Dooyeweerd than is usual in English-speaking countries, but in the second sense it has a more restricted, technical meaning.

Sphere Sovereignty – A translation of Kuyper's phrase souvereiniteit in eigen kring, by which he meant that the various distinct spheres of human authority (such as family, church, school, and business enterprise) each have their own responsibility and decision-making power which may not be usurped by those in authority in another sphere, for example, the state. Dooyeweerd retains this usage but also extends it to mean the IRREDUCIBILITY of the modal aspects. This is the ontical principle on which the societal principle is based since each of the societal "spheres" mentioned is qualified by a different irreducible modality.

* Subject – Used in two senses by Dooyeweerd: (1) "subject" as distinguished from LAW, (2) "subject" as distinguished from OBJECT. The latter sense is roughly equivalent to common usage; the former is unusual and ambiguous. Since all things are "subject" to LAW, objects are also subjects in the first sense. Dooyeweerd's matured conception, however, does not show this ambiguity. By distinguishing between the law-side and the factual side of creation, both subject and object (sense (2)) are part of the factual side.

Subject-Side – The correlate of LAW-SIDE, preferably called the factual side. Another feature of the factual subject-side is that it is only here that individuality is found.

Substratum – The aggregate of modalities preceding a given aspect in the modal order. The arithmetic, spatial, kinematic, and physical, for example, together form the substratum for the biotic. They are also the necessary foundation upon which the biotic rests, and without which it cannot exist. See SUPERSTRATUM (and the DIAGRAM on p.165).

Superstratum – The aggregate of modalities following a given aspect in the modal order. For example, the pistical, ethical, juridical and aesthetic together constitute the superstratum of the economic. See SUBSTRATUM.

* Synthesis – The combination, in a single philosophical conception, of characteristic themes from both pagan philosophy and biblical religion. It is this feature of the Christian intellectual tradition, present since patristic times, with which Dooyeweerd wants to make a radical break. Epistemologically seen the term synthesis is used to designate the way in which a multiplicity of features is integrated within the unity of a concept. The re-union of the logical aspect of the theoretical act of thought with its non-logical 'Gegenstand' is called an inter-modal meaning-synthesis.

* Time – In Dooyeweerd, a general ontological principle of intermodal continuity, with far wider application than our common notion of time, which is equated by him with the physical manifestation of this general cosmic time. It is, therefore, not coordinate with space. All created things, except the human HEART, are in time. At the law-side time expresses itself as time-order and at the factual side (including subject-subject and subject-object relations) as time duration.

Transcendental – A technical term from the philosophy of Kant denoting the a priori structural conditions which make human experience (specifically human knowledge and theoretical thought) possible. As such it is to be sharply distinguished from the term "transcendent." Furthermore, the basic (transcendental) Idea of a philosophy pre-supposes the transcendent and central sphere of consciousness (the human HEART). This constitutes the second meaning in which Dooyeweerd uses the term transcendental: through its transcendental ground-Idea philosophy points beyond itself to its ultimate religious foundation transcending the realm of thought.

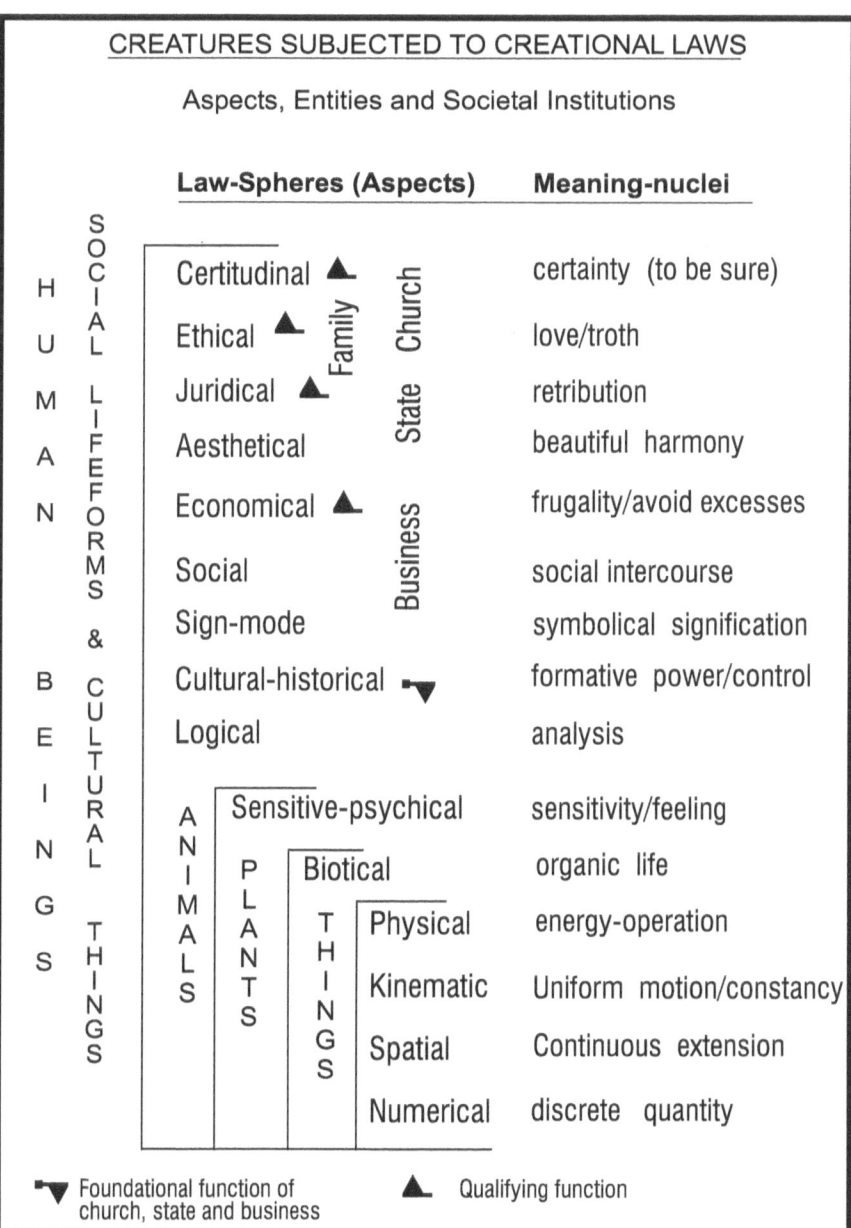

Index

A
adequate causation 40–44, 56
Althusius, J. 24, 105–106, 135
Ambrose 10
Aristotelianism 5, 12
Aristotle 7–9, 11–12, 15–16, 32, 69, 124, 126, 131, 134, 137
Augustine 10–12, 31, 149

B
Bergson, H. 75
Berolzheimer 25
Beyssens 26
Beza 24
Bismarck 14, 28
Bodin, J. 22, 103–108, 110–111, 150
Brunner, E. 121–122, 132–133

C
Calvinism 3–6, 8, 10, 12, 14, 16, 18–20, 22, 24–26, 28, 30, 32, 34, 36–38, 123, 139
Cathrein, V. 26, 31–32
causae secundae 16
Cicero 9
civil law 36, 67, 84, 92–98, 107, 110, 112, 119
civil private law 45, 52, 54, 89, 93, 97–98
civitas Dei 11
civitas terrena 11
Comte, A. 25, 97
conditio sine qua non 40–41, 43–44, 48, 65, 67,
coordinational relationships 64
corpus Christianum 13
criminal law 27, 30, 32, 42, 44–45, 51, 54, 56–57, 62, 67, 69

cultural-historical development 76, 87

D
Duguit, L. 97, 113
Durkheim, E. 25

E
ecclesiastical law 52, 54, 94–95, 112, 114, 118–119
Ehrligh, E. 80
Eigeman 139
Elster 4
enkapsis 88
entelechy 7
epistemology 5, 17–18
expropriation 21

F
Fascism 122, 126, 150, 153
Filmer 22
forms of participation 56
foundational function 83–84, 149

G
Galileo, G. 49, 106
Gegenstand 17–18, 21
Gerson 22
Gierke, Otto von 110–113, 139
Golden Age 10
Graswinckel 22
Greek Stoicism 6
Groen van Prinsterer 4
Grotius, H. 20, 30, 69, 91, 93, 107, 137–138
Gurvitch, G. 75–81, 86–87, 113–114

H
Haering, Theodor L. 88
Hegel 154

Index

Heidenhain 88
Heller, H. 102
High Scholasticism 12–13
Hitler, A. 138
Hobbes, Th. 27, 91, 107–108, 136, 138
human rights 94, 96–97
Hundeshagen 37
Hottomannus 24

I
individualism 9–10, 34, 92, 137
individuality-structure 54, 80, 147
instrumental commission 56
inter-communal relations 85–86, 88
inter-individual 85, 88
ius gentium 12, 92–94, 96
ius publicum 97–98, 107

J
James, W. 75
Jellinek, G. 25, 33, 37, 111, 113
jural morality 68

K
Kallikles 154
Kant, I. 5, 17, 19–20, 26, 30–31, 39, 49–50, 137–138
Kaufmann 14
Kelsen, H. 20–21, 69, 102, 113
Kohler 25
Kohnstamm 44
Krabbe 25, 113
Kuyper, A. 4–5, 37, 123, 133, 141–143

L
Languet 24
law-spheres 18–19, 32, 35, 37, 142–146, 151
legal order 12, 19–21, 23–25, 27, 29–31, 35, 37, 46, 57, 59, 65–66, 91, 107, 109, 114
legal theory 5–6, 20–21, 32, 106
Leibniz, G.W.F. 50

Leviathan 97, 107
lex naturalis 6, 9, 11–12, 15
Locke, J. 107, 138
logos 10–11, 17–18
Lohman S. de 4, 23
Lotze, H. 69
Lowie, R.H. 68, 78, 87
Luther, M. 13–15, 22, 24, 26, 28, 30, 130, 132
Lutheranism 13–14, 19, 22, 28

M
Machiavelli 154
Machtsstaat 154
Magnus, Albertus 12
Maritain, J. 101
Mayer 57
meaning-nucleus 55, 65, 68–70, 81–82
Melanchton 15
Mill, J.S. 40, 50

N
National-Socialism 122, 126, 150, 153
Natural law 8, 10, 19
Newton, I. 49, 106
Nietzsche, F. 154
nominalism 16–17, 22, 131–133, 137
non-political relationships 88

O
Occam, W. 16, 22
organized communities 85–86, 91
ownership 21, 142

P
pacta sunt servanda 21
part-whole relation 88
pater familias 9, 93, 153
Philo 10
Plato 6, 11
political theory 3–6, 22, 26, 28, 38, 106, 132–133, 135, 149–150

populus Romanus 9
positive law 6, 12, 19–22, 25, 27, 29–30, 36, 38, 80, 89, 103–105, 107, 109, 111, 115, 119
Preusz, H. 101, 112–113
prima causa 16
princeps legibus solutus est 9, 23–24
property law 21, 35
providentia Dei 16
public law 9–10, 27, 34, 36, 84, 89, 92, 97, 112, 118–119, 151, 153
Pufendorff, S. 138

Q
qualifying function 53, 82–84, 95, 98, 146–150

R
Rechtsstaat 138–139, 150–151, 154
religious root-unity 68, 134, 143–144, 153–154
res publica 105, 110
Rickert, H. 25, 50
Roman Catholic 4–5, 13, 21, 26, 31–32, 121–122, 125, 128–130, 135, 149, 152
Roman jurists 9, 93–94
Roper, D. 66
Rousseau, J.J. 27, 107–108, 137–138

S
Salmasius 22
Schilling 12
Schelling, F.W.J. 22, 108
Schopenhauer, A. 19
Seerveld, C. 66
Seneca 9–10, 24
Sombart, W. 4
sovereignty in its proper orbit 116, 118–119
sovereignty of God 10, 15
sovereignty of reason 19, 21

speculative metaphysics 17
sphere-sovereignty 4, 18–19, 25, 29–30, 33, 35–36, 58, 128, 135–136, 139–142, 144–146, 149, 151–155
sphere-universality 144–145
Stahl, J. 3–4, 14, 19, 22–23, 26–27, 29–31
Stammler, R. 26, 29, 36, 81
Stoic philosophy 6
suum cuique tribuere 8, 10

T
theologia naturalis 15
Thomas Aquinas 5, 12, 31, 125, 128, 130–131, 134, 148–149
Thomism 18–19, 32, 131
totality-structures 52–54
Traeger, W. 41, 43
transcendental realism 18
Treitschke 14
Troeltsch, E. 4, 37

U
undifferentiated communities 77, 87

V
van der Vlugt 5
van Eck, D. 44
Van Idsenga 23
Volksgeist 96, 109–110
Von Bernardi 14
von Buri 40–41, 43
Von Hertling 26
Von Kries 40–42, 56
Von Pesch 26

W
Weber, M. 4, 50
Windelband, W. 25
Wiskeman 4
Wolff, C. 33

Z
Zwingli, U. 15

I

www.ingramcontent.com/pod-product-compliance
Lightning Source LLC
Chambersburg PA
CBHW032038290426
44110CB00012B/859